Forgotten Trails

Forgotten Trails

Historical Sources of the Columbia's Big Bend Country

Ron Anglin

Edited with contributions by
Glen W. Lindeman

WSU
PRESS

Published by Washington State University Press
Pullman, WA 99164-5910

In collaboration with the Grant County Historical Society
and the Washington Centennial Committee of Grant County

Washington State University Press, Pullman, Washington 99164-5910
© 1995 by the Board of Regents of Washington State University
All rights reserved
First printing 1995

Library of Congress Cataloging-in-Publication Data
    Anglin, Ron.
        Forgotten trails : historical sources of the Columbia's Big Bend country /
    by Ron Anglin ; edited with contributions by Glen W. Lindeman.
            p.   cm.
        Includes bibliographical references (p.   ) and index.
        ISBN 0-87422-116-1 (pbk.)
            1. Grand Coulee Dam Region (Wash.)—History.   2. Grand Coulee Dam
    Region (Wash.)—Description and travel.   3. Trails—Washington (State)—
    Grand Coulee Dam Region.   I. Lindeman, Glen W.   II. Title.
    F897.C7A54   1995
    979.7'31—dc20   95-18896
                                                                              CIP

Cover painting: "The Columbia Sinkiuse," by Keith Powell, P.O. Box 788, Grand Coulee, WA 99133. In circa 1820, a band of Sinkiuse in the Upper Grand Coulee leaves a lakeside campsite where the women have been collecting tule stems for making basketry and mats. Steamboat Rock is visible in the far distance (to the north). Having dressed in their best finery and decorated the horses with feathers and paints, the cavalcade of riders is journeying south to visit a village of kinfolk located in the lakes area of the lower coulee, a few miles below Dry Falls. Artist Keith Powell has researched historic photographs of Sinkiuse men to depict the faces of the warriors in the foreground.

Contents

Acknowledgments

As A LAND MANAGER at the Columbia National Wildlife Refuge I often was asked, "Just what do the Cariboo or White Bluffs trails have to do with the Columbia Basin today?" My answer to this question is bound up in my professional training and career. I was taught to observe the things that take place around me each day and to relate them to my job, which is that of a steward of the land. I do not feel that I, or anyone for that matter, can manage a parcel of land without knowing and understanding its history.

So many times state and federal land management personnel are transferred from one geographic location to another, then asked to manage new areas, though they may have no prior knowledge of them. In most cases people try to relate to and manage the new areas as though they were the same as the ones left behind. In parts of the country that have high rainfall this generally is not too detrimental to the area, but in a desert this can be a disaster. A desert is a very fragile system and most humans have only a superficial understanding of it. They, for the most part, look upon it as a hostile environment.

For many years a large portion of the population of Washington state all but forgot about the Columbia Basin. This in turn has led to the destruction of most of the former campgrounds and burial sites of the original inhabitants—the Columbia Salish.

Some people will ask, "What difference does it make?" I can only answer these critics by saying that these Salish Indians were able to exist for thousands of years in this desert environment and we in our infinite wisdom learned very little from them. With the passing of most elements of their culture, mankind lost something that can never be replaced.

Hopefully, new land managers who come to the Columbia Basin and read this manuscript will gain an insight into just what their responsibilities are. They should also understand that if they are going to encourage development along or near these old trails, the chances are great that they will uncover relics of times past. It is their obligation to protect these objects for future generations.

To sum up, I believe Richard J. Myshak, a former Regional Director of the U.S. Fish and Wildlife Service in Portland, Oregon, said it well:

> I must strive to touch the land gently and care for it as a steward so that those who follow may see that my mark on the land was one of love and respect, not cruelty or disdain.

This book, *Forgotten Trails*, owes its existence to the economic conditions of the late 1970s and early 1980s, which delayed transfers and promotions within the U.S. Fish and Wildlife Service, giving me time to complete the gathering of material for the manuscript. The book also owes its existence to the encouragement and assistance of a large number of people from the local community, colleges and universities, historical societies, and state, federal, and private agencies.

First, I would like to express my thanks to former Washington State Senator Nat Washington. He was always there to give me a word of encouragement when I became bogged down on this project.

Secondly, I am grateful to the people of the community of Othello, Washington, who have always been supportive of my work: to Maxine Taylor, who read the first very rough draft; to Bev McDonald and Bev Boley of the city library for locating materials and loaning me books for months at a time; to Mrs. Joel Cramer for typing the first readable draft of the manuscript; and to Gladys Para, a local historian, who shared with me her files and knowledge of the Columbia Basin and the Othello area.

I would also like to thank Dr. Robert H. Ruby of Moses Lake, Washington, who was most helpful in explaining how to put a manuscript of this size together and where to send it for review.

To Janice Peterson, an archaeologist with the U.S. Fish and Wildlife Service, who gave me a place to stay when I was in Portland, Oregon, doing research.

To Mrs. Virginia Beck Michel, a daughter of professor George F. Beck, who spent untold hours searching through her father's papers looking up items for me.

To Victoria Taggart, clerk typist at the Umatilla National Wildlife Refuge, for working nights and weekends to help me bring this manuscript together.

There is no library or archive that can be successfully probed without the help and intimate knowledge of the staff at these places. My appreciation goes to: Layne Woolschlager and Elizabeth Winroth of the Oregon Historical Society, Portland, who went out of their way in assisting me; to Nancy Pryor and the staff in the Washington Room, at the Washington State Library, Olympia; to Larry Dodd at the Northwest Library at Whitman College, Walla Walla; and to Doug Olson of the Eastern Washington State Historical Society Library, Spokane.

Thanks also to all of the fine people of the Lake Chelan, Adams, Grant, Franklin, and Okanogan county historical societies, the Montana and Idaho historical societies, the Royal Ontario Museum of Canada, and the Stark Museum in Texas.

I wish to express gratitude to my wife Kathleen who put up with all my piles of research notes spread over the house for months and years at a time, and finally to Marie Baldridge, the former clerk at the Columbia National Wildlife Refuge, who was always there to encourage me to complete this study.

Ronald M. Anglin
Fallon, Nevada

Editor's Preface

Included here are travelers' tales from a time when the Big Bend country was a wild, untethered land occupied by the Sinkiuse and Wanapam tribes. Given this far frontier's remoteness during most of the nineteenth century, it is remarkable that so many astute and highly literate persons journeyed this way on the trails and riverways. In their wake, they left journals, diaries, letters, and other accounts. In this book, these frontier people—the traders from Canada, the Indians, and a host of American travelers—largely speak for themselves. *Forgotten Trails* is a fine tribute to Ron Anglin for his determined, long-term quest to collect these valuable sources.

The Big Bend's frontier era was as flamboyant and exciting as similar epics in other, more celebrated, regions of the Old West such as Montana, the Dakotas, or Colorado. Basic historical stages in the Columbia Basin (i.e., the sequence from exploration, to the fur trade, to gold rushes, to Indian resistance, to the cowboy's empire, etc.) were similar to what occurred on the western Great Plains and in the Rockies. In effect, the Big Bend story, though obviously having unique regional variations, represents a microcosm of the history of the Old West.

In addition to the many "historical" accounts presented here, *Forgotten Trails* also includes incomparable selections by "modern" authors and historians. Deserving special note in this regard are Ted Van Arsdol of Vancouver, Washington, for his outstanding coverage of gold rush travelers in the critical year of 1858 (see chapter VII), and Nat Washington, of Ephrata, Washington, for an irreplaceable firsthand account from one of the last old-time Sinkiuse Indians (see chapter III). Likewise, Stuart McIntyre, of Sacramento, California, has provided his grandfather's extremely entertaining description of the great 1906 horse roundup (see chapter XII). All three of these individuals graciously granted permission for their unique materials to be reproduced at length in *Forgotten Trails*.

Two other contemporary writers also are extensively cited and deserve particular mention: Bette E. Meyer, for her coverage of the White

Bluffs road during the late 1860s Montana gold rush (see chapter IX); and Bruce Mitchell, for describing the U.S. Army's establishment and abandonment of Camp Chelan in 1879-80 (see chapter X). Special thanks also are due to art collector Curt Campbell of Spokane for use of a fine painting depicting Sinkiuse warriors, and to Laura Arksey and Karen DeSeve, who provided valuable assistance at the Research Library and Archives, Eastern Washington State Historical Society, Spokane.

In *Forgotten Trails*, the primary focus remains on firsthand historical accounts about the Big Bend's trails and travelers, beginning with the Indians and the Lewis and Clark Expedition (1805-06). Next came Canadian and American fur traders in the 1810s, and arriving in following decades were missionaries, miners, packers, herders, soldiers, rivermen, teamsters, agents, surveyors, artists, and scientists. Also significant in history, but receiving somewhat less attention in *Forgotten Trails*, are the ranchers, farmers, and town builders who permanently settled the Big Bend country in the 1890s-1910s. In this regard, space limitations prohibited full coverage; to tell the detailed story of turn-of-the-century ranching, homesteading, steamboating, railroading, and community life would entail an entire volume in itself!

Likewise, some well-known incidents in Big Bend history not directly related to the theme of trails and travelers are left out of *Forgotten Trails*, again largely due to space restrictions. Importantly, these stories already have been well told by other authors. For example, the celebrated pursuit and arrest of Chief Moses by a posse in December 1878 has been thoroughly described in two Big Bend area classics: A.J. Splawn's *Ka-Mi-Akin* (1917), and *Half-Sun on the Columbia* (1965) by Robert H. Ruby and John A. Brown.

Though *Forgotten Trails* contains excellent maps, it is recommended that readers utilize county maps or a state atlas for additional reference. The *Washington Atlas & Gazetteer* (DeLorme, 1988) is a good selection in this regard and available at retail outlets. With an atlas, routes can readily be followed in interesting detail. A good example of this would be the important Hudson's Bay Company trail north from old Fort Walla Walla to the Grand Coulee and on to Fort Okanogan. However, take note that since the late 1940s irrigation seepage from the Columbia Basin Project has created numerous lakes and ponds. Thus, new lakes appear on modern maps that did not exist in the nineteenth century. Seepage also has altered many of the natural bodies of water that were present.

Forgotten Trails is fully referenced with endnotes and a bibliography for those readers desiring to further investigate specific aspects of Big Bend history. In addition, the primary and secondary historical materials collected by Ron Anglin have been donated to the Eastern Washington State Historical Society library in Spokane and can be viewed there. The collection includes extensive excerpts from periodicals, books, and other secondary sources, as well as copies of photographs, maps, newspaper articles, and numerous primary written materials gathered from both public and private sources in the Pacific Northwest and elsewhere. A majority of this collection, but by no means all of it, has been utilized in the publication of *Forgotten Trails*.

In closing, I wish to thank Director Thomas H. Sanders and Associate Director Mary B. Read of the Washington State University Press, as well as Nat Washington of the Grant County Historical Society, for continued support of this highly involved project. It truly is due to them that this significant contribution to the historical literature of the Big Bend country is being released to the public.

Glen W. Lindeman, Editor
WSU Press
Pullman, Washington

Branding Irons

Depictions of authentic turn-of-the-century Big Bend livestock brands are presented at the start of each chapter in *Forgotten Trails*.

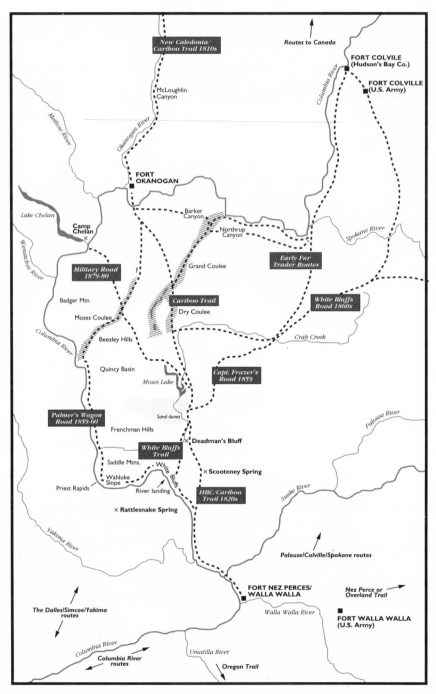

Primary historic routes in the Big Bend country, up to 1880.

I
Introduction

O N A VERY HOT, DRY, DUSTY day in August 1978, I was standing with a group of men in the ruts of the old White Bluffs road about 10 miles west of Othello. One of the men present said that he had been told that a 60-foot-long steamboat was hauled by horses over this road a hundred years before. Turning slowly from left to right, I beheld before me the dry, sagebrush covered scablands of eastern Washington. Through the mirage I could just see the Saddle Mountains. The old White Bluffs ferry landing was located 10 miles further south on the Columbia River, where this road originated.

I had to wonder after hearing that statement why anyone in his right mind would have ever attempted something as insane as hauling a boat through this country. As it turned out, this was only the first of many stories I was to hear concerning this old road from White Bluffs, and about another old route in the locality, called the Cariboo trail. Among the many things I learned later, U.S. Army troops in 1879 had cut the steamboat *Chelan* in half, and hauled it and the machinery and boiler by wagon teams north to Lake Chelan.

Most people living in what is now the western portion of the Columbia Basin, or more rightly termed the Big Bend country, owe their livelihood to the U.S. Bureau of Reclamation's Columbia Basin Project, and I am no exception. I moved to the Othello area in January 1978 to assume the duties of Assistant Manager of the U.S. Fish and Wildlife Service, Columbia National Wildlife Refuge (CNWR). In the last several decades, the Columbia Basin Project has so completely altered the landscape of the Columbia River valley and the western portion of the basin for the benefit of man that a person familiar with this country prior to the beginning of the project would not recognize it today, except for its major topographical features. Likewise, a person familiar only with the area today cannot visualize what it must have looked like in the past except for those same features. Much of this region has been changed from a land once dominated by bunchgrass and sagebrush, i.e., a shrub steppe (meaning a grassland without trees), to a landscape that now looks more like a Midwestern farming area than a desert.

As all persons have a habit of doing, I thought the history of the Big Bend country began when I moved into the area. It was hard for me to believe that anyone would have been here before the development of irrigation. But, as I was to learn, such was not the case. The state of Washington is unique in that it was settled from west to east, whereas most of the United States was settled from east to west. No major immigrant wagon route from Missouri and the Midwest, such as the Oregon Trail, passed directly through here. The Big Bend country was an obstacle to early travelers from the settlements west of the Cascades, who were traveling north into the Canadian interior or east into what later became the states of Idaho and Montana.

The routes used by these early travelers had been laid out by Indian inhabitants 10,000 to 12,000 years earlier. Archaeologists are only now beginning to understand who these earliest people were. What we do know is that their trails had to be direct. Their campsites or waterholes were located 5 to 10 miles apart within easy walking distance, because all travel was by foot. Horses did not appear in the basin until the early 1700s.

At the time of the first contact with whites, the Big Bend country was primarily the home of the Columbia Salish, otherwise known as the Sinkiuse, while another group, the Wanapam, resided on the mid Columbia. They were a hunting/gathering people who acquired their annual subsistence during a seasonal round of food gathering activities. The Sinkiuse territory extended from the north slope of the Saddle Mountains northward to the borderlands of the Wenatchee and Okanogan tribes. The boundary to the west was the Columbia River, and, to the east, a vaguely understood line between Othello and Washtucna. The south slope of the Saddle Mountains, or Wahluke slope as it is known today, was part of the homeland of the more sedentary, river-oriented Wanapam Indians.

Even after the Sinkiuse acquired horses, they still followed their ancestral footpaths across the Big Bend. They seem to have made little use of the travois, but instead preferred to pack all of their possessions on horseback, which seems odd considering that they incorporated so many other elements of the Plains Indians' life-style (e.g., the tipi, mode of warfare, etc.). However, when one takes into account the rugged terrain they had to travel over, it is easy to see why. Up until the turn of the century, it was not unusual to find lodge poles still standing at old abandoned camp sites along these trails; in fact, Indians were still using these trails well into the 1920s, or so it has been reported.

It was not until the spring and summer of 1980 that I read my first article concerning the Cariboo and White Bluffs routes. At the time, I was working on a management plan for the proposed Eagle Lakes National Wildlife Refuge in Franklin County. This area was never acquired for a refuge, but, during the course of this project, I learned that Eagle Lake originally had been called Scooteney Spring. I went on to find several other spellings for the spring—Scooten, Skootenai, and Skookum—but I was never able to learn the derivation of the name.

In the course of my research, I found out that this spring was located about two days' journey on a trail from the Hudson's Bay Company's Fort Nez Perces, also known as Fort Walla Walla, located at the junction of the Walla Walla and Columbia rivers. (Lake Wallula behind McNary Dam has inundated the original site of the fort.) The trail followed along the river northward from Fort Nez Perces, and then across the Big Bend country. I learned that at different times this route was known by such names as the Hudson's Bay Company trail, the Hudson's Bay express route to Fort Okanogan and Fort Colvile, the Walla Walla-Okanogan trail, the Okanogan trail, the Similkameen trail, and, its most common name, the Cariboo trail.

One thing led to another and I found that three other men had tried to work out and write down the history of these routes. The first was William Compton Brown, a turn-of-the-century Okanogan judge. Brown interviewed descendents of the men who had been employed at the Hudson's Bay Company's Fort Okanogan in the later years of its operation. He published his findings in an article titled "Old Fort Okanogan and the Okanogan Trail" in the March 1914 issue of the *Quarterly of the Oregon Historical Society*.

The second individual was Theo (Theophilus) H. Scheffer. Scheffer had joined the U.S. Office of Biological Survey, the forerunner of the U.S. Fish and Wildlife Service, in 1910 and retired in 1937. After his retirement, he became very much interested in the early history of the Grand Coulee area before it was affected by the formation of the Columbia Basin Project's Banks Lake. During the late 1940s and early 1950s, Scheffer wrote up his findings in Sunday supplement articles in the Spokane *Spokesman-Review*. It was my good fortune to find copies of these articles along with some letters he wrote to historical societies.

Scheffer focused mainly on the section of the Cariboo trail extending south from Fort Okanogan across the Big Bend to about Moses Lake;

whereas Judge Brown's interest in the route was mainly north from Fort Okanogan into Canada. Upon examining their work along with historic maps of eastern Washington dating from the 1850s to the 1880s, it did not take me long with my understanding of the basin's topography to determine the only direction the Cariboo trail could have taken from Fort Walla Walla. It was then that I discovered that the Cariboo trail and the White Bluffs road came together in a locality on the Columbia NWR called Marsh Unit 1. When I found this out, I was hooked.

The third individual was George F. Beck. Beck was a professor of geology at Central Washington State College (now Central Washington University) in Ellensburg, but his second love was the history of the Big Bend country. Around 1980, I read an article by Beck from the 1949 Ritzville *Journal-Times* titled "The Four Old Wagon Trails," which dealt with the history of the White Bluffs road (see appendix). Raised at Marlin, Washington, Beck was very familiar with the White Bluffs road north of Moses Lake. His article was probably one of the most complete short histories of the route published up to that time.

Continuing my research, before I knew it I had accumulated piles of information dealing with these routes. Some of this material was new, but a lot of it was not. What I tried to do in gathering material for this manuscript was to explain what I have learned about the history of these routes, to clear up some of the misinformation that has come down to us over the years, and, finally, to provide a firm base on which future historians can build. Only you as the reader can tell if *Forgotten Trails* has successfully completed this task.

The sternwheeler *Mountain Gem* docked on the Columbia's west shore opposite to the White Bluffs, 1902. Two years later, the *Mountain Gem* ventured into the Hells Canyon area on the upper Snake River to supply a booming copper mining camp. By autumn 1905, the steamer again returned to work the Columbia and lower Snake waterways. *Click Relander*

II
The Big Bend Country

THE COLUMBIA BASIN'S Big Bend country includes all of Douglas and Grant counties and most of Lincoln, Adams, and Franklin counties of eastern Washington, an area of more than 9,000 square miles. It derives its name from "the Big Bend" of the Columbia River, which bounds the area on the northwest, west, and southwest. The Big Bend is further bordered by the Spokane River watershed to the northeast, by the Palouse River system on the east, and by the lower Snake River drainage to the southeast. The average elevation of this region is approximately 1,100 feet above sea level.

Plateaus, broad basins, and low foothills predominate in the Big Bend. Although its general features are those of a tableland sloping gently southwest, there is much diversity in its surface details, largely caused by the effects of ancient glacial outwashing on the structurally variable basalt.

The eastern two-fifths of the Big Bend—the eastern uplands—consist of rolling hills sloping generally to the west. The plateaus along the western border of the Big Bend, on the other hand, stand at several levels and are interrupted by the Frenchman Hills and the Saddle Mountains. The northern edge of the Big Bend includes the southern fringe of a hilly mass of highlands intersected by north-south floodwater drainageways cut through structural divides. The westernmost segment of these highlands consists of the Waterville Plateau and the Beezley Hills. Much of the northern portion of the Big Bend is composed of outwash material from the Lower Grand Coulee, known as the Coulee fan. A small enclosed plain, the Quincy Basin, extends south 20 to 30 miles from the Beezley Hills to the Frenchman Hills.

The Quincy Basin slopes generally to the south and east, so that drainage flows toward the eastern end of the Frenchman Hills where the Quincy Basin abuts the western slope of the eastern upland. There, drainage collects to form Moses Lake. The Frenchman Hills have a steep north face,

The Big Bend drainage in the state of Washington.

but a long and somewhat irregular southern face, called Royal Slope. Natural drainage skirts around the east end of the Frenchman Hills and flows generally west via lower Crab Creek to the Columbia River, a distance of about 35 miles.

To the south of the Lower Crab Creek drainage rise the Saddle Mountains, similar to the Frenchman Hills in character. This ridge's southern incline, called the Wahluke Slope ("soaring up like birds"), slants to the Columbia River, which flows easterly in the lower portion of the Columbia Basin. The Wanapam Indian term for this slope was Wanuke ("going on foot up hill"). At the eastern end of the Saddle Mountains, a ridge curves to the south, declining in elevation to form a somewhat irregular bench sloping to the Columbia and Snake rivers. The principal drainage through this latter area is Esquatzel Coulee, which fans out over a gravel outwash north of Pasco and on down to the Columbia at its confluence with the Snake.

The Columbia Basin Project, located within the Big Bend country, is a multiple purpose Bureau of Reclamation development providing irrigation, power generation, flood control, navigation, recreation, and fish and wildlife benefits. The major feature of the project is Grand Coulee Dam, situated at the head of the Upper Grand Coulee on the Columbia (river mile 596.6, about 95 miles west of Spokane). Located in Grant, Adams, and Franklin counties, the entire project area, including the East High locality, contains about 2,400,000 acres, of which 1,097,000 acres are considered irrigable. To date, about 560,000 acres have received water. It is unlikely, however, that this will be greatly increased in the foreseeable future. If ultimately completed, the water distribution system will have about 600 miles of major canals, 4,200 miles of laterals, and 3,600 miles of wasteways and drains.

About 20 million years ago, the landscape of the Columbia Basin consisted of mountains, valleys, streams, and lakes. During the warm, moist early Miocene epoch, redwood or Sequoia (now found only in California) extended as far north as southern British Columbia. Apparently, the Sequoia-dominated forest communities, growing on hillsides, mountains, and in well drained lowlands, were characterized by three floral elements:

1. A western element, which is still found in modern redwood forests, consisting of alder, pepperwood, tan oak, dogwood, hazel, maple, and Oregon grape, together with border forests of ash, live oak, madrone, hackberry, cherry, sycamore, rose, and willow. It seems probable that another important component of the basin's ancient forest was Metasequoia, a redwood tree now restricted to the mountains of China.

2. A portion of an eastern element (which is absent from modern western forests) was composed in part of elm, chestnut, hickory, magnolia, hornbean, basswood, persimmon, and redbud. These species occurred on slopes in mixtures with the western components of the vegetation. Other species (which are found in present-day eastern temperate forests) grew near ponds and swamps and along streams, and included cypress, red gum, black gum, cottonwood, willow, and alder. On the highest and driest terrain, several kinds of oak probably dominated.

3. The third element consisted of such species as maidenhair tree (Ginkgo) and Tree of Heaven; trees that are now endemic only to Asia although they have been widely reintroduced in North America as ornamentals.

Due to the extensive basaltic flows that later covered this region, fossil remains of Miocene animals are extremely rare and thus difficult to find. Ground sloths, rhinoceros, and precursors of Pleistocene horses, camels, carnivora, deer, bear, and other mammals probably lived here during this epoch.

Grand Coulee Dam stands on solid granite—the oldest rock in the Big Bend region—which forms the hills east and north of the dam. This rock was squeezed up into the earth's crust from deep below about 60 million years ago; at that time, it was white-hot liquid or molten rock. It did not rise all the way to the surface, but came to rest a few thousand feet down, cooling and solidifying into its present form. During the next 30 million years, the granite was exposed by erosion of the overlying rock and by movement in the earth's crust.

Most travelers passing through the basin today have noticed scenic, geological features that are unique to this region. These are the channelled scablands, an intricate series of deep troughs cut in the Columbia River basalt. During late Miocene and early Pliocene times, tremendous volumes of basaltic lava—the Columbia River basalt group—were extruded across the Columbia plateau region. These molten lava flows covered thousands of square miles. Some of the flows are believed to have traveled over 200 miles from their source vents.

These vents were in fact huge cracks, many miles deep in the earth's crust, and the molten lava flowed out and over the land much like a hot brown syrup. After inundating many miles of the terrain, outpourings stopped, and the lava cooled into nearly flat basalt deposits. This was repeated again and again over a great period of time. In the Big Bend, the basalt's depth is unknown except in a couple of places, but the maximum thicknesses normally are probably about 5,000 feet. In the Grand Coulee Dam area, where both the granite and basalt are exposed, it has been determined that the basalt is more than 1,000 feet thick near Coulee City. But, incredibly, in the Saddle Mountains, natural gas well diggers have drilled down through more than 16,000 feet of basalt.

Molten lava occupies a greater volume than solidified lava, thus, as the fresh lava slowly cooled and crystallized, a hexagonal pattern of shrinkage joints commonly developed at right angles to the cooling surface. These joints break up the lava features and are called "columnar jointing," and can frequently be seen in basalt outcroppings in the area. Where basalt encroached upon ponds or lakes, however, the quickly-quenched lava formed rounded blobs called "pillows" instead of columnar joints. In a portion of the western Big Bend, lava engulfed swampy forested terrain, but, because of the water, the molten rock formed pillows and did not completely consume the vegetation. In 1934, professor George F. Beck recognized one of these old swamps, and this area is now set aside as Ginkgo Petrified Forest State Park, at Vantage.

Lava outpouring continued for millions of years (between 16 and 6 million years ago). Meanwhile, a new mountain range—the Cascades—began experiencing erosion, while the eastern part of the state sagged under sediments and the weight of the basalt flows. Sedimentary deposits were laid down atop basalt surfaces, and then were covered by subsequent lava flows.

The uplift which created the Cascade Range began in the late Pliocene and continued into the early Pleistocene. The Big Bend became increasingly arid after the late Pliocene because the rising Cascades formed an effective barrier to the eastward movement of moisture-laden air masses from the Pacific Ocean. As this rain shadow effect increased, all of the streams except the ancestral Columbia and Snake rivers diminished in flow or finally disappeared.

During this time there were several periods of glaciation along the northern rim of the basin. Intermingled with the glacial activity, large deposits of fine, windblown dust called "loess" thickly mantled the basaltic floor of the basin. The massive, structureless silt deposits are believed to be derived largely from older eroded material. This material is now believed to have been laid down in an extensive Miocene lake along with volcanic ash from eruptions in the Cascade Range. Loess deposits are clearly evident in the Ringold formation at White Bluffs on the Columbia River. It was also during this period that the flat lying basalt flows were folded into hills, valleys, and broad, shallow basins—e.g., the Frenchman Hills, Quincy Basin, and the Saddle Mountains.

In the latter part of this age, huge glaciers formed in Canada and moved south, sending great fingers of ice down the valleys into northern Washington. One of these ice masses, the Okanogan lobe, extended southward on a wide front, blocking the Columbia River. The ice not only dammed the Columbia, but completely filled its canyon from the Okanogan River to the Grand Coulee. The glacial ice was about 2,500 feet thick over what is now the Grand Coulee Dam area. Geological evidence indicates that this glacial intrusion remained west of the Grand Coulee; and, its most southerly advance was at a point just a few miles west of Coulee City, where it extended about two miles south of present day U.S. Route 2.

Meltwater from the southern edge of the ice sheet formed lakes in the valleys that had been blocked by the tongues of ice spilling across the southwesterly sloping plain of central Washington. Rivers flowed on top of, and under, the ice sheets and out into the basin. The resulting outwash of glacial floodwaters helped form eastern Washington's extensive channelled scablands and coulees, mainly in three great drainages. These include:

1. The Cheney/Palouse drainage, extending southwesterly from Spokane to the Snake River.

2. The Crab Creek drainage, which heads in the Reardan vicinity and continues southwest into the Quincy Basin.

3. The Grand Coulee drainage, starting at Grand Coulee on the Columbia River and entering the Quincy Basin at Soap Lake. This also includes Moses Coulee, heading in central Douglas County and extending southwesterly to the Columbia River.

These drainages later became the routes for trail systems across the basin—e.g., the Cheney/Palouse corridor contained the Spokane-Walla Walla trails, and Crab Creek and the Grand Coulee were used for the Wallula-Okanogan routes.

The existence of these unique coulees, scablands, and their associated sand and gravel deposits are due primarily to the passage of several catastrophic ice-age floods, which were released from the watershed of the Clark Fork River in Montana, where "Glacial Lake Missoula" had formed. The Pend Oreille lobe of the ice sheet had blocked the Clark Fork at the mouth of Cabinet Gorge (east side of what is now Lake Pend Oreille, in far northern Idaho), damming the river. Consequently, the impounded water filled tributary valleys for many miles into Montana. Holding an estimated 500 cubic miles of water (half the volume of present-day Lake Michigan), the lake's surface eventually stood at 4,150 feet above sea level, giving it a depth of 2,000 feet at the ice dam.

Whenever the ice dam collapsed, hundreds of cubic miles of water immediately were released across northern Idaho to scour out Washington's scablands. The dam's collapse appears to have occurred in part because of warm climatic cycles, lasting for centuries or millennia, which weakened the dam, causing its cataclysmic bursting. A readvance of ice would again close the gap, creating another Lake Missoula. It is believed that there were at least seven major floods down the Pend Oreille-Spokane valley, five of which spilled across the Columbia Plateau. Two of them occurred when no ice dam stood at the mouth of the Okanogan River and therefore affected only the Columbia River valley. (More recent investigation, however, suggests that there may have been other floods—perhaps 40 or more altogether.) Floods appear to have occurred as recently as 15,000 to 12,800 years ago.

When the huge lake's 500 cubic miles of water was released, it had only one place to go: southwestward across Rathdrum Prairie and down the Spokane valley, which by this time was probably ice free. As the lake basin drained in Montana, the water had to pass through the narrow parts of the Clark Fork canyon, where current velocities are calculated to have

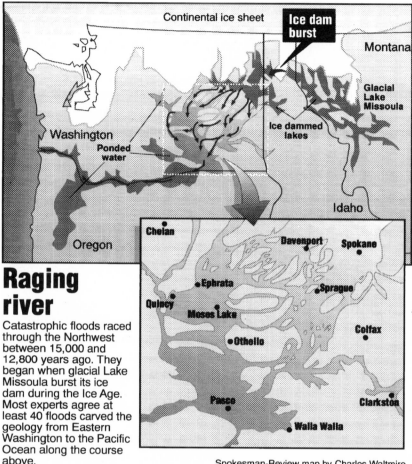

Continental ice sheet

Ice dam burst

Montana

Glacial Lake Missoula

Washington

Ice dammed lakes

Ponded water

Idaho

Chelan

Davenport   Spokane

Ephrata   Sprague

Quincy

Moses Lake

Colfax

Othello

Oregon

Pasco   Clarkston

Walla Walla

Raging river

Catastrophic floods raced through the Northwest between 15,000 and 12,800 years ago. They began when glacial Lake Missoula burst its ice dam during the Ice Age. Most experts agree at least 40 floods carved the geology from Eastern Washington to the Pacific Ocean along the course above.

Spokesman-Review map by Charles Waltmire

reached 45 or more miles per hour. The maximum rate of flow is estimated to have been 9.5 cubic miles per hour (a rate of 386 million cubic feet per second), or about 10 times the combined flow of all the rivers in the world today. For comparison, the rate of flow of the world's largest river, the Amazon, is 6 million cubic feet per second, and today the Columbia averages about 255 thousand cubic feet per second.

As noted earlier, the Columbia Basin's great lava field is shaped somewhat like a giant saucer, tilted to the southwest. When the floodwater reached the basin and started down this sloping surface, the enormous volume, velocity, and turbulence of the water provided great erosional energy, sweeping away the soil and exposing the jointed basalt underneath. The current was so turbulent and so powerful that it was able to pluck out and transport great blocks of basalt, some measuring more than 30 feet across, while cutting deep canyons into the bedrock.

The longest and deepest of these scabland canyons is the Grand Coulee. The coulee begins at the Columbia River at the north end of Grant County, where its head is a notch, cut in the gorge's wall 650 feet above the river. The coulee extends southwest for a distance of about 50 miles, ending at Soap Lake.

In carving out the Grand Coulee and its smaller associated coulees—Dry, Long Lake, Lenore, and a number of lesser coulees—the great floods eroded away many cubic miles of rock. Some of this material in the form of sand, gravel, and boulders was deposited below the mouth of the Grand Coulee in the Quincy Basin. However, a substantial volume was washed southward down the Columbia and out of the area.

Grand Coulee actually is two canyons, separated by low, but nevertheless coulee-dominated, terrain at its mid-point. The upper coulee is altogether about 25 miles long with essentially continuous canyon walls, approximately 800 to 900 feet high. At its head, the upper coulee is 3 miles wide gradually widening to nearly 5 miles at Steamboat Rock, and then narrowing to about 1 1/2 miles as it opens out on the Hartline Basin. The floor is now largely covered by the Equalizing Reservoir (Banks Lake) of the Bureau of Reclamation's Columbia Basin Project. Banks Lake is retained by earth and rock fill Dry Falls Dam at Coulee City. Three miles below Coulee City, at the coulee's mid-length, the bottom of the canyon drops over 400 feet at 3-mile-wide Dry Falls, marking the place where the Columbia River once poured in a mighty cataract.

Below this point is the Lower Grand Coulee. The eastern wall of the Lower Grand Coulee continues on at about the same level as the brink of Dry Falls, but the western wall, a monocline, rises in places to over 1,000 feet high and can be seen from many miles to the eastward as a black, broad escarpment. The lower coulee's floor contains beautiful, rock-walled lakes.

The Drumheller Channels is another enormous spillway and a spectacular tract of butte-and-basin scabland. It is an almost unbelievable labyrinth of interconnecting channels, rock basins, and small abandoned cataracts. Today, earth and rock fill O'Sullivan Dam blocks the Drumheller Channels, capturing the flow of Crab Creek and the return water from irrigation in more northerly parts of the Columbia Basin Project. The reclaimed water in Potholes Reservoir is reused for irrigation. Only one channel in the plexus, the route now followed by Lower Crab Creek, has a continuous gradient across this 50 square mile area; its route almost surely once had open rock basins, which have since been leveled up by the creek's sand and gravel deposits in postglacial times. The average descent across this tract of country is between 30 and 50 feet per mile. And, of course, there are other grand flood channels—the Othello Channels, Moses Coulee, and the Cheney/Palouse scabland tract—in the Columbia Basin.

Some 6,700 years ago, long after the last glaciation, Mt. Mazama (Crater Lake) in central Oregon erupted and added a mantle of volcanic ash to the Big Bend country. Wind-borne soil (loess) has continued to be reworked by both wind and water erosion, and today varies from a few feet to over 100 feet in depth across the basin. Sand and gravels, deposited by glacial outwash, are widely distributed throughout the area in the form of terrace deposits and old filled-in channels.

Two large tracts of sand dunes also exist in the Big Bend. One tract, southwest of Moses Lake, blocks the Crab Creek channel and forms Moses Lake. This is why most of the early maps of eastern Washington show Moses Lake as either bigger or smaller, or it is not even shown at all, because the dunes that made the lake were constantly being formed or eroded away depending on the weather in any given year. The second great tract of sand dunes is northeast of Pasco. Lesser expanses of sand can be seen in other localities.

Since the retreat of the glaciers over 10,000 years ago, the climatic conditions in the Columbia Basin have been interpreted as falling broadly into three subsequent periods. First came the Anathermal—a post-glacial climate—cooler and moister than at present. It was followed by the Altithermal or "Thermal Maximum," a much warmer and drier period of extreme conditions. And finally came the Medithermal, or recent period, when conditions were cooler and moister, approximating the present climate. The basin's climate today is semiarid, having hot summers and moderately cold winters.

Important factors influencing the climate are the region's topography and the prevailing westerly winds from the Pacific Ocean. Maritime and continental weather patterns surge and ebb across the Columbia Basin. The northern Rockies and the ranges in southern British Columbia usually protect eastern Washington from most of the severe winter weather moving south out of central Canada. Valleys separating the north-south ranges near the Canadian border, however, sometimes do permit arctic air to penetrate the Columbia Basin. Occasionally, surges of cold air from the more severe storms will bring several days of unusually low temperatures in mid-winter, or result in damaging freezes in late spring or early fall. Strong winds accompanying storm systems coming from the Pacific in the spring or fall can cause sky-darkening, blowing dust.

The original plant communities in the basin prior to the coming of the horse in the 1700s appear to have been bluebunch wheatgrass and Sandberg bluegrass, as the principal grasses, and big sagebrush and bitter-brush, as the principal shrubs. Variable amounts of needle-and-thread, Thurber needle-grass, cusick bluegrass, or squirrel tail may have been present, but collectively their coverage never equaled that of the bluebunch wheatgrass and Sandberg bluegrass.

These are quite different from plant communities found on the Great Plains, where the predominant grasses are rhizomatous, meaning that they form a sod—a continuous dense mat of stems and roots. In the Columbia Basin, on the other hand, and, for that matter, across the whole inter-mountain West, grasses are predominantly bunchgrasses, i.e., plants that grow in groups of erect stems in tufts, or bunches.

Another feature of these grasslands is a prominent, fragile layer of mosses and lichens thriving on the ground's surface. This thin crust of slow-growing and very small organisms forms a matrix around the base of shrubs, bunchgrasses, and other plants native to the region. The mosses and lichens are quite conspicuous in most areas, but even minimal impact by large animals can destroy this living crust, providing sites for coloniza-tion by weeds or other introduced species, e.g., cheatgrass.

The vegetation of the basin, unlike that of the Great Plains, evolved largely in the absence of large hoofed herbivores. Thus, with the introduc-tion of horses in the early 1700s, and cattle, sheep, and other livestock in the 1800s, the native plant community has been seriously impacted.

References

J. Harlen Bretz, *Washington's Channeled Scablands*, State of Washington, Division of Mines and Geology, Bulletin 45, 1959.

A Brief Geological Description of the Columbia Basin Project, U.S. Department of the Interior, Water and Power Resources Service, 1980.

Helmut K. Buechner, "Some Biotic Changes in the State of Washington, Particularly during the Century 1853-1953," *Research Studies of the State College of Washington* 21 (2), June 1953, 154-92.

The Channeled Scablands of Eastern Washington, The Geologic Story of the Spokane Flood, U.S. Department of the Interior, Geological Survey, USGS-72-2 (R-1), 1976.

Climatological Summary 1942-1960, Othello, Washington, U.S. Department of Commerce, Weather Bureau, in Cooperation with the State of Washington, Department of Commerce and Economic Development.

R. Daubenmire, *Steppe Vegetation of Washington*, Washington State University, Washington Agricultural Experiment Station, Technical Bulletin 62, 1970.

Jerry R. Galm, et al., *A Cultural Resources Overview of Bonneville Power Administration's Mid-Columbia Project, Central Washington*, Eastern Washington University Reports in Archaeology and History, 100-16, Archaeological and Historical Services, Cheney, 1981.

M.J. Grolier and J.W. Bingham, *Geology of Parts of Grant, Adams, and Franklin Counties, East-Central Washington*, State of Washington, Department of Natural Resources, Division of Geology and Earth Resources Bulletin 71, 1978.

Richard N. Mack, "Invaders at Home on the Range," *Natural History* 15 (February 1984), 40-47.

Joseph G. McMacken, *The Grand Coulee of Washington and Dry Falls in Picture and Story*, 8th ed. (Spokane, 1950).

Bette E. Meyer, "Grit and Grass: A Historical Geography of Adams County, Washington," *Northwest Science* 45 (1), 1971.

Michael Parfit, "The Floods That Carved the West," *Smithsonian* 26 (April 1995): 48-59, 167.

Washington State Study Team for the Pacific Northwest River Basins Commission, *The Big Bend Basin Level B Study of the Water and Related Land Resources*, December 1976.

"Sees-Use" of the Sinkiuse (Columbia) tribe; note the dentalium, bead, and bear claw finery. Photo by Major Lee Moorhouse, circa 1900. *Historical Photographs Collections, Washington State University Libraries*

III
The Original Inhabitants

THE HISTORY OF MAN in the Big Bend country naturally begins with the people who first lived on the land. Archaeological investigations reveal that Native Americans occupied the Columbia Basin by at least 11,250 years ago. The oldest archaeological artifacts found so far in the Big Bend area (or in the entire Inland Northwest for that matter) were discovered in 1987 at the Richey-Roberts site in East Wenatchee. Here, 11,250-year-old "Clovis" points and tools were uncovered as workers dug an irrigation trench in an apple orchard.

The large, handsomely crafted points, up to nine inches long, were distinctively fluted at the base for fitting to a foreshaft. Clovis finds, which are rare across North America, have the distinction of being the oldest undisputed artifacts yet found in North America; the East Wenatchee site is among the most outstanding of these unique sites.

The name "Clovis" is derived from a famous site near Clovis, New Mexico, where, in the 1930s, ancient stone tools were first scientifically documented. Clovis points were made and utilized by peoples who are thought to have arrived from Asia via the Bering land bridge (Beringia) by at least 11,500 years ago at the end of the Pleistocene. Beringia had formed as land in the North Pacific when a vast amount of water from the earth's oceans became locked up in huge continental ice sheets covering most of Canada, northern Europe, Siberia, as well as the high mountain ranges of the world and the polar regions. Ocean levels fell worldwide, draining shallow seas to expose Beringia and other continental shelves that previously had been underwater.

After colonizing Beringia from Asia, these early immigrants (known as Paleo-Indians) apparently continued southward down a dry corridor between ice sheets in western Canada that had opened by about 12,000 years ago. They were migratory hunters, entering a landscape occupied by ice age elephants, giant ground sloths, an antique breed of long-horned bison, caribou, horses, camels, and other large mammals that roamed the

New World. These Paleo-Indians spread rapidly, occupying North America within several hundred years; Clovis sites in the western United States date between 11,000 and 11,500 years ago, and a few centuries later in the eastern United States.

As the ice age ended, releasing water back into the oceans, Beringia again receded beneath the waves, shutting off human immigration by land from Asia into America. By then, the first Paleo-Indians had colonized the New World, utilizing their distinctive and beautiful stone tool technology, which never was surpassed or duplicated by any of the cultures that later succeeded these early colonists. A striking aspect of the Clovis stone technology is that it was universally utilized by all occupants of the continent for several hundred years.

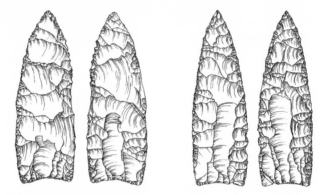

The East Wenatchee Clovis points date from 11,250 years ago. Illustrations by Sarah Moore, from *Cornucopia* [Washington State University] (Fall 1988): 16.

In time, many of the ice-age mammals disappeared—horses, camels, mammoths, etc.—due to rapidly changing environments or over-hunting, or a combination of causes, as the climate became more similar to what we are accustomed to today. Eventually, the Clovis technology of the early Paleo-Indians disappeared, as diversified new hunter and gatherer cultures evolved in response to the varied local environments that characterized the post ice-age period.

Stone is one of nature's most durable materials, and the magnificent tools made by the continent's early occupants are scattered today in a thin veneer across North America, and rarely found. They remain from ancient camps, caches, burials, hunting and ceremonial sites, or are simply laying on the surface of the ground. All too often, these rare finds are retrieved by farmers, construction workers, artifact hunters, and other persons without training in archaeology, and, consequently, essential scientific information about the sites is irretrievably lost. Despite widespread acknowledgment of their critical importance, relatively little is known about the first Paleo-Indians.

Isolated finds (in ones, twos, etc.) of Clovis points and artifacts have occurred at a couple of dozen locations across the continent, but there have been only five documented discoveries of large "caches." East Wenatchee's Richey-Roberts site has the distinction of being one of these latter rare finds. Approximately 35 Clovis stone and bone tools were recovered there in 1987-88 by Washington State University archaeologists and other Paleo-Indian experts from across the United States, resulting in the excavation of the only Clovis cache that has been studied in place (*in situ*) by professional archaeologists.[1] It is the only Clovis cache that has been removed from the ground under rigorous scientific scrutiny, where radiocarbon dates and a solid regional stratigraphic picture have been obtained. The cache lay in association with well-dated volcanic ash that spewed from Glacier Peak in the Cascade Range 11,250 years ago. Additional excavations have followed at the Richey-Roberts site.

There are, of course, other key archaeological sites in the region revealing the presence of early Native Americans. During the 1960s, for instance, WSU archaeologists uncovered the oldest, well-documented "human" remains ever discovered in the Pacific Northwest. The Marmes rockshelter site, situated in Franklin County near the confluence of the Palouse and Snake rivers, is at least 10,000 years old. The excavation's long record of human occupation and burials interspersed in an unusually clear stratigraphic sequence has been of particular value to archaeologists.

Most of the human burials found at the Marmes site had been ceremonially interred by their relatives, but there were exceptions. Nearly 7,000 years ago, two adult bodies had remained unburied where they lay, until covered by volcanic ash from the massive eruption of Mt. Mazama (a cataclysm occurring 6,700 years ago forming Oregon's Crater Lake caldera, located hundreds of miles to the southwest). Numerous shell beads made from the gastropod Olivella were found scattered throughout the upper portion of the stratum beneath the two unburied adults. These shells obviously came from the Pacific Coast, indicating the existence of trade routes with coastal inhabitants as far back as before the Mt. Mazama cataclysm. Further archaeological evidence revealed that these contacts continued through later time periods without serious interruption.

Beginning in the 1960s, another important Big Bend archaeological dig was conducted in Lind Coulee, near Warden. At this 8,000-year-old site, WSU archaeologists revealed remains of a type of ice-age elk weighing 700 pounds, as well as an extinct form of bison (Bison Antiques), which was considerably larger than modern bison. Lind Coulee may have been a summer campsite for an extended group of perhaps four or five families, or about a score of individuals. Unlike the Marmes site, Lind Coulee did not contain human burials.

When the ice-age climate began warming approximately 10,000 or so years ago, ancient bison, wooly mammoths, horses, and other large Pleistocene mammals became extinct. As the ice front receded, more modern animal forms, especially of bison and antelope, entered the region. This newer fauna, however, seems not to have spread much beyond the warmer and drier parts of the Columbia Basin, and appears to have dwindled steadily after the onset of the Altithermal (or "Thermal Maximum")—a period of much dryer and warmer climatic conditions occurring between about 8,000 and 4,000 years ago.

Thus, the niche for grazing ungulates seems to have been fairly well occupied in late glacial times, but then progressively became abandoned. Eventually, Indians came to depend increasingly on root and berry gathering and fishing, and their villages were for the most part concentrated along streams where salmon could be readily obtained in season.

Bison became extinct in the Columbia Basin about 2,000 years ago. However, there were reports in the early 1800s of individual or small numbers of bison moving into the Grand Coulee area, but they were quickly killed or died off. These wandering Plains animals probably worked their way westward from Montana via the Clark Fork valley. By the time the first white men came into the area, antelope were relatively few and confined to the driest parts of the steppe. Deer remained common in the forest border regions, the sagebrush country, and the riparian thickets, while bighorn sheep occupied the cliffs and talus slopes of the coulees and the Columbia River valley. Elk also frequented the sagebrush coulees and the foothills of the Cascades.

Originally, the Indian cultures in the region apparently were quite similar. The early inhabitants probably lived in small bands of several extended families, and decorated their bodies and clothing with paints, dyes, pieces of fur, and beads and other ornaments. As time passed, however, changes accrued. Initially, a prominent weapon was the atlatl, a spear-like throwing device, but later the bow and arrow was adopted. Climates changed, lake and stream waters decreased or dried up, food supplies altered or disappeared, and groups adapted or remained isolated. New migrations came causing cultural stimulation or alteration, and contact with nearby peoples further enhanced change. At the time of white contact, the tribes occupying the Big Bend country were part of the distinctive Plateau cultural area.

The Plateau Culture

Tribes with a Plateau cultural affinity thrived in the environment between the Cascade Range and the Rocky Mountains, an area including eastern Washington, southeast British Columbia, northern Idaho, western Montana, and northeast Oregon. Early in the twentieth century, archaeologists considered the Indian cultures of the Columbia Basin to be merely part of a transitory zone between the distinct and elaborate Northwest Coast peoples to the west and the Plains cultural area to the east. Ongoing research and scholarship, however, soon indicated that the Plateau Indians' cultural traditions and environmental adaptations were distinct for the region.

Following World War II, with new data derived from archaeological excavations along the Columbia and Snake rivers, regional archaeologists presented various chronological syntheses to explain the origin and development of Plateau culture since Paleo-Indian times and up to the early historic period. Plateau culture, as it existed at the time of white contact, is extensively documented and understood today, and descendants of these tribes continue to reside in relatively large numbers in the region. Archaeologists, of course, continue to excavate sites and conduct other scholarly research and investigations, and the possibility of exciting, new discoveries remains entirely possible for the Big Bend area in the future.[2]

More specifically, the tribes directly occupying the Big Bend—the Wanapam and the Sinkiuse (Columbia)—are designated as having been part of the "Southern Plateau" cultural area. Other Southern Plateau tribes with homelands bordering on the Big Bend country included the Cayuse, Walla Walla, Yakima, Wenatchee, Chelan, Methow, Southern Okanogan (Sinkaietk), Nespelem, Sanpoil, Lower Spokane, and Palouse (Palus). Additional neighboring groups visited the area from time to time for subsistence gathering and for social and trading purposes; these included the Wishram, Klickitat, Nez Perce, Colville, and the Middle and Upper Spokane.[3] Among the traditional peoples of eastern Washington, languages

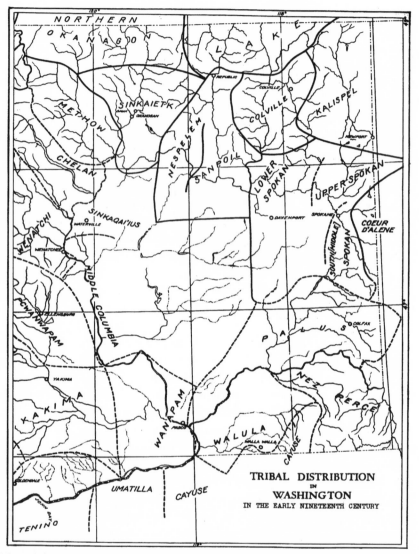

The southwestern Big Bend country was the homeland of the river-focused Wanapam, whereas the horse-oriented Columbia or Sinkiuse (here spelled Sinkaqai'ius) occupied the central and northern Big Bend. The Sinkiuse shared abundant, springtime root grounds with neighboring tribes. Adapted from Leslie Spier, *Tribal Distribution in Washington* (1936).

and dialects from two main linguistic stocks were spoken: Sahaptin in the south, and Salish to the north.

In the wintertime, Plateau bands normally resided in semipermanent villages along the banks of major streams at lower, more temperate elevations. When springtime came, portions of the population, especially women, moved to the uplands, where they often established temporary camps, while gathering roots and other vegetal foods that became seasonally available. Meanwhile, other people remained on the rivers at winter village sites or in special fishing camps, utilizing scaffolds, weirs, baskets, nets, and spears to catch large quantities of migratory salmon. The enormous yearly spring and late summer salmon runs up the Columbia were essential for subsistence; the failure of which could spell disaster.

In the Big Bend, vast amounts of nutritious Lomatium, bitterroot, and other roots vital to the traditional diet of the Plateau tribes were gathered. (Modern Indians from nearby reservations continue to collect these foods in the Big Bend country, but on a lesser scale, of course.) Salmon was dried and, along with stored roots, provided the main dietary staples for winter.

This pattern continued through the summer and early fall as migratory fish runs continued and various plants and roots matured in the uplands and plateaus (along with berries in the Cascade and Bitterroot ranges, the Blue Mountains, and the Okanogan highland). In the autumn, a portion of the population around the Big Bend's periphery remained in temporary hunting camps in the mountains, mainly stalking deer and elk. With the coming of snow, all of the population returned to winter village sites to wait out the cold weather and to participate in extensive wintertime ceremonial rites and celebrations.

For many centuries, large partially underground pit houses, covered over with poles, mats, sand, or dirt, and circular in shape, were common dwellings, frequently housing an extended group of relatives. However, another type of dwelling—the mat lodge—was commonly adopted prior to the arrival of white explorers. Standing above ground, much in the shape of modern A-frame structures, these long, oblong lodges were composed of wood-pole framing, and usually covered with strong, flexible tule mats.[4] Poles sometimes were attached on the outside to hold mats in place or to quickly remove them in case of fire. Mat lodges normally sheltered several families at a time. Smaller conical, tepee-like structures of the same materials also were common. All of these dwellings were functional, comfortable, and relatively easy to maintain.

Before their first contact with whites, the Plateau Indians had acquired horses, either through trade or by raiding their traditional enemies to the south—the Paiutes and Shoshone. The original source for Indian horses in North America was the Spanish-controlled settlements of the Southwest. Shoshonean tribes in the upper Snake River plain had acquired horses from that direction by about the end of the 1600s, and, in another two or three decades, the Sahaptin-speaking Nez Perce, Palouse, and Cayuse, and the Salish-speaking Sinkiuse, Spokane, and Flathead (of western Montana) had in turn acquired their own herds.[5] Horses thrived and multiplied in the valleys and on the rich bunchgrass plains. They soon became an integral part of Indian life, but generally more so in the southern part of the Plateau cultural area than to the north.

Whereas travel previously had been restricted to the limitations of humans on foot, the horse allowed Plateau tribesmen greater movement while hauling larger loads, and they traveled as far east as the Great Plains to hunt bison. Not all chose to visit the Plains, but for those who did, they subsequently acquired, to some extent, the Plains Indians' urge for glory and the chase, as well as the fighting capacity to counter the powerful, aggressive Blackfoot of Montana.

This in turn induced the adoption of the rituals, techniques, and honors associated with such activities. Frequently, Salishan and Sahaptin bands, particularly the Sinkiuse, Spokane, Coeur d'Alene, Pend Oreille, Palouse, Nez Perce, and Cayuse, joined together for protection in the annual journeys to the Plains. In the Plateau, the skin tepee became prevalent; and buffalo robes, Plains accoutrements, and horses became popular items at the trading fairs at Rocky Ford Creek in the Big Bend, Wenatchee flat, The Dalles, the mouth of the Snake River, and other intertribal gathering places, where Indians met to barter, gamble, gather roots, fish, or visit.

The historical geographer Donald W. Meinig has skillfully described the effects of the Plateau Indians' adoption of the horse in his monumental study of the region, *The Great Columbia Plain: A Historical Geography, 1805-1910* (1968):

> This new mobility improved hunting efficiency, enlarged the economic area, extended trading contacts, and intensified warfare with traditional enemies to the south and east. Expeditions to the buffalo range . . . now became annual affairs, often marked by intermittent fighting with Plains culture tribes. Increased contacts with these alien peoples brought further changes. The Indians of the Columbia took over many of the Plains "horse culture" characteristics, especially the techniques

and rituals associated with warfare. Wealth and prestige became bound up with horses and war. Access to the buffalo and increased range and efficiency of hunting enhanced economic security, and this in turn allowed larger groups to live together. Numerous autonomous fishing villages tended to amalgamate into organized bands, necessitating political and social change . . .

At the opening of historic time these changes had been under way for little more than half a century. They were still in progress and unevenly spread over the region, and the peoples of the Great Columbia Plain mirrored the full gradation of differences which had appeared. Along the southeast, the Nez Perces and Cayuse, who had obtained horses first and who occupied areas where a combination of low protected valleys and high, thickly grassed plains provided superb year-around grazing, were . . . deeply altered. Each was a linguistic unit composed of several large bands; each band owned hundreds of horses, fishing was less important, buffalo expeditions were major annual events, and trading contacts within and beyond the Plain were extended.[6]

Other eastern Washington tribes adopting large herds of horses and Plains Indian cultural traits (e.g., peace chiefs, war chiefs, etc.) included the Yakima, Klickitat, Walla Walla, Palouse, Spokane, and Coeur d'Alene. Horses likewise were utilized by the Kittitas, Wenatchee, Okanogan, and other small regional bands. Generally, however, farther north "the intensity of change decreased, the number of horses held were fewer, and the veneer of new, imported cultural characteristics became shallower."[7] Most importantly to the history of the northerly section of the Big Bend country, the Sinkiuse, the dominant tribe in the area, acquired many horses, became buffalo hunters and noted warriors, and were strongly influenced by the Plains culture.[8]

At the time of the arrival of whites, intertribal relations were relatively good among most Plateau groups; however, there was a limited amount of open conflict in some cases. For instance, mounted bands of young Sahaptins from the south (e.g., the Nez Perce) occasionally raided Salishan-speaking groups in the north, such as the Okanogan, Sanpoil, and Nespelem. Friction between the Nez Perce and the Coeur d'Alene also sometimes occurred to the east in the Palouse. From the Indian oral tradition, it appears that these conflicts between the Sahaptins and Salishans may have been more intense in the previous century.

Sometimes, Chinookan groups from the lower Columbia paddled hundreds of miles upstream to capture Plateau Indians and take them back as slaves. Among the eastern Washington tribes, however, the incidence of slavery was rare, except among those groups having close trade contacts with coastal peoples through gaps in the Cascade Range. The Cayuse, however, attacked the Klamath, Shasta, and other peoples along the Oregon-California border, capturing slaves to be traded at intertribal trading fairs, particularly at The Dalles. Sometimes, the Cayuse also raided Indian groups in Oregon's Willamette Valley.

Elsewhere, along the Plateau's southern border, the Cayuse, Nez Perce, and other Sahaptins exchanged intermittent hit-and-run raids with the Paiute, Shoshone, and Bannack of southeast Oregon and southwest Idaho. This ages-old intertribal warfare was the most serious and deep rooted in the region. In fact, the Sahaptin name for these enemies was "Tewilka," meaning "enemy to be fought."

In the culturally conservative riverine fishing villages in the west-central and northern Big Bend, strict local autonomy, rather than larger tribal groupings, was the rule, particularly among the Wanapam in the Priest Rapids area of the mid-Columbia, and among the Sanpoil and Nespelem on the northern edge of the Big Bend. Village leaders were selected mainly for their personal attributes and out of family tradition, and not because of wealth or other aggressive influences.

At the fishing places, a shaman ("medicine man") served as "salmon chief" or overseer to regulate and control the prescribed rituals, set times for fishing, and divide the catch. Some basic equality existed between men and women, which permeated elements of the culture. For example, guardian spirit quests were open to anyone; and women, as well as men, could become shamans, although men were more common in these positions. (White fur traders, in their initial explorations, named Priest Rapids for a male Wanapam shaman.) Among these remarkable people there was the recognition that some ailments (and the cures for them) were perfectly natural. This belief was unusual among most indigenous peoples, who believed all sickness was caused by malignant spirits and dark magic. Plateau shaman were not paid unless they successfully cured a sick person.

Thus, a relative egalitarianism, peacefulness, and harmony were constant social themes among the occupants of the traditional riverine villages in their stark, but intriguing localities. In fact, right up to modern times, some of the Wanapam have been able to remain largely unmolested on their lands, cordially left in peace by government officials, while retaining much of their ceremonial culture.

Elsewhere in the Southern Plateau in the late 1700s and early 1800s, horse-oriented peoples such as the Sinkiuse, Walla Walla, Yakima, Nez Perce, Spokane, Coeur d'Alene, and others of course exhibited more distinctive "tribal" tendencies, largely due to the new Plains influences. But even among these latter peoples, much of the basic core of the Plateau mythological and spiritual beliefs, their concepts of social equity, and the ancient gathering economy remained intact at the time of white contact.

Nomadic Life of the Sinkiuse

In the fall of 1956, local historian/archaeologist Nat Washington of Ephrata interviewed and went on field trips with Billy Curlew, an old-time Sinkiuse Indian from the Colville Reservation. As a youngster, Curlew had roamed freely with his people over the Big Bend country before the arrival of white ranchers and homesteaders. From notes recorded in conversations with Curlew, Nat Washington prepared a brief, but excellent, description of Indian life in the Big Bend area in pre-reservation days (prior to 1884). This unique document is presented here:

> Billy Curlew was about 94 when he made his last trip to the homeland of his people in the Grand Coulee/Columbia Basin country in 1956. Billy, whose Indian name was Kul Kuloo, was born at the big tsuka-lo-tsa digging camp at Ephrata, known to the Sinkiuse as Tuc-Ta-Hyaspum . . . He said the Indian war of 1858 had only been over a few years when he was born.
>
> The Columbia River (Umpa-quotwa) was the wintering place of the Sinkiuse and the site of their permanent villages. One large winter village was located below the mouth of Moses Coulee, and another just a few miles south of Vantage. In Billy's time the Vantage camp was the largest and it occupied both sides of the river.
>
> There were sound reasons for wintering on the river. Driftwood furnished the best source of firewood in the entire area, and the deep canyon afforded the best protection from the winter winds. Driftwood also furnished the large poles necessary for their longhouses which were covered with woven tule mats. Some of the houses were 40 feet long and would accommodate three or four families.
>
> In addition to the large camps mentioned, the Sinkiuse had smaller winter camps on almost every flat river bar on both sides of the river from Wenatchee south to Beverly.
>
> During the late fall, winter and early spring, most of the travel was up and down the river between the various winter villages. For this travel the dugout canoe was the favorite transportation. The Sinkiuse were excellent boatmen and many of them were expert crafts-men in the difficult art of canoe making . . . the Indians usually crossed [rivers] in a canoe, leading their swimming horses. If no canoe was available the Indian would cross by holding on to his swimming horse.

In the spring the migration would start. Horses would be rounded up from the winter range. Tepees, and all the family equipment would be loaded . . . and everyone but the very old would head for the main camp at Ephrata (Tuc-Ta-Hyaspum) in the center of the tsuka-lo-tsa country . . .

There are many roots . . . but the [root] . . . called tsuka-lo-tsa by the Sinkiuse was by far the most plentiful. The tsuka-lo-tsa root [Lomatium Canbyi], next to Salmon, was the largest source of food . . . [The Sinkiuse] gathered other roots, but none were as important as the tsuka-lo-tsa.

The tsuka-lo-tsa grew in most parts of central Washington, but its greatest concentration was on the hills running north from Quincy to about Coulee City, and extending into the coulees and flat lands to the east as far as Moses Lake and Wilson Creek.

The tsuka-lo-tsa matured earliest on the southern and eastern slopes of the Beezley hills so the first main camp of the many tribes who traveled to the tsuka-lo-tsa ground was near the area's best water supply. This was along the small stream that came down the canyon west of Ephrata and meandered across the flat on which the city is now built.

Although the tsuka-lo-tsa grounds were in Sinkiuse country, . . . the Sinkiuse allowed many friendly neighboring tribes to come and dig and carry on a big inter-tribal [gathering] . . . While the women were busy digging and cooking roots, the men spent their time playing stick games and racing and trading horses.

The tribes which gathered at Tuc-Ta-Hyaspum were Sinkiuse, Yakima, Kittitas, Wenatchee, Okanogan, Methow, Palus, Wanapam [Sanpoil, Nespelem], and western Nez Perce. Each tribe camped in its own area, but members of the various tribes intermingled freely. The big inter-tribal camp would consist of hundreds of tepees. Most of them would be on the flat, but many were pitched on both sides of the creek in the canyon.

In those days there were many trees in the canyon and there was a large grove on the flat where the stream meandered.

After most of the tsuka-lo-tsa near the main camp was gathered, the women would leave the main camp and establish satellite camps within a radius of 10 miles wherever there were small springs where the tsuka-lo-tsa could be steamed in cooking pits. In addition to the large main camp at Tuc-Ta-Hyaspum, there were several smaller camps near Soap Lake.

After the tsuka-lo-tsa roots had been gathered and cooked and dried, the Indians moved their main camp four or five miles to Rocky Ford on Rocky Ford Creek to a spot near where the ranch house of the Tom Drumheller ranch is now located [in 1957]. This was formerly the ranch house of Lord Blythe, an early day stockman. This camp was known far and wide among Indians of the Northwest as Entapas-Noot. Next to the Dalles it was the most important inter-tribal trading place in the Northwest.

The Sinkiuse and the other tribes came to trade the dried tsuka-lo-tsa for the things they needed. Indians from the Rocky Mountains (the Flathead, Crow, Snake), and Indians from the Plains (the Sioux), came to trade buffalo and deer hides, and dried buffalo and deer meat. There was also a brisk trade in horses and other items. The Sinkiuse and the Indians from the Columbia and Snake rivers camped on the west side of the creek and the Indians from farther east camped on the east side.

After the trading was completed at Entapas-Noot, the Sinkiuse would head for the big camp in the bitterroot country on the south slope of Badger Mountain, near the head of Rock Island Creek.

After breaking camp at Badger Mountain . . . the more adventurous . . . would head for the buffalo country in Blackfoot territory east of the Rockies. A few men and boys would head back to the lakes in the Grand Coulee to catch young ducks and geese, but the main band would take off for the salmon fisheries on the Columbia and Wenatchee rivers.

In late summer most of the Indians scattered in small camps on the east slope of the Cascades in the Wenatchee and Entiat valleys and were engaged in hunting deer or bear or picking berries. A few of the expert boat builders would spend the fall in making dugout canoes from the cedar trees near Lake Wenatchee.

When the nights started getting cold, the Sinkiuse would come down out of the mountains and make for the winter villages along the Columbia, and thus complete their yearly migration cycle.[9]

(For further details about Billy Curlew and the Sinkiuse of the Big Bend country, see chapter XIII.)

Mesa Top Cliff Dwellers

In recent decades, the long-term efforts of amateur archaeologist Nat Washington resulted in the discovery of a significant and unexpected type of archaeological site in the coulees and channeled scablands of eastern Washington. In 1973, Washington released a report titled "Mesa Top Cliff Dwellers of Eastern Washington,"[10] presenting strong evidence that at some period (or periods) in the prehistoric past, Native Americans occupied the tops of many of the area's cliff-walled mesas.

The report's title emphasizes the conclusion that there is a reason why the mesa-top dwellers of the American Southwest and the mesa-top peoples of eastern Washington each located villages on flat-topped, cliff-walled mesas. It is generally agreed that the southwestern cliff dwellers built their dwellings on mesas to better protect themselves from marauders. Likewise, Washington believes the evidence is strong that tribal peoples in eastern Washington built many of their dwellings on mesas for the same reason.

At some of eastern Washington's mesas, the natural defenses provided by sheer, basalt walls would have provided all of the protection that was needed against raiders. A few of these highly defensible mesas are so difficult to climb, Washington concludes, that the people occupying them probably used ladders that could be pulled up in case of an attack. However, at a number of mesas, it appears that the natural rock walls alone, though formidable, were not fully unassailable and needed to be augmented at vulnerable points by the strategic placement of hand-laid rock breastworks.

Washington reported locating 55 of these utilized mesas. The majority are in the Big Bend area, but some are situated as far east as the coulees and scablands of western Whitman County. Washington reported 31 defensible mesas that bore strong evidence of having served as seasonal or semi-permanent occupation sites. Another 24 mesas were defensible, but were too small or otherwise unsuited for habitation. (Each of the 24 unhabitable mesas appears to have served purely as a defensive refuge, or natural fortification, for Native Americans residing in habitation sites on adjacent lower terrain. When danger threatened, these people sought safety by quickly climbing to the mesa tops. Thus, these mesas served prehistoric Indians in much the same manner as log blockhouses later served early white settlers on the frontier.)

Washington believes that the use of so many defensible mesas—either as protected seasonal or semi-permanent dwelling sites, or simply as refuges as needed—casts serious doubt on the widely held belief among archaeologists that eastern Washington, and the Big Bend country, was a peaceful area which rarely saw hostilities in prehistoric times. He suggests that the prevalence of dwelling sites on defensible mesa tops can be used as a reliable guide to measure the intensity of major conflict in the Big Bend country. From the ethnographical and historical record, of course, it is known that conflict sometimes did occur in the eighteenth and early nineteenth centuries between some Plateau groups as well as with tribes from nearby regions. It is reasonable to assume that other conflicts occurred in earlier centuries also.

(It also can be speculated, but without being proven, that the southerly migrating Athabascan forebears of the fierce Apache and Navajo *may have passed* through the Big Bend country a number of centuries ago in their epic journey from what is now Canada to the American Southwest. In the Southwest, of course, they became notorious raiders. Linguistic studies have shown that the Apache and Navajo originally were closely related to the Athabascans of north-central Canada. *Whether or not* these people actually passed through eastern Washington when moving south has yet to be verified.)

Excavations on Big Bend mesa tops by professional archaeologists, undertaken in response to Washington's report, have clearly indicated occupation by prehistoric peoples for significant periods of time.[11] The results strongly support Washington's position that defensible mesas had been used for seasonal or semi-permanent occupation. Still to be fully answered is the question of whether or not the mesas served as dwelling sites primarily to provide protection against attack, or for some other reason. The reports of professional archaeologists conducting these excavations indicate there is persuasive evidence that defense indeed had been a factor in the selection of mesas as occupation sites; but whether defense was the main and controlling determinant will not be fully resolved without further archaeological research.[12]

In presenting his views on the defensive use of mesas, Washington relies not only on artifacts, physical evidence, and archaeological interpretation, but also on ethnographic information gained directly from a knowledgeable elder of the Sinkiuse tribe and from Sanpoil informants. Washington began investigating mesa tops in 1957 because of his confidence in information received in the spring of that year from Billy Curlew, a highly reliable and respected Sinkiuse.

As a boy in the pre-reservation days, when roaming freely over the Big Bend country with his parents and other tribal members, Curlew learned from older people that a number of flat-topped high places had been utilized in the past as strongholds (or forts) for protection against enemy raiders. In talking to Washington, Curlew specifically identified a low mesa south of Ephrata as a place which his people had pointed out as having been used for defensive purposes. Such mesas were called tsmee-toos by the Sinkiuse.

This particular tsmee-too, though quite low, is the highest point for miles around. Its natural defensibility had been augmented with impressive breastworks around its entire perimeter, providing the only defensive sanctuary in the vicinity of the highly productive root grounds between Moses Coulee and Crab Creek. This feature was important enough to the

Sinkiuse to have been named Tsluk-slo-ku-min. It was the only mesa found by Washington in which its defensibility relied more on breastworks than cliffs; and only one other mesa retained such an impressive array of breastworks. Washington identified Tsluk-slo-ku-min as mesa number 1 in his report.

Curlew also was told that the most feared raiders were the Blackfoot of Montana, who retaliated for Sinkiuse horse stealing raids conducted against the Blackfoot during the Plateau Indian's annual buffalo hunts on the Great Plains. Conflict with the Blackfoot, of course, largely developed after the Sinkiuse acquired horses, probably before the mid 1700s.

Two elderly Sanpoil, Henry Covington and Jimmy James, who had roamed much of the northern Big Bend area during root digging times when they were boys, likewise told Washington that their parents had informed them about Big Bend mesas being utilized for defensive purposes. The Sanpoil, of all the Columbia Basin peoples, are reputed to have been among the most non-warlike and pacifistic; apparently, however, this did not prevent them from sensibly utilizing defensible mesas when danger threatened.

Many of the mesas recorded in Washington's report are located in Grant County—either in or near the Grand Coulee and its tributary canyons, in the coulees associated with the Crab Creek and Lower Crab Creek drainages, in the Columbia River canyon, and in the extensive scablands north and east of Moses Lake in the eastern part of the county. Some tsmeetoos also are located in Moses Coulee and its side canyons in Douglas County, while others can be seen in the western scablands of Adams and Lincoln counties. A few more stand east of the Big Bend country, in eastern Lincoln County and western Whitman County.

The following characteristics apply to most of the fortified mesas:

1. They exhibit nearly vertical walls, with few feasible routes up to the top. The preferred type have a single, narrow, and easily-defended ledge or defile leading to the top, which required persons to use both hands when ascending and, in some cases, the use of a ladder.

2. They are located along or near traditional travel routes, either north/south or east/west through the Big Bend country (e.g., along the Upper Grand Coulee, or along the Crab Creek/Lower Crab Creek drainage).

3. A good source of water is normally nearby.

Unlike the adobe and stone dwellings of the Southwest cliff dwellers, people occupying mesas in the Big Bend undoubtedly utilized traditional pit houses, tepee-like structures, or A-frame lodges. Most structures would have been covered with tule matting, while lesser numbers of structures may have utilized deer, buffalo, or antelope hides for coverings.

Douglas Osborne, in a 1967 report titled *Archaeological Tests in the Lower Grand Coulee, Washington,*[13] reported that archaeological sites in the Grand Coulee showed much evidence of cultural connections and trade with groups both to the far north and the south. In discussing the importance of further archaeological study in the Grand Coulee locality, Osborne stated, "this is particularly important in view of the high probability that the Coulee was an ancient highroad, and that trade items and influences from both north and south and perhaps from elsewhere may be found therein."

The ancient north-south trail system through the Big Bend that Osborne called a "highroad" (Cariboo trail) traversed the most productive part of the extensive Big Bend root grounds. This area produced some bitterroot along with great quantities of various varieties of Lomatium, chiefly Lomatium Canbyi (called tsuka-lo-tsa by the Sinkiuse). As Billy Curlew related above, tsuka-lo-tsa grew most profusely and matured earliest in the Beezley Hills and the hills extending northerly to about where present-day U.S. Route 2 crosses the Grand Coulee near Coulee City.

This rich food supply became available for digging in early March when the stored winter provisions of most Indians was at its lowest. These nutritious roots provided the richest early spring source of vegetable food in the entire region east of the Cascade Range. Roots could be harvested at various elevations in the Big Bend from early March until late May. It can be speculated that, at times over the centuries, these valuable root fields possibly might have been the focus of contention between groups, necessitating the storage of food stuffs and occupation on top of mesas.

There is much evidence that a well-traveled prehistoric east/west trail also passed through the Big Bend, following the southwesterly course of Crab Creek/Lower Crab Creek, which begins at present-day Reardan and ends far to the southwest at the Columbia River near Beverly. A number of occupied mesas are in this rather vast area, some of which are located along Lower Crab Creek between the now-deserted settlement of Corfu and the Columbia. This locality is known to have been a place where Indian hemp was obtained, which was widely used by Native Americans in making cordage.

Though archaeologists have contributed much to an overall understanding of Big Bend prehistory, Nat Washington's discoveries illustrate the fact that many questions yet remain to be answered.

Endnotes

1. Peter J. Mehringer, Jr., "Clovis Cache Found: Weapons of Ancient Americans," *National Geographic* 174 (October 1988): 500-03.
2. For a complete overview of Big Bend archaeology, see Jerry R. Galm, Glenn D. Hartmann, Ruth A. Masten, and Garry Owen Stephenson [Bonneville Cultural Resources Group], *A Cultural Resources Overview of the Bonneville Power Administration's Mid-Columbia Project, Central Washington*, Eastern Washington University Reports in Archaeology and History, No. 100-16, Cheney, Washington, 1981.
3. Verne F. Ray, "Native Villages and Groupings of the Columbia Basin," *Pacific Northwest Quarterly* 27 (April 1936): 99-152; and Leslie Spier, *Tribal Distribution in Washington*, General Series in Anthropology, No. 3, Menasha, Wisconsin, 1936. See also, Eugene S. Hunn, *Nch'i-Wana "The Big River": Mid-Columbia Indians and Their Land* (Seattle: University of Washington Press, 1990).
4. For a discussion of the types of structures utilized at habitation sites in the Southern Plateau, see Harvey S. Rice, "Native Dwellings of the Southern Plateau," in *Spokane and the Inland Empire: An Interior Pacific Northwest Anthology*, ed. by David H. Stratton (Pullman: Washington State University Press, 1991), 82-107.
5. Francis Haines, "The Northward Spread of Horses among the Plains Indians," *American Anthropologist* 40 (January-March 1938): 112-17.
6. D.W. Meinig, *The Great Columbia Plain: A Historical Geography, 1805-1910* (Seattle: University of Washington Press, 1968), 24-25.
7. *Ibid.*, 24.
8. James H. Teit, *The Middle Columbia Salish* (Seattle: University of Washington Publications, 1928), 94, 118, 120, 123.
9. Nat W. Washington, "The Nomadic Life of the Tsin-Cayuse as Related by Billy Curlew (Kul Kuloo) in the Fall of 1956 to Nat Washington, Jr.," typewritten unpublished manuscript, Ephrata, Washington, 4 pages.
10. Nat W. Washington, "Mesa Top Cliff Dwellers of Eastern Washington," 1973, unpublished report, privately circulated, Ephrata, Washington. Also on file, Department of Anthropology, Washington State University, Pullman.
11. See William C. Smith, *Archaeological Explorations in the Columbia Basin: A Report on the Mesa Project, 1973-1975*, Department of Anthropology, Central Washington University, Ellensburg, Washington, 1977; and Ruth A. Masten, *A Report on Archaeological Testing at Salishan Mesa (45GR455), Grant County, Washington*, Eastern Washington University Reports in Archaeology and History, No. 100-54, Cheney, Washington, 1988.
12. *Ibid.*
13. Douglas Osborne, *Archaeological Tests in the Lower Grand Coulee, Washington*, Occasional Papers of the Idaho State University Museum, No. 20, Pocatello, Idaho, 1967.

Fort Walla Walla, located at the junction of the Walla Walla and Columbia rivers above Wallula gap, as it appeared in 1853. Canadian fur hunters established a post here in 1818, originally naming it Fort Nez Perces. *Pacific Railroad Explorations and Surveys, Vol. 12*

IV
Quest for Furs

AFTER ADOPTION OF the horse, the next outside force destined to change Native American lifeways forever was the arrival of the white man in his quest for furs, geographical knowledge, and empire.

In September 1805, the U.S Army's Lewis and Clark Expedition (officially known as the Corps of Discovery and led by captains Meriwether Lewis and William Clark) entered the region from the east, inaugurating the utilization by whites of the Snake-Columbia waterway as a travel route. In addition to the two captains, the party included 29 men (mainly enlisted soldiers, but also two interpreters and Clark's Black manservant, York), a Shoshone woman (Sacagawea) and her baby, and Meriwether Lewis's large, black Newfoundland dog named "Seaman."

After making a difficult crossing of the snowy Bitterroot Mountains, the party carved out five dugout canoes near present-day Orofino, Idaho, and set out downstream on the rapid-strewn Clearwater and Snake rivers toward the Columbia, directed much of the way by Nez Perce guides.

Lewis and Clark at the Forks

On October 16, 1805, the party reached the Snake-Columbia confluence, encamping the next two nights at a location near, or in, what is today Sacajawea State Park.[1] At this ancient intertribal gathering place, the men rested while refurbishing their wool and leather clothing, flintlock firearms, and other equipment. Hundreds of Indians—apparently Yakima, Palouse, Walla Walla, "Sokulks" (Wanapam), or other Sahaptins—occupied a village just ¼ mile away on the Columbia. A chief came, leading 200 men from the camp in a ceremonial and friendly greeting, and others approached later to visit and trade with the strange newcomers. The presence of Sacagawea, the wife of one of the expedition's French Canadian interpreters, proved especially beneficial for the Corps of Discovery in the

Plateau region, since a woman seen traveling with a group of men was a sign of peace.

Though whites had never before visited the region, Lewis and Clark noted that the inhabitants wore red and blue cloth, glass beads, and copper and brass ornaments of European and American manufacture. These goods had been acquired through intertribal trading networks—the origin being fur trade posts located to the east on the Great Plains, the Spanish settlements far to the south, or trading vessels, mainly American and British, that had plied the inlets and harbors of the Northwest Coast in the last two decades. (Many of these sailing vessels were from the Boston, Massachusetts, area. Consequently, in time, tribes in the Northwest referred to Americans as "Bostons." The British, on the other hand, were commonly known as "King George Men," after their regent, King George III.)

The next day, William Clark and two men paddled up the Columbia, observing the mouth of the Yakima River from a distance. With the great fall salmon run in progress, a multitude of fish were visible to a depth of 15 or 20 feet in the Columbia's clear flowing water. Clark also sighted mat lodges and fish-drying scaffolds at various locations, and was told by the Indians that great quantities of dead salmon were being gathered from the shore and dried for fuel for cooking.

On October 18, 1805, after again expressing their friendship to the Indians, the Corps of Discovery set out down the Columbia with two elderly Nez Perce chiefs, Twisted Hair and Tetoharsky, who for some time had accompanied the expedition as guides and messengers of goodwill to tribes further west. Twisted Hair and Tetoharsky, who of course understood the languages of other Sahaptin-speaking groups, served as translators for Lewis and Clark, communicating with the white men in sign language. On this day, the explorers observed other Indian fishermen at their lodges and fishing scaffolds along the Columbia's shoreline and on islands, and Indian horses were seen idly grazing in Wallula Gap near the Walla Walla's mouth. These are scenes frequently described in the narratives of other explorers and fur traders who followed Lewis and Clark.

After traveling about 21 miles, the expedition encamped on the Columbia's south shore near the present Washington-Oregon boundary line, hoping to use willows and a drift log for fuel, but which, unfortunately, would not burn. With only driftwood usually available, a shortage of firewood often plagued both the Native Americans and early whites in the nearly treeless mid-Columbia locality. That evening, Yelleppit (or Yellept), the "Great Chief" of the Walla Walla tribe, came downriver with

20 men, including some lesser chiefs, to camp nearby and converse with the explorers. Earlier that day, Yelleppit hailed Lewis and Clark from an island fishing village as the explorers floated by. Had the captains known the village had firewood, they would have landed.

Yelleppit made a striking impression on the explorers. Clark described him as "a bold handsom Indian, with a dignified countenance about 35 years of age, about 5 feet 8 inches high and well perpotioned."[2] Yelleppit asked the white men to remain until mid-day of the 19th so that his people at the village could come downstream to visit. The captains excused themselves, noting that they would stay with his people two or three days on the return journey; winter was approaching and the explorers needed to be on their way. Launching their canoes, the party departed. Reaching the Dalles area a week later, Twisted Hair and Tetoharsky turned back because of the long-term hostility that existed between their people and the tribes of the Columbia River gorge. In November 1805, the Corps of Discovery finally reached the mouth of the Columbia, erecting a small stockade (Fort Clatsop) on the Oregon side of the Columbia estuary to spend the winter.

Returning east the following spring, they discarded their canoes at the Dalles and traded for Indians horses. Loading supplies and equipment on horseback, they led their pack train along the north side of the river, accompanied by a few Nez Perce companions who happened to be in the area and wished to travel back to their homeland. After passing Umatilla Rapids, they left the Columbia and crossed nine miles over the Horse Heaven Hills to avoid traversing through rugged Wallula Gap, and returned to the river just above the gap. Near here, the expedition camped for two nights, April 27-28, 1806, at Yelleppit's village of 15 mat lodges standing on the Columbia's west bank nearly opposite to the Walla Walla River.

Communication with the Walla Walla remained limited to sign language until it was discovered that Sacagawea could speak in her native tongue with a captive Snake woman in the village. Consequently, the Shoshoni-speaking slave translated for the Walla Walla chief, while Charboneau, Sacagawea's husband, interpreted between his wife and Lewis and Clark. (Sacagawea spoke her native Shoshoni tongue, and Minitari, a Plains language, but she did not know English.) Thus, speech passed back and forth in succession through the Walla Walla, Shoshoni, Minitari, and English or French languages (i.e., translated in turn, between Yelleppit, the Shoshone woman, Sacagawea, Charboneau, and Lewis and Clark, and back again). The captains too noted that sore eyes were a common affliction for inhabitants of this sun-drenched and wind-swept environment; Captain Clark dipped into the medicine stores and administered to the needs of the Indians the best he could.

As evidence of the goodwill generated by this encounter, Yelleppit presented Clark with "a very eligant white horse," requesting a kettle in return. Unable to spare any of the expedition's cookware, Clark instead gave his own sword, 100 balls and powder, and other items to the chief. The gift of ammunition indicates that Yelleppit (and probably some other warriors as well) had adopted the use of guns sometime prior to the Lewis and Clark Expedition's visit. Two lesser headmen also gave the whites a pair of fine horses, receiving in return a pistol, powder and balls, and other articles.[3]

At this time the Indians told the explorers about an overland route leaving the Columbia at the Walla Walla's mouth, passing in an easterly direction through the grassy hills north of the Blue Mountains, and reaching the Snake near its confluence with the Clearwater. By taking this trail, the expedition would save 80 miles as compared to following directly up the Snake to the Clearwater. Known as the "Nez Perce" or "Overland" trail, this route was much used by Indians, and, eventually, by fur traders, miners, stockmen, settlers, and other frontiersmen. It traversed through portions of the Walla Walla, Touchet, Tucannon, Pataha, and Alpowa drainages, passing through the sites of the modern towns of Prescott, Waitsburg, Dayton, and Pomeroy before reaching the Snake-Clearwater confluence.

The commanders quickly decided to take this shorter road. On the morning of April 29, 1806, after a night of dancing and fiddle playing in the village amongst several hundred Walla Walla and Yakima Indians, the explorers transported their baggage to the east bank of the Columbia in canoes provided by Yelleppit. The men had crossed the horses the day before, but it took several hours to round up the strayed animals; soon an Indian guide informed the commanders that it was too late in the day to reach a suitable camping place.

Consequently, the party encamped on the north side of the Walla Walla, about one mile from the Columbia, probably near the present shoreline of the McNary Dam reservoir. Here, the captains observed an Indian fishing weir standing in the Walla Walla River. Carefully pieced together with poles and willow withes, it was being used at the time to catch what the explorers called "mullet." That night the explorers had to forego dancing and other amusement with Yelleppit's people because of high winds and rain.

The next morning, April 30, 1806, the men with their cavalcade of 23 packhorses set out for the distant Snake-Clearwater junction. As they left the mid-Columbia area, the commanders dutifully noted that the Walla Wallas were the "most hospitable, honest, and sincere people" that they had yet encountered on their long two-year journey.

David Thompson and Canada's North West Company

Following the Corps of Discovery's return east on the Lolo trail over the Bitterroots, the next white explorers to arrive in the region were fur traders from Canada. In the early nineteenth century, the Montreal-based North West Company had developed into a serious rival of the famed Hudson's Bay Company (HBC) in Canada's eastern forests and lake country and along the bordering eastern Great Plains.

On Canada's far western Plains, however, the Nor'Westers held the field to themselves with little HBC interference. Consequently, they had established a chain of trading posts westward across the Plains and were poised to extend their activities into the Rockies and the Columbia watershed. This they did accomplish in 1807, despite tacit, and sometimes overt, resistance from the Blackfeet on the western Plains. The Blackfeet did not want the white traders to supply guns and other trade goods to their traditional enemies, the Flathead, Kootenai, Nez Perce, and other Salish and Sahaptin tribes residing beyond the mountains.

In 1807, the Nor'Westers' David Thompson (b. 1770), who served the North West Company as explorer, cartographer, and ambassador of goodwill to the tribes, pushed across the Rocky Mountains, establishing Kootenae House at the headwaters of the Columbia River in what is now southeast British Columbia. And, in the next three years, other new posts were built by the Nor'Westers in the Columbia drainage for the Indian trade: Kullyspell House (1809) in north Idaho, Saleesh House (1809) in northwest Montana, and Spokane House (1810) at the junction of the Spokane and Little Spokane rivers, located a few miles northwest of present-day Spokane.[4]

As the Nor'Westers continued their westward advance, the company's line of communication back across the continent to Montreal was becoming extremely lengthy. It became clear to the Canadians that a route to the Pacific needed to be found in order to send out furs and bring in supplies by sea. However, due to the complex, mountainous geography of what is now southeast British Columbia and northern Washington, Idaho, and

Montana, it took Thompson—a well-trained and highly capable geographer—four years (1807-11) to indisputably determine the main, navigable trunk of the Columbia River.

Not until the summer of 1811, five years after Lewis and Clark returned to St. Louis, was David Thompson[5] able to make preparations to set out downriver from Kettle Falls to explore the lower Columbia, establish cordial relations with the tribes along the way, and assess trading and fur hunting prospects. Thus, Thompson and his small party would be the first white men known to have traveled the full length of the Columbia River through the Big Bend country.

From recently established Spokane House, Thompson began his journey by proceeding by horseback to Kettle Falls. Here, on July 3, 1811, at 6:30 A.M., his party launched a "cedar boat," which Thompson had directed his men to build there especially for exploring the Columbia down to the sea. Accompanying Thompson were seven company employees: Michael Beaurdeau, Pierre Pareil, Joe Cote, Michel Boulard, and Francois Gregoire, all French Canadians, and Charles and Ignace, both of whom were Iroquois. In addition, two Sanpoil Indians acting as interpreters and guides joined them for the first part of the journey. (This complement of men reflected a general characteristic of the Canadian fur trade: i.e., the leaders were British, and the common workers were French Canadians and Indians.)

After traveling nearly 90 miles the first day and running through "many eddys and small whirlpools," the party of 10 encamped at an Indian village at the mouth of the Sanpoil River, where they were hospitably greeted by the congenial Sanpoil with dancing and singing. Before retiring, Thompson made a number of keen observations about these people when the dust from many feet "fairly obscured the dancers though we stood only about 4 feet from them as they danced on a piece of dusty ground in the open air."[6]

Interestingly enough, Thompson learned that the area's Native Americans already were familiar with whites. The Mid-Columbia Indians had heard reports about white men from other tribes. Some also probably had had direct contact with the Lewis and Clark Expedition at the forks, and with the Canadians at the Nor'Westers' posts to the northeast or with American and British traders in sea-going vessels on the coast; interior tribespeople frequently traveled via the Yakima, Methow, or Similkameen watersheds through the Cascades to visit coastal peoples.[7]

Next day, after proceeding to the Box Canyon locality, Thompson reported that the rapids forced the men to unload the canoe and it

was run down hereto, but in doing this they ran too close to a drift
tree on a rock which . . . struck Ignace [one of the Iroquois boatmen]
out of the stern of the canoe, although he had never swam in his life he
swam so as to keep himself above the waves till they turned the canoe
around to take him up . . . All this day the current has been very strong
with many rapids and whirlpools . . . Latterly this country, though
still meadows, showed much rock . . . There are no woods but a chance
tree, and then of straggling fir.

Ignace's dunking resulted in this rapid in the Box Canyon vicinity being
known as "La Rapide d'Ignace" by Canadians during the fur trade era.

Early the next day, July 5, the explorers stopped to converse with a
large encampment of Nespelim Indians, but a heavy rain ended the meeting. At mid-afternoon, however, Thompson noted that the men,

returned singing us a song of a mild air as the women had welcomed
us with one also, having smoked a few pipes and discoursed of the
country which they discribed as a hilly meadow with a very few trees
of fir . . . Of course there can be no beaver, they have bears and rats
with a few sheep and black tailed deer. Horses they have many and the
country appears good for them. We discoursed of the river and people
below us, after which they offered to dance for our good voyage and
preservation to the sea and back again. We accepted their offer.[8]

After passing the Okanogan River on July 6 (see appendix 2),
Thompson's party again was ceremonially greeted by Indians, in this case
the Methow. The next day, approaching Rock Island Rapids, Thompson
stopped to visit another large Indian encampment. Throughout the journey he recorded a wealth of information about the native inhabitants, and
his journal on this day, July 7, is typical:

a large band of Indians . . . received us all dancing in their huts [mat
lodges], one of which was about 80 yards long and the other 20 yards
d[itt]o. there were about 120 families. I invited them to smoke and
the 5 most respectable men advanced and smoked a few pipes. We
asked them to invite the others which they readily did but it was 20
[minutes] before we could get them to all sit down. They put down
their little presents of berries, roots, etc., and then continually kept
blessing us and wishing us all manner of good visiting them, with
clapping their hands and extending them to the skies. When any of us
approached their ranks they expressed their good will and thanks with
outstretched arms and words, followed by a strong whistling aspira-
tion of breath. I discoursed awhile with them and they seemed thankful for the good I offered them of trading their superfluities for articles
they stood much in need of. A very respectable old man sat down by

me thankful to see us and smoke of our tobacco before he died, he often felt my shoes and legs gently as if to know whether I was like themselves. A chief of the countries below [downriver] offered to accompany me. He understood the language of the [Sahaptin-speaking] people below, which I gladly accepted, and we embarked him, his wife and baggage . . . We had much trouble to get away, as they very much wished to detain us all night, and when we went they all stretched out their hands to heaven, wishing us a good voyage and a safe return . . . Many of these people, like the others, have shells in their noses . . . Though poor in provisions they were all hearty in health and tolerably well clothed for the country, a few buffalo robes etc.

Some Plateau Indians in this time period pierced the nasal septum at the bottom of the nose to hold ornaments. Thus, Thompson's comment about "shells in their noses," refers to narrow, tubular, ivory-like dentalium shells (also known as *hiqua*), one or two inches long, which were held in the pierced nose. Rows of dentalium likewise decorated clothing or were used as necklaces. Dentalium, found in the offshore waters of Vancouver Island and gathered with great difficulty by coastal tribes, was a very valuable commodity of exchange in the Pacific Coast intertribal trade network. Interestingly, within a few decades, the custom of piercing the nose appears to have all but died out in the Plateau, particularly among the southern tribes, including the Nez Perce whose French name virtually means "pierced nose."

After proceeding 65 miles altogether this day, Thompson's party encamped near the mouth of Crab Creek, passing "a bad night with mosquitoes and a high wind." After rigging a mast and sail on the boat the next morning, July 8, they set out a few miles to the "high waves" of the Priest Rapids locality, where "62 men and their families" greeted the explorers in the usually friendly fashion:

They made us a present of 4 salmon, much berries, etc., of which we took only part, also of 2 very small salmon . . . Here the chief came to visit us on horseback, then returned with word to the camp, as the current drove us down half a mile below them. He returned with another and with an old white headed man . . . He showed no signs of age except his hair and a few wrinkles in his face, he was quite naked and ran nearly as fast as the horses. We could not but admire him. I invited the horsemen to invite all their people to smoke, which they set off to do in a round gallop, and the old man on foot ran after them and did not lose much ground. They all came and sat down and smoked and discoursed as usual. What I said the chief repeated to his people and another so repeated after him, both very loud. The women then advanced, singing and dancing in their best dress, with all of them shells in their noses, two of them naked but no way abashed, they advanced all the time the men smoked and like the rest [of the upriver tribes in] something of a religious nature. When done I paid them for their present of which I took only part, but the pounded roots were made in neat cakes . . . They are of the Shawpatin nation and speak that tongue. Here my last guide showed his service interpreting with an audible voice, and seemed a sensible, respectable man.

After the morning meeting with the "Solkuks" or Wanapam people, the Canadians again shoved off, floating past the White Bluffs. At 5:30 that afternoon, they "put ashore" 1/2 mile from the mouth of the Snake River, meeting "about 150 men with their families" at this traditional intertribal camping spot in today's Pasco vicinity. Thompson again discoursed in the usual manner with the inhabitants. Noting that these people exhibited much of the Plains Indians' features, he also commented that "they did not appear to make so much use of the nose ornament as" the upriver tribes.

Casting off at 6:10 A.M. the next day, the explorers paddled ½ mile to the mouth of the Snake River and put ashore. At this key geographical point in the Inland Northwest, Thompson "erected a small pole with a half sheet of paper well tied about it, with these words":

Know hereby that this country is claimed by Great Britain as part of its territories, and that the N. W. Company of Merchants from Canada, finding the factory for this people inconvenient for them, do hereby intend to erect a factory in this place for the commerce of the country around. D. Thompson. Junction of the Shawpatin River with the Columbia. July 9th, 1811.[9]

Thompson's announcement is a reminder of this era's vast international struggle for control of the west coast of North America. Both the United States and Great Britain, as well as Russia and Spain, eyed gaining sole possession of the Pacific Northwest region. Fur traders, as discoverers and pioneers, were as much agents of imperial expansion as the official explorers like Lewis and Clark. Interestingly enough, Thompson carried a copy of Sergeant Patrick Gass's journal (Gass's account of his experiences as a member of the Lewis and Clark Expedition had appeared in print in 1807, just one year after the American explorers had returned to St. Louis).[10]

Regarding the phraseology of Thompson's proclamation, the term "factory," of course, meant trading post, and the "Shawpatin River" is the Snake River. Early white fur traders frequently identified the Snake by this name ("Shawpatin" or other similar spellings), since the Nez Perce, Palouse, Walla Walla, and other tribes of the lower Snake River vicinity were Sahaptin speakers. However, the Snake also sometimes was identified with an alternate designation, the "Lewis River," in recognition of Captain Meriwether Lewis. The eventual name for the stream—Snake River or sometimes "Shoshone" River—originated when white fur hunters in southern Idaho in the 1810s encountered the Snake (or Shoshone) Indians residing on the upper part of the river.

The Columbia, on the other hand, was named in 1792 by its seagoing discoverer, Captain Robert Gray of the Boston trading ship *Columbia Rediviva*. The Columbia was also called the "Oregon River" or the "Great River of the West" by some early fur men and writers; and, occasionally that portion of the Columbia flowing down to the junction with the Snake was referred to as Clark's (or Clarke's) River, for Captain William Clark. It should be remembered, of course, that Indian groups had their own names for these rivers.

After posting his proclamation, Thompson continued downstream, meeting a group of Indians near the mouth of the Walla Walla and their principal chief, apparently Yelleppit, who Thompson described as "a stately good looking man of about 40 years and well dressed." The chief, who exhibited "an American medal of 1801, Thomas Jefferson, and a small flag of that nation" given by Lewis and Clark, directed his band of "soldiers," "cousins," and "women" to greet the Nor'Westers with smoking, dancing, and food. After a "very friendly" four-hour visit with him and "two old respectable chiefs," the explorers continued through Wallula Gap to the Umatilla area. There Thompson sighted Mt. Hood in the far distance, a "conical mountain right ahead alone and very high, seemingly a mass of snow."

The Astorians

Reaching the mouth of the Columbia six days later on July 15, 1811, Thompson saw a unique spectacle—a large group of fur traders from a rival American fur company constructing a trading post (Fort Astoria) on the south shore. These men had arrived by sea only a few months earlier. Though most of the newcomers were Canadians (with lesser numbers of Americans), they were all employees of an American firm, the Pacific Fur Company, organized and financed by John Jacob Astor, the great New York entrepreneur. Astor had earned considerable wealth in the fur trade of the Great Lakes region, and now had ambitiously sent out his lieutenants to develop a system of trading posts across the continent.

Thompson was not surprised by their presence here. The Nor'Westers had anticipated and heard rumors about such a venture, and, while journeying down the Columbia, Thompson had been told by Indians that an American ship (the *Tonquin*) had disembarked fur traders at the river's mouth. The Astorians themselves likewise knew, in indefinite terms, that North West Company traders were conducting operations west of the continental divide and had been doing so for several years. Still, the Astorians were startled to see Thompson's boat approaching, flying the British flag, but they received him "in the most polite manner."

The Astorians were determined to send an expedition up the Columbia to establish posts in the interior. For several days after Thompson's arrival, the Astorians and Canadians played a cat and mouse game for information, all done very cordially and on a friendly basis of course, before it was decided that they would proceed together upriver for mutual protection. Consequently, on July 22, 1811, the two parties cast off into the Columbia.

The Pacific Fur Company contingent was led by 45-year-old David Stuart, a Highland Scotsman, and included clerks Alexander Ross, Ovide de Montigny, Francis Pillet, and Donald McLennan, two or three Canadian voyageurs, two Indians, and two Hawaiians who had been recruited from the native population when the *Tonquin* had stopped in Hawaii on the Pacific voyage. (Beginning at this time, supply vessels beating toward the Columbia River frequently stopped in Hawaii, then called the Sandwich Islands, to replenish water and food stocks, and take on native laborers, or "Kanakas," for the Pacific Northwest fur trade. It is noteworthy that vessels likewise stopped in California on occasion in this era.)

The joint parties continued together through the Columbia River gorge where danger from pillage by unfriendly Indians was greatest. These tribal groups were accustomed to being the middlemen in the intertribal trade network that extended up and down the Columbia, and they were becoming aware that the whites would be excluding them from this lucrative position in regard to trade goods.

Thompson's party traveled light. Stuart's group, on the other hand, was burdened with 1,500 lbs. of trade merchandise loaded in coastal Chinook canoes unsuited for upriver work. Reaching relative safety in the Dalles vicinity, Thompson and his experienced men, with their more manageable boat, forged ahead of Stuart, and several days later beached at the Indian encampment at the Snake-Columbia confluence. Having experienced rather rough treatment from the Columbia gorge tribes, Thompson expressed his gratitude for reaching friendly Indians: "Thank Heaven for the favors we find among these numerous people."

At 7:30 A.M. on August 6, the Canadians turned their boat up the Snake, and on August 8 reached the mouth of the Palouse River, where they planned to proceed overland to Spokane House. The Nor'Westers had been informed earlier about this route by Indians. On arriving at the Palouse, Thompson noted:

> At end of course, put ashore at the mouth of a small brook [Palouse River] and camped, as this is the road to my first Post on the Spokane lands [Spokane House]. Here is a village of 50 men, they had danced till they were fairly tired and the Chiefs had bawled themselves hoarse. They forced a present of 8 horses on me, with a war garment.[11]

After concluding his friendly councils with the Palouse tribe, Thompson set out the next day up the Palouse River on the well-traveled Indian road to the Spokane country that followed the Cheney-Palouse flood channels.[12] (A year later the Pacific Fur Company's John Clarke also would lead a party of Astorians over this same route to establish a post on the Spokane River.[13] It is interesting to note that this trail in later years became the "Colville Road" to the Spokane and upper Columbia areas and also the route of the "Mullan Road" which branched off to Montana; it would play a key role in the economic and commercial development of eastern Washington. In the nineteenth century, Indians, fur hunters, miners, soldiers, stockmen, packers, and other frontiersmen by the thousands traveled this way to and from points in the Inland Northwest and the northern Rocky Mountains.)

Thompson, his task accomplished, never revisited the lower Columbia, but thereafter focused his activities in the northern Inland Northwest and Canada. Later, from 1816 to 1826, Thompson was involved in the survey of the U. S./Canadian border in the Midwest region.

Now, we return to Stuart's men on the Columbia, who were pulling oars in their two heavy Chinook dugout canoes, and sometimes hoisting sails to harness the wind. On August 12, 1811, passing through Wallula Gap seven days after Thompson's party, the Astorians reached the Walla Walla, "a beautiful little river, lined with weeping willows." Here, according to the expedition's excellent chronicler, clerk Alexander Ross, a large band of Indians were encamped, who expressed a wish that we should pass the day with them. We encamped accordingly; yet for some time not an Indian came near us . . . in the midst of our perplexity we perceived a great body of men issuing from the camp, all armed and painted, and preceded by three chiefs. The whole array came moving on in solemn and regular order till within twenty yards of our tent. Here the three chiefs harangued us, each in his turn; all the rest giving, every now and then, a vociferous shout of approbation when the speaker happened to utter some emphatical expression. The purport of these harangues was friendly, and as soon as the chiefs had finished they all sat down on the grass in a large circle, when the great calumet of peace was produced, and the smoking began. Soon after the women, decked in their best attire, and painted, arrived, when the dancing and singing commenced—the usual symbols of peace and friendship; and in this pleasing and harmonious mood they passed the whole day.

The men were generally tall, raw-boned, and well dressed; having all buffalo-robes, deer-skin leggings, very white, and most of them garnished with porcupine quills. Their shoes were also trimmed and painted red;—altogether, their appearance indicated wealth. Their voices were strong and masculine, and their language differed from any we had heard before. The women wore garments of well dressed deer-skin down to their heels; many of them richly garnished with beads, higuas, and other trinkets—leggings and shoes similar to those of the men. Their faces were painted red . . . The tribes assembled on the present occasion were the Walla-Wallas, the Shaw Haptens [probably Yakima or Nez Perce], and the Cajouses [Cayuse]; forming altogether about fifteen hundred souls. The Shaw Haptens and Cajouses, with part of the Walla-Wallas, were armed with guns, and the others with bows and arrows . . . The plains were literally covered with horses, of which there could not have been less than four thousand in sight of the camp.[14]

Ross's account indicates that the Indians of the southern Columbia Basin were acquiring guns at this time, probably mostly from the North West Company's posts to the northeast. Pushing on the next day, Stuart's party arrived at the Snake-Columbia confluence in the evening, and received a friendly, all-night reception in another "immense" Indian encampment. Arising early the next morning, Ross whimsically reported:

what did we see waving triumphantly in the air, at the confluence of the two great branches, but a British flag, hoisted in the middle of the Indian camp, planted there by Mr. Thompson as he passed, with a written paper, laying claim to the country north of the forks, as British territory.

The proclamation, of course, did not deter the Astorians from proceeding on, up the Columbia.

While in the vicinity of the forks, Ross recorded other interesting observations about the locality:

> At the junction of their waters, Lewis's River [the Snake] has a muddy or milk-and-water appearance, and is warm; while [the "larger"] Clarke's River [the Columbia] is bluish, clear, and very cold. The difference of colour, like a dividing line between the two waters, continues for miles below their junction. These branches would seem, from a rough chart the Indians made us, to be of nearly equal length from the forks— perhaps 700 miles—widening from each other towards the mountains, where the distance between their sources may be 900 miles . . .
>
> The only European articles seen here with the Indians . . . were guns, and here and there a kettle, or a knife; and, indeed, the fewer the better. They require but little, and the more they get of our manufacture the more unhappy will they be, as the possession of one article naturally creates a desire for another, so that they are never satisfied.

The Stuart party would be the second group of white men to travel the full length of the Columbia in the Big Bend country. Ross's description of the mid-Columbia area is unsurpassed in the early historical literature, and we will quote from him extensively on the journey northward:

> On the 16th, we left the forks and proceeded up the north branch [the Columbia] . . . About twelve miles up, a small river entered on the west side, called Eyakema [the Yakima]. The landscape at the mouth of the Eyakema surpassed in picturesque beauty anything we had yet seen. Here three Walla-Walla Indians overtook us on horseback, and to our agreeable surprise delivered us a bag of shot which we had left by mistake at our encampment of last night . . . if I recollect well, a similar circumstance, attesting the probity of the Walla-Wallas, occurred when Lewis and Clarke passed there in 1805 [actually 1806].[15] We saw but few Indians to-day, and in the evening we encamped without a night watch, for the first time since we left Astoria. General course, north.
>
> On the 17th, we were paddling along at daylight. On putting on shore to breakfast, four Indians on horseback joined us. The moment they alighted, one set about hobbling their horses, another to gather small sticks, a third to make a fire, and the fourth to catch fish. For this purpose, the fisherman cut off a bit of his leathern shirt, about the size of a small bean; then pulling out two or three hairs from his horse's tail for a line, tied the bit of leather to one end of it, in place of a hook or fly. Thus prepared, he entered the river a little way, sat down on a

stone, and began throwing the small fish, three or four inches long, on shore, just as fast as he pleased; and while he was thus employed, another picked them up and threw them towards the fire, while the third stuck them up round it in a circle, on small sticks; and they were no sooner up than roasted. The fellows then sitting down, swallowed them—heads, tails, bones, guts, fins, and all, in no time, just as one would swallow the yolk of an egg. Now all this was but the work of a few minutes; and before our man had his kettle ready for the fire, the Indians were already eating their breakfast. When the fish had hold of the bit of wet leather, or bait, their teeth got entangled in it, so as to give time to jerk them on shore . . . fire produced by the friction of two bits of wood was also a novelty; but what surprised us most of all, was the regularity with which they proceeded, and the quickness of the whole process, which actually took them less time to perform, than it has taken me to note it down.

On August 17 and 18, 1811, Stuart's party passed by the White Bluffs, referring to the area as "the marl hills," and reached Priest Rapids. Continuing in Ross's own words:

a long range of marl hills interrupts the view on the east side of the river. Here two dead children were presented to us by their parents, in order that we might restore them to life again, and a horse was offered us as the reward. We pitied their ignorance, made them a small present, and told them to bury their dead. As we advanced along the marl hills . . . Here and there were to be seen, on small eminences, burial-places . . . a few small sticks always point out the cemetery.

On the 18th, we reached the end of the marl hills. Just at this place the river makes a bend right south [actually southwest] for about ten miles, when a high and rugged hill confines it on our left. Here . . . a little under the brow of the hill, a strong and rocky rapid presented itself in the very bend of the river. Having ascended it about half way, we encamped for the night.

Here a large concourse of [Wanapam] Indians met us, and after several friendly harangues, commenced the usual ceremony of smoking the pipe of peace: after which they passed the night in dancing and singing. The person who stood foremost in all these introductory ceremonies, was a tall, meagre, middle-aged Indian, who attached himself very closely to us from the first moment we saw him. He was called Ha-qui-laugh, which signifies doctor, or rather priest . . . We named the place "Priest's Rapid," after him [The "priest" joined the party as a guide and herder of the horses that the Astorians acquired on their journey toward the Okanogan River] . . .

The Priest's Rapid is more than a mile in length, and is a dangerous and intricate part of the navigation. The south side, although full of rocks and small channels, through which the water rushes with great violence, is the best to ascend.

On the 19th, early in the morning, we started, but found the channel so frequently obstructed with rocks, whirlpools, and eddies, that we had much difficulty in making any headway. Crossing two small portages, we at length, however, reached the head of it, and there encamped for the night, after a very hard day's labour, under a burning sun. From the head of Priest's Rapid, the river opens again due north . . . rattlesnakes are very numerous. At times they may be heard hissing all around, so that we had to keep a sharp look-out to avoid treading on them; but the natives appeared to have no dread of them. As soon as one appears, the Indians fix its head to the ground with a small forked stick round the neck, then extracting the fang or poisonous part, they take the reptile into their hands, put it into their bosoms, play with it, and let it go again. When anyone is bitten . . . the Indians tie a ligature above the wounded part, scarify it, and then apply a certain herb to the wound . . .

On the 20th we left the Priest's Rapid, and proceeded against a strong ripply current and some small rapids, for ten miles, when we reached two lofty and conspicuous bluffs [Sentinel Bluffs], situate[d] directly opposite to each other, like the piers of a gigantic gate, between which the river flowed smoothly. Here we staid for the night, on some rocks infested with innumerable rattlesnakes, which caused us not a little uneasiness during the night . . .

Early on the 21st, we were again on the water [in what is now the Vantage vicinity]. The country on the east side is one boundless rough and barren plain; but on the west, the rocks, after some distance, close in to the water's edge, steep and rugged, and the whole country behind is studded with towering heights and rocks . . . We saw but few natives to-day, but those few were very friendly to us.

On August 22, Stuart's party reached the Rock Island Rapids vicinity where one of the canoes, spinning dangerously out of control, shot back down a chute, grounding on a rock. A line thrown to the men allowed their escape and saved the boat. Encamping below the white water, they spent "the remainder of the day in drying goods, mending the canoe, and examining the rapids." The next day, after passing Rock Island Rapids by portaging and pulling tow lines, they were greeted in customary style by a large encampment of Indians at the Wenatchee flats.

Continuing north of the Wenatchee's mouth, they sighted "the ibex [bighorn sheep], the white musk goat [mountain goat], and several deer, and supped on a half devoured salmon, which a white-headed eagle had very opportunely taken out of the river." Shortly, after meeting other large groups of tribesmen, most notably at the mouths of the Chelan and Methow rivers, they were informed

> that there were whites before us, but a long way off. The Indians showed us a gun, tobacco, and some other articles, which they said they had purchased from the whites ahead, which confirmed the report. We therefore at once suspected that it must be a party of the North-Westerns; and here Mr. Stuart, for the first time, began to think of finding a suitable place to winter in.

Reaching the Okanogan River on August 31, 1811, they proceeded two miles upstream to pitch their tents.

> A great concourse of Indians followed us all day, and encamped with us. After acquainting them with the object of our visit to their country, they strongly urged us to settle among them. For some time, however, Mr. Stuart resisted their pressing solicitations, chiefly with the view of trying their sincerity; but, at last consenting, the chiefs immediately held a council, and then pledged themselves to be always our friends, to kill us plenty of beavers, to furnish us at all times with provisions, and to ensure our protection and safety.
>
> During this afternoon we observed, for the first time . . . above the horizon, and almost due west, a very brilliant comet, with a tail . . . The Indians at once said it was placed there by the Good Spirit ["or Great Mother of Life"] . . . to announce to them the glad tidings of our arrival; and the omen impressed them with a reverential awe . . .
>
> On the 1st of September 1811, we embarked, and descending the Oakinacken again, landed on a level spot, within a half a mile of its mouth . . . which operation concluded our long and irksome voyage of forty-two days.[16]

Here, on the Okanogan's east bank, the men erected a single building "sixteen by twenty feet, chiefly constructed of drift wood," with a cellar for storing trade goods. Upon its completion, David Stuart, clerk Ovide de Montigny, and two men proceeded up the Okanogan valley with packhorses laden with goods for a reconnaissance and trading trip into the Shuswap Lake and Thompson River country of what is now central British Columbia. Expecting to be gone a month, little did they know at the time that they would journey 350 miles north and winter among the numerous Shuswap Indians. Meanwhile, the remainder of the upriver party returned to Astoria, leaving Alexander Ross in sole charge at Okanogan for the winter.

Surrounded by a large Indian encampment, Ross's only companion in the trading house for 188 days was "a little Spanish pet dog from

Monterey, called Weasel." Ross recorded detailed observations about the culture, customs, and subsistence patterns of the Okanogan Indians, which, unfortunately, space does not allow to repeat here. At the Okanogan post, contacts and trade with the local Indians proved excellent. Nevertheless, suffice it to say that Ross, a solitary sojourner, felt feelings of extreme isolation:

> Only picture to yourself, gentle reader, how I must have felt, alone in this unhallowed wilderness, without friend or white man within hundreds of miles . . . Every day seemed a week, every night a month. I pined, I languished, my head turned gray, and in a brief space ten years were added to my age. Yet man is born to endure.[17]

Causing even greater apprehension for Ross was the fact that he had expected Stuart to return in 30 days, but, due to circumstances, Stuart's party did not reappear at Okanogan until the following spring when Weasel's barking alerted Ross of their return.

After his arrival, Stuart recounted his journey to Ross:

> After leaving this place . . . we bent our course up the Oakinacken, due north, for upwards of 250 miles, till we reached its source; then crossing a height of land fell upon Thompson's River, or rather the south branch of Fraser's River, after travelling for some time amongst a powerful nation called the She Whaps. The snow fell while we were here in the mountains, and precluded our immediate return; and after waiting for fine weather the snows got so deep that we considered it hopeless to attempt getting back, and, therefore, passed our time with the She Whaps and other tribes in that quarter. The Indians were numerous and well disposed, and the country throughout abounds in beavers and all other kinds of fur; and I have made arrangements to establish a trading post there the ensuing winter. On the 26th of February [1812] we began our homeward journey, and spent just twenty-five days on our way back. The distance may be about 350 miles.[18]

It is important to note that Stuart and his three companions on their northward exploration, "were the first white men that ever traveled through the Okanogan valley."[19] Of course, this route following the natural north-south passageway along the meandering Okanogan River was hardly a new one. With various deviations, it had been used by Indians for many centuries.

Fur Trade Rivalry, 1811-13

Thus, in 1811, American and Canadian adventurers forged the fur trade's primary river and land routes in the Inland Northwest, setting the stage for the vigorous commercial and territorial rivalry to follow. After the snows melted in early 1812, scores of Pacific Fur Company men came up the Columbia to assist Ross at Okanogan and build a trading post at "She Whaps."

Other Astorians boated up the Snake to the mouth of the Palouse, and from there proceeded overland to the Spokane area where they brashly established a competing trading post adjacent to the Nor'Westers Spokane House. Elsewhere, Astorians pushed up other Columbia tributaries to challenge the Canadians for the Indian trade of the Coeur d'Alene, Kootenai, and Flathead districts. Also, an Astorian party proceeded to the Snake-Clearwater confluence, where it established a short-lived post among the Nez Perce. Meeting the challenge, the North West Company instituted competitive, but fair, trading practices and built a post (Kamloops) across the South Thompson River from the Astorians' She Whaps trading house. Also in this time period, a small group of Astorians carrying dispatches to the East forged a route across the Rockies and Plains to St. Louis, via South Pass and the Platte River. This route, with some changes, later became famous as the "Oregon Trail."[20]

In summary, the basic pattern of British and American communication and transportation links in the Pacific Northwest were established and persisted for nearly four decades to come. As the modern historical geographer, D.W. Meinig, has so aptly explained in *The Great Columbia Plain*:

> Almost simultaneously Thompson and the Astorians laid out the key lines of strategy for Britain and the United States. The one was anchored in Fort William [on Lake Superior] (later to be shifted to York Factory [on Hudson Bay]), the other in St. Louis; each followed the rivers across the plains (the Saskatchewan-Athabasca, and the Missouri-Platte), each threaded a strategic corridor across the summit of the continent (Athabasca Pass and South Pass), then curved to contact the outspread sources of the upper Columbia and the Snake, and finally merged into the [Columbia River] trunk route through the Cascade Range to the sea. For forty years these were the overland arteries through which the commercial and political interests of the [two] nations were maintained.[21]

In this era, numerous fast-moving fur trade parties, both large and small, boated up and down the waterways of the Columbia and Snake. Readily taking to land routes as well, they utilized horse trails along the Okanogan, Spokane, and Palouse rivers, through the Grand Coulee, in the Palouse Hills, and along Lewis and Clark's "overland" road south of the Snake.

In addition, traders used other Indian trails to visit the Yakima and Walla Walla valleys to trade for Indian horses. The rival companies needed large numbers of mounts for transporting trade goods and baggage throughout the region, and also sometimes to serve as a supply of food for men at the posts. Irishman Ross Cox, an Astorian clerk, noted that the number of horses owned by the various tribes in the interior depended upon the nature of the country. Among the Spokane and Flathead, where conditions for raising horses were merely adequate, there were just enough horses to fulfill the needs of the Indians; every colt on reaching proper age was broken for the saddle. On the other hand, on lands inhabited by the Walla Walla, Nez Perce, and other Sahaptins of the southern Columbia Basin, where there were well-watered, grassy plains and sheltered valleys, thousands of horses thrived and ran free; it was not uncommon for a man to own several hundred horses.

The Yakima valley, as well as the Walla Walla valley, provided a setting for great gatherings of the tribes with their vast pony herds. In the Yakima country, different groups of "horse" Indians congregated every summer to engage in wholesale trading and socializing. Ross, an early eyewitness to this great rendezvous, sighted as many as 9,000 horses grazing on the river bottom at one time.[22]

Competition between the Nor'Westers and Astorians continued at a vigorous pace throughout 1812, but the repercussions of international developments far away suddenly changed everything. Word came in January 1813 across the Canadian Plains that long standing disputes between the United States and Great Britain (over the commerce of the seas, and British encroachment on American territory and interests in the Great Lakes region) had erupted into open hostilities—the War of 1812.

Despite this shocking news that their home countries were at war, relations between the Americans and Canadians in the Pacific Northwest remained amenable. However, after the previous year's fierce competition, the stock of trading goods in both companies' warehouses were largely depleted. Throughout the winter, both sides impatiently waited for supply ships, but they did not come. (Typical goods used in the Indian trade included tobacco, guns, balls, shot, powder, gun flints, axes, knife blades, buttons, beads, needles, thimbles, awls, thread, blankets, flannel shirts, combs, rings, and copper and brass kettles. Steel or iron digging sticks, used by Native American women in digging roots, also became an important trade item.)

The trade remained stalemated, with the rivals keeping a watchful eye at the mouth of the Columbia for the first sail to come into view, anxious as to whether it would be an American or British vessel. Meanwhile, the Nor'Westers and Astorians decided to temporarily divide up the Indian trade. This impasse finally broke in August 1813, when word arrived that a British war frigate intended to seize Fort Astoria. The Astorians, now in a perilous situation, decided to sell out to their Canadian rivals so as to prevent a complete loss of holdings should a warship arrive. Consequently, lengthy negotiations began over the transfer of the Astorians' assets, and the Nor'Westers made preparations to take over Fort Astoria and the Pacific Fur Company's other interior posts.

In late November, the naval sloop *Raccoon*, commanded by Captain Black of the Royal Navy, crossed the dangerous Columbia River bar. Two weeks later, on December 13, 1813, Black ceremonially took possession of the Astorian post for Great Britain, renaming it Fort George for King George III. Black's actions proved to be a mere formality, since the post already had been handed over to the Nor'Westers. His task completed, Captain Black shortly turned the *Raccoon* back out to sea.[23]

For those Astorians desiring to return east, the North West Company agreed to take them across the Canadian Plains with the next annual brigade in the spring of 1814. Most of the Astorians, however, also were given the opportunity to join the North West Company if they wished, and serve in the region. Consequently, many of them, particularly the French Canadians, and several of the clerks and partners including Ross Cox and Alexander Ross, transferred loyalties to the Nor'Westers.

After the summer of 1813, the North West Company had no further competition from the Americans in the Inland Northwest; the young republic's fur hunters remained bottled up in St. Louis due to Indian hostility in the upper Mississippi valley and other consequences of the War of 1812. Fort George remained the Nor'Wester's principal depot on the Pacific Coast, with ocean-going ships bringing in supplies and exporting furs. Meanwhile, overland communication to Montreal was maintained by an annual overland express to Fort William on Lake Superior.

Relocation of Fort Okanogan, 1816

Upon gaining possession of Fort Okanogan, the North West Company immediately began utilizing the Astorians' Okanogan valley route to supply and receive furs from Kamloops and the Thompson River district. The Nor'Westers also had other posts located even farther north—in the Peace River and upper Fraser River watersheds. Simon Fraser had pioneered the fur trade there, establishing trading houses in 1805-06. Among these far northern posts were Fort McLeod, Fort St. James, and Fort Fraser, which drew furs from a vast area called "New Caledonia" (the northern interior of present-day British Columbia). Consequently, Fort Okanogan now became the supply and transfer point for New Caledonia as well as Kamloops. Later, in 1821, Fort Alexandria would be constructed as a storage depot on the Fraser River, about midway between the most northern forts and Kamloops.

Though structures had been added at Fort Okanogan in the five years since its founding by the Stuart party, the location's inadequacies became apparent to the Nor'Westers. Consequently, a party under clerk Ross Cox arrived at Okanogan on April 30, 1816, as a detachment of the annual upriver brigade. Cox was charged with the duty of moving the post 1¼ miles southeast, nearer the mouth of the Okanogan. Here are excerpts from his narrative:

> The immediate vicinity is poorly furnished with timber, and our wood-cutters were obliged to proceed some distance up the river in search of that necessary article, which was floated down in rafts. We also derived . . . immense quantities of drift-wood which was intercepted in its descent down the Columbia by the great bend which that river takes above Oakinagan . . . our men used such dispatch, that before the month of September we had erected a new dwelling house for the person in charge, containing four excellent rooms and a large dining-hall, two good houses for the men, and a spacious store for the furs and merchandise, to which was attached a shop for trading with the natives. The whole was surrounded by strong palisades fifteen feet high, and flanked by two bastions. Each bastion had, in its lower story, a light brass four-pounder [cannon]; and in the upper, loop-holes were left for the use of musketry . . .
>
> Owing to the intense heat the men were obliged to leave off work every day at eleven, and did not resume until between two and three in the afternoon . . . In the interval they generally slept . . .
>
> The horses . . . suffered severely from [mosquitoes] . . . and the horseflies. We caused several fires of rotten wood to be made in the prairie . . . and round which they instinctively congregated to avail themselves of the protection afforded by the smoke . . . I have often observed the poor animals, when the smoke began to evaporate, gallop up to the fort, and neigh in the most significant manner for a fresh supply of damp fuel; and on perceiving the men appointed for that

purpose proceed to the different fires, they followed them, and waited with the most sagacious patience until the smoke began to ascend and disperse their tormentors . . .

The climate of Oakinagan is highly salubrious. We have for weeks together observed the blue expanse of heaven unobscured by a single cloud. Rain, too, is very uncommon . . .

Several dreadful whirlwinds occurred during the summer . . . When the men observed these sudden and dangerous squalls rising, they threw themselves prostrate on the ground, to avoid the clouds of sand and dust, which otherwise would have blinded them . . .

The natives of Oakinagan are an honest, quiet tribe. They do not muster more than two hundred warriors; but as they are on terms of friendship with the Kamloops, Sinapoils, and other small tribes in their rear, and as the Columbia in front forms an impassable barrier against any surprise from their old enemies the Nez Percés, they have in a great degree forgotten the practice of "glorious war."

The post was destined to remain at this location throughout much of the heyday of the fur trade. Between 1831 and 1837, however, the post was again moved, and rebuilt on the Columbia at a site having a better shoreline for a boat landing and ferry site. Much more, of course, will be yet mentioned about Fort Okanogan.[24]

Fort Nez Perces, Founded 1818

Another fur trade post playing a key role in Big Bend history was Fort Nez Perces, later known as Fort Walla Walla, erected at the Walla Walla-Columbia confluence in 1818. The post also was sometimes called Fort "Numipu" (after the Nez Perce name for themselves, meaning "the People"), though the Nez Perce were only visitors in this locality; this was more correctly the homeland of the Cayuse and especially the Walla Walla.

The establishment of this post was due largely to the efforts of Donald McKenzie, a former Astorian who had been a key explorer and highly capable field leader in the Snake River country of central and southern Idaho. After the demise of the Pacific Fur Company, McKenzie had returned east with important dispatches for Astor. Then, after transferring his loyalty to the Nor'Westers, he was assigned to the Columbia in 1816 to take charge of the interior trade, particularly the leadership of brigades sent into the dangerous Snake country of southern Idaho.

"A man of huge stature, weighing over 300 pounds; tireless, fearless, and a skilled rifleman able to 'drive a dozen balls consecutively at one hundred paces through a Spanish dollar,' he was" respected by the Indi-ans,[25] whom he treated fairly. McKenzie stands out as a man of vision and action in this period, when such qualities were unexplicitly becoming rare among the North West Company's leadership in the Pacific Northwest.

In 1818, McKenzie and 97 men built Fort Nez Perces on the east bank of the Columbia, about ½ mile north of the Walla Walla's mouth. It was destined to be one of the most significant posts in the history of the West. Seven years earlier, of course, David Thompson had recognized the strategic importance of this locality when he posted his proclamation at the mouth of the Snake, about 10 miles north. The brigades outfitted at Fort Nez Perces, with coordination from Spokane House and other re-gional posts, were among the first to explore and trap much of present-day eastern Oregon, Idaho, northern Nevada and Utah, and western Wyo-ming and Montana.

Furthermore, the mouth of the Walla Walla was a key crossroads. Converging here were numerous lines of communication across the region and the West, including: the bateau routes up and down the Columbia and Snake rivers, the Oregon Trail extending eastward over the Blue Moun-tains to southern Idaho and the Rockies and eventually St. Louis, the "Over-land" trail to the Nez Perce country, and routes northward across the Columbia Basin to Okanogan and the Spokane country (more will be said about these latter trails, of course, in following chapters). Also of great importance, Indian horses were plentiful and relatively easily acquired here.

Fort Nez Perces was stoutly fortified, with corner bastions and a 12-to 15-feet-high stockade. Alexander Ross, first in charge here, called it the "Gibralter [*sic*] of the Columbia," the strongest fort west of the Rockies. "At each angle was placed a large reservoir sufficient to hold two hundred gallons of water as a security against fire, the element we most dreaded in the designs of the natives."[26]

Special defensive precautions were taken because the local tribes, par-ticularly the Cayuse, were the most powerful and warlike in the region, though usually the warriors remained on fairly good terms with the fur traders. By this time, hostilities sometimes surfaced between Native Ameri-cans and fur traders in these southern areas, though relations remained better in the northern Big Bend area. Raiding Paiute, Bannack, and Shoshone from southeast Oregon likewise proved to be something of a threat to the fur traders, as well as, of course, to their traditional enemies, the local Sahaptin tribes. Armaments included cannon, swivel guns, a primitive mortar, 60 stands of muskets and bayonets, boarding pikes, and hand grenades. An inner stockade further protected the dwellings and storehouses, should the outer wall be breached. Trade was conducted through a small window in the stockade wall.

Meinig, in his usually succinct manner, has summed up the establishment and importance of Fort Nez Perces:

> It would have been difficult to find a more bleak and unattractive site: a barren gravel terrace overlooking the Columbia, but a view blocked on the south and west by basaltic walls, and to the east extending over the drab sandy sagebrush plain of the lower Walla Walla Valley. The almost constant wind, channeled violently up between the black ramparts of the river corridor, drove sand and dust into everything and, as attested by many a journal account, was to imbed itself upon the memories of a host of travelers in subsequent decades. Little wonder that few wished to forego the pleasant valley of the Spokane for such a spot. But [McKenzie] . . . was governed by strategy, not beauty, and from that standpoint Fort Nez Perces was superb. Under the Astorians the lower Walla Walla Valley had been the main rendezvous for parties departing for and arriving from the several peripheral districts. The North West Company not only inherited this traffic pattern but now enlarged its significance by focusing the whole of New Caledonia southward to the Columbia [via the Okanogan River]; the intentions of opening up the Snake River country to the southeast would provide added emphasis. Increasing trouble with the Indians necessitated transforming it from an informal rendezvous into a permanent post. It was "the most hostile spot on the whole line of communications," wrote Ross . . . Furthermore, it was a location significant to the Indians themselves as a major meeting and trading ground, and as the site of their first encounter with whites where Lewis and Clark made an informal treaty of friendship. This was not just another post, therefore, but the key strategic position west of the Rockies.[27]

Duties for the men at the post varied: they strived to maintain peaceful relations with the local tribes, assisted the annual brigades and other parties paddling up and down the river, outfitted and received the Snake country expeditions, and traded for and maintained a supply of horses. Being in direct contact with the tribes having the largest herds, the procurement of mounts eventually became the post's most essential function. Orders perennially came in from officials at Fort George, Spokane House, and other posts to trade for all the horses that could be obtained, and there was frequent concern over the fact that not enough might be available. In fact, providing the 100 to 200 head a year needed to support the several interior parties proved difficult at times.

The Indians—keen, intelligent traders themselves—fully understood the fur traders' need for mounts and capitalized on this knowledge. This in turn cut deeply into fur trade profits, since the Indians here obtained almost all of the trade goods they needed in exchange for "horses," rather than for the "beaver pelts" so dear to the fur traders' hearts.

Endnotes

1. Documentation for the Lewis and Clark Expedition at the Snake-Columbia junction is extensive. See, Roy E. Appelman, *Lewis and Clark: Historic Places Associated with Their Transcontinental Exploration, 1804-06* (Washington, D.C.: National Park Service, 1975), 164 map, 181, 206; Elliott Coues, ed., *History of the Expedition under the Command of Lewis and Clark*, (New York: Dover, 1965 [rep. ed.]), Vol. 2: 629-50 and Vol. 3: 970-80; Patrick Gass, *A Journal of the Voyages and Travels of a Corps of Discovery* (Pittsburgh, 1807), 151-52, 204-06; Milo M. Quaife, ed., *The Journals of Captain Meriwether Lewis and Sergeant John Ordway . . .* (Madison: State Historical Society of Wisconsin, 1916), 300-01, 347-49; and Reuben Gold Thwaites, ed., *Original Journals of the Lewis and Clark Expedition, 1804-1806* (New York: Antiquarian Press, 1959 [rep. ed.]), Vol. 3: 129-35, Vol. 4: 327-47, Vol. 7: 175-76, and Vol. 8: map 31, part 2.

    In recent years, the various expedition journals have been combined in an excellent multi-volume series: see, Gary E. Moulton, ed., *The Journals of the Lewis and Clark Expedition*, published by the University of Nebraska Press, Lincoln.
2. Thwaites, *Original Journals of the Lewis and Clark Expedition, 1804-1806*, Vol. 3: 134.
3. *Ibid.*, Vol. 4: 331-32.
4. D.W. Meinig, *The Great Columbia Plain: A Historical Geography, 1805-1910* (Seattle: University of Washington Press, 1968), 36-39, 55.
5. The overall detail, accuracy, and thoroughness of Thompson's accounts (see below) are only equalled in the mid-Columbia region's early historic literature by the Lewis and Clark chronicles. No portrait or photograph of this famous Canadian explorer are known to exist.
6. T.C. Elliott, ed., "Journal of David Thompson," *Quarterly of the Oregon Historical Society* 15 (March 1914): 46. In addition to Thompson's journal, see J.B. Tyrrell, ed., *David Thompson's Narrative of His Explorations in Western North America, 1784-1812* (Toronto: Champlain Society, 1916). Thompson wrote his narrative in his later years, expanding on the journals he had kept while active in the fur trade from 1784 to 1812.
7. William C. Brown, "Old Fort Okanogan and the Okanogan Trail," *Quarterly of the Oregon Historical Society* 15 (March 1914): 11-12.
8. Elliott, "Journal of David Thompson," 48-49. See also, William D. Layman, "Hawkbells: David Thompson in North Central Washington," *Columbia: The Magazine of Northwest History* (Winter 1991): 12-19.
9. *Ibid.*, 53-57.
10. *Ibid.*, 60. Patrick Gass's journal, privately printed in 1807, was the first of the Lewis and Clark Expedition annals to be published. The Gass book preceded by seven years

the release of Meriwether Lewis's and William Clark's official account of the journey, which appeared in 1814. See, Gass, *A Journal of the Voyages and Travels of a Corps of Discovery* (1807); and Nicholas Biddle, comp., *History of the Expedition Under the Command of Captains Lewis and Clark*, 2 Vols., ed. by Paul Allen (Philadelphia, 1814).

11. T.C. Elliott, ed., "Journal of David Thompson," *Quarterly of the Oregon Historical Society* 15 (June 1914): 121.

12. Tyrrell, *David Thompson's Narrative of His Explorations in Western North America, 1784-1812*, 525-28.

13. Ross Cox, *The Columbia River*, ed. by Edgar I. and Jane R. Stewart (Norman: University of Oklahoma Press, 1957 [originally published 1831]), 89-106; and Washington Irving, *Astoria, or Anecdotes of an Enterprise Beyond the Rocky Mountains*, ed. by Edgeley W. Todd (Norman: University of Oklahoma Press, 1964 [originally published 1836]), 433-35.

14. Alexander Ross, *Adventures of the First Settlers on the Oregon or Columbia River* (London, 1849), 126-27. Ross's two volumes of his reminiscences—his *Adventures . . .* cited here, covering the years 1810 to 1813, and *The Fur Hunters of the Far West*, for 1813 to 1825—originally were published in London in 1849 and 1855 respectively. Ross's two volumes, along with those of Astorian clerks Ross Cox (*The Columbia River*) and Gabriel Franchere (*Adventure at Astoria*), plus Washington Irving's *Astoria*, are essential to an understanding of Inland Northwest history in the early fur trade era. All five books recount a thrilling period, making for insightful and informative reading about one of the unique regions of the West.

15. Ross, *Adventures of the First Settlers on the Oregon or Columbia River*, 132. The Astorians, like Thompson, probably were familiar with Sergeant Gass's *Journal*.

16. Ross, *Adventures of the First Settlers on the Oregon or Columbia River*, 133-42.

17. *Ibid.*, 146.

18. *Ibid.*, 151.

19. Brown, "Old Fort Okanogan and the Okanogan Trail," 14; also see, A.G. Harvey, "David Stuart: Okanagan Pathfinder and Founder of Kamloops," *British Columbia Historical Quarterly* 9 (October 1945): 277-88.

20. Philip Ashton Rollins, ed., *The Discovery of the Oregon Trail: Robert Stuart's Narratives* (New York: Charles Scribner's Sons, 1935); and Gabriel Franchere, *Adventure at Astoria, 1810-1814* (Norman: University of Oklahoma Press, 1967), 72. The account by Franchere, an Astorian clerk, first appeared in the French language at Montreal, in 1820.

21. Meinig, *The Great Columbia Plain*, 44-45.

22. Ross, *The Fur Hunters of the Far West*, 23.

23. Elliott Coues, ed., *The Manuscript Journals of Alexander Henry, Fur Trader of the Northwest Company, and of David Thompson, Official Geographer and Explorer of the Same Company, 1799-1814* (Minneapolis, 1897), 770.

24. Cox, *The Columbia River*, 229-31, 233. Also see, "Fort Okanogan: Fur Empire Outpost," *Okanogan County Heritage* 15 (Spring 1977): 28-30.

25. Dorothy O. Johansen and Charles M. Gates, *Empire of the Columbia: A History of the Pacific Northwest*, 2nd Ed. (New York: Harper and Row, 1967), 107.

26. Ross, *The Fur Hunters of the Far West*, 144-46.

27. Meinig, *The Great Columbia Plain*, 62. Also see, Theodore Stern, *Chiefs and Chief Traders: Indian Relations at Fort Nez Perces, 1818-1855* (Corvallis: Oregon State University Press, 1993).

Sir George Simpson, Governor of the Hudson's Bay Company during the heyday of the nineteenth-century western fur trade. *Oregon Historical Society*

V
A New Era

FOR NEARLY A decade, the North West Company alone conducted the fur trade in the Inland Northwest, free from intrusions by Americans, or from the Nor'Westers great Canadian rival, the Hudson's Bay Company (HBC). By the early 1820s, the HBC had yet to effectively push operations west of the Canadian Plains; while the Americans, based out of St. Louis, focused their attention on the Missouri, Platte, and Green River drainages in the central Rockies.

But the winds of change were stirring. Internal dissension, between the Nor'Westers' Montreal-based merchant proprietors and the wintering partners in their wilderness outposts, damaged the firm's effectiveness. More significantly, a virtual state of warfare resulting in a considerable loss of life broke out between the Nor'Westers and the HBC over the fur trade, particularly in the Red River country of the eastern Plains. Even though the Pacific Northwest remained far removed from actual hostilities, efficiency and organization at Fort Nez Perces and other western posts suffered from neglect, as the energy and focus of the normally adventuresome Nor'Westers' was consumed by the wasteful, decade-long conflict. The British crown finally stepped in to stop this ruinous disruption of the wilderness economy, forcing a coalition of the bitter rivals in an agreement signed by the principal representatives of each company in London in 1821.

The resulting organization generally adopted the more efficient features from either company, as the enlarged HBC took in all but the most recalcitrant of its former enemies. In fact, ex-Nor'Westers actually outnumbered HBC men in the important leadership positions at the frontier posts. The compromise was intended to last 21 years, but by 1825 the combination had reconciled itself to the hegemony of the HBC.

The new organization's administration was in the hands of men usually wintering at the wilderness trading posts, and included 25 chief factors and 28 chief traders who were, more often than not, Scots. Chief factors were senior to chief traders. (The old-fashioned term "factor" means, in this case, one who handles important monetary and business affairs.) An annual governing council at a post on Hudson Bay—attended by the governor, chief factors, and chief traders in charge of fur trade districts— set policy for the upcoming year. As was the case with Astor's Pacific Fur Company and the old North West Company, most of the firm's rank and file workers in the interior (the hunters, laborers, boatmen, etc.) were French Canadians. However, also occupying these positions, in lesser numbers, were men from the Iroquois, Abnaki, Nipissing, and other eastern tribes. These tribal peoples, of course, had played prominent roles in the eighteenth century wars between France and England and in the American Revolution. Now, as their eastern homelands succumbed to advancing settlers, many of them preferred the wilderness freedom of Canada's far western realms. Often independent minded and difficult to manage, these eastern Indians nonetheless proved hardy, brave, and resourceful.

Sir George Simpson and the HBC

In the merger with the North West Company, the HBC, of course, acquired a virtual monopoly of the Interior Northwest fur trade. As already noted, the fur trade in the Pacific Northwest region—called the Department of the Columbia—had slid in efficiency, proving unprofitable. But a new era was about to begin in 1824 with the arrival of George Simpson, the flamboyant, vitriolic HBC Governor based out of London, but now on an inspection tour of his realm.[1]

"Simpson—intelligent and energetic, possessing an almost incomparable power to drive himself, willing to turn his coat in order to keep in favor with his superiors in London, and capable of harshness as inexorable as the wilderness in which his company operated" had worked tirelessly in the service of the HBC since 1810.[2] He was an efficient, Machiavellian-type administrator, who within only a few years had become the sole head of the company in Canada and the architect of its policies—in fact, practically its dictator.

Simpson in 1824, having set affairs in order in Canada's Hudson Bay country, in the far northern forests, and on the northern Plains, turned his attention to the far-off Columbia River country. On August 15, 1824, Simpson left the HBC's headquarters at York Factory on the west side of Hudson Bay to cross the continent on his first inspection tour of the HBC's new holdings in the Pacific Northwest. During this journey across the continent, he subjected to piercing scrutiny every employee, post, route, portage—in fact, any and all aspects of the fur trade system.

Two months later, his party struggled through rain, sleet, and snow across Athabasca Pass in the great Canadian Rockies. Even the indomitable governor was impressed by his first contact with these mountains, which he described as "stupendous." Once in the Columbia River country, however, he felt that practically every station was overstaffed with personnel and overstocked with luxury provisions. As he stated in his diary after an inspection of Spokane House:

> The good people of Spokane District and I believe of the interior of the Columbia generally have since its first establishment shewn an extraordinary predilection for European Provisions without once looking at or considering the enormous price . . . they may be said to have been eating Gold; such fare we cannot afford in the present times, it must therefore be discontinued . . . The articles of Provisions and Luxuries are in themselves . . . of little value but when the Expence of conveying them to their destination is taken into account that acquired value is a matter of very serious consideration.
>
> I do not know any part of the Country on the East side of the Mountain [Cascades] that affords such resources in the way of living as Spokane District; they have abundance of the finest Salmon in the World besides a variety of other Fish within 100 yds. of their Door, plenty of Potatoes, Game if they like it, in short every thing that is good or necessary for an Indian trader; why therefore squander thousands uselessly in this manner? . . . I have therefore given intimation that they had better Hoard the European provisions and Luxuries they have got now in Store as their future supplies will be very scanty.

From Spokane House, Simpson's party paddled quickly on down the Columbia, reaching Fort Okanogan (see appendix 2) on November 1, 1824, where the governor observed:

> This Post is agreeably situated in a fine plain . . . the Soil is much the same as at Spokane and produces the finest potatoes I have seen in the Country. Grain [and corn] in any quantity might be raised here . . . In regard to Provisions and Luxuries not one oz. is required for this place beyond the established allowance as excellent fish can be got in abundance with little cost or trouble, and at merely the expense of a little ammunition the table of the Gentleman in charge can be occasionally supplied with Game.

Continuing down the Columbia, the party floated past the "Pischouse" (Wenatchee) River and bolted through Rock Island Rapids and Priest Rapids. In passing over the latter on November 3, Simpson reported: "by a blunder of my foreman who . . . took the wrong lead we narrowly escaped being upset; it was such a close shave that I began to peel for a swimming match."

His account continues with these interesting observations of the Columbia's Big Bend:

> In the course of to Day passed some Hundreds of Indians all busily employed in laying up Salmon for the Winter. Since leaving Okanagan there is scarcely a Tree or Shrub to be seen and Fire Wood is so scarce that the Brigades passing frequently burn the pallisades that surround the Graves of the Natives; this is a most unwarrantable liberty and would on the other side of the mountain [east of the Rockies] be considered the grossest insult that could be offered and accordingly resented by the Natives; but the Indians here are so passive and well disposed that they take little notice thereof, we should not however impose on their good nature as it cannot fail of giving offense and I mean to issue instructions that it be discontinued in future as it might some Day lead to serious quarrels.

Two hours after sunset, the party put ashore to encamp, probably somewhere just above or in the White Bluffs locality. Shortly, they were unexpectedly approached by 60 Nez Perces "who smoked and were very friendly." Simpson, noting that the Indians "mustered strong," perhaps became overly anxious and suspicious. After eating, he abruptly ordered his party to embark in the darkness, leaving the Indians ashore, and they paddled all night, arriving at Fort Nez Perces at sunrise.

Here, Simpson continued his tirade against the lackadaisical condition of local fur trade operations. Fort Nez Perces, where large, powerful bands of Walla Walla, Cayuse, and Nez Perce frequently gathered to trade horses with the whites, had a relatively large complement of employees—11 men and their Indian wives and families:

> Large quantities of Luxuries and European provisions are annually consumed at a prodigious cost and for no other good reason than that they are preferred to the produce of the Country which is cheap and abundant; while this ruinous system continues it is not surprising that the Columbia Department is unprofitable.

Thus, with each successive visit to a post, Simpson's indignation at extravagance mounted. It culminated with his arrival at Fort George at the Columbia's mouth, where the stockade, bastions, and two cannon presented, an air or appearance of Grandeur & consequence which does not become and is not at all suitable to an Indian Trading Post. Everything appears to me on the Columbia on too extended a scale *except the Trade* and when I say that that is confined to Four permanent Establishments the returns of which do not amount to 20,000 Beaver & Otters altho the country has been occupied upwards of Fourteen Years I feel that a very Severe reflection is cast on those who have had charge of the management of the Business . . . I cannot help thinking that no economy has been observed, that little exertion has been used, and that sound judgment has not been exercised but that mismanagement and extravagance has been the order of the day. It is now however necessary that a radical change should take place and we have no time to lose in bringing it about.

Simpson especially disapproved of the expensive utilization of brigades of three or four boats and 35 to 40 men at a time partly for the purpose of distributing domestic goods at the upriver posts. Included among these items from London, Boston, or California were butter, cheese, pickles, sauces, vinegar, sugar, pepper, tobacco, brandy, rum, wine, tea, bar iron, glass, saddlery, fishing gear, soap, firearms and associated equipment, and a great variety of textile and apparel goods. And, to make matters worse in Simpson's eyes, the posts could even make a lavish use of local resources, such as at Fort Nez Perces for instance:

> As an example of the Waste and extravagance of Provisions some time ago no less than Seven Hundred Horses were slaughtered for the use of this Establishment in three Years besides Imported Provisions and it has been left for me to discover that neither Horse Flesh nor Imported Provisions are all required as the River with a Potatoe Garden will abundantly maintain the post.[3]

Changes followed quickly. By early 1825, the governor, true to his Scottish soul, "loosed a chilly wind of austerity which swept through the whole department, blighting the ideas of luxurious living and wasteful practices in the fur trade as effectively as a springtime Chinook wind cleared the Columbia Valley of ice and snow." To further continue in the eloquent words of noted Northwest historian J. Orin Oliphant:

> Henceforth efficiency and economy would replace slovenliness and extravagance. Henceforth both the gentlemen and the lesser servants of the Hudson's Bay Company not only would work to expand the fur trade and make it more efficient, but also would accept as a legitimate activity any pursuit that promised to lessen the cost of such trade.

Henceforth there would prevail the notion, until then considered odd, that the resources of both land and water should be so exploited that they would not only meet the needs of the department for food, but also provide a surplus of pork, beef, grain, butter, fish, and other articles for an export trade. Thus in the middle 1820's there was generated, among other things, a pressing concern about agricultural pursuits and the breeding of livestock in the valley of the Columbia.[4]

Among the most significant of Simpson's reforms was his insistence upon self-sufficient agricultural development, the better utilization of transportation and accounting strategies, and the building of two new posts: Fort Vancouver in 1824-25, and Fort Colvile in 1825-26. These strategically located forts were destined to direct operations in the Department of the Columbia, as well as New Caledonia (which extended from central British Columbia north to the Arctic).

The HBC's vast Department of the Columbia soon generally came to be called the "Oregon Country" by people in the East and in England. Claimed by both Great Britain and the United States, the disputed Oregon Country comprised the entire greater Pacific Northwest region from the Russian settlements in the north to Mexico-controlled California in the south, and from the crest of the Rocky Mountains west to the Pacific Ocean.

Simpson was convinced that if a permanent boundary settlement was finalized with the United States, the area south of the Columbia (present-day Oregon, the Big Bend, the Palouse, etc.) would go to the Americans, while the lands north of the river (i.e., western Washington, the Cascade Range, the Yakima Valley, and the Okanogan highland) would come under British hegemony. (This expectation never materialized, of course, because the 49th parallel eventually became the international boundary through diplomatic agreement in 1846.)

At any rate, Simpson authorized the shift of department headquarters in 1825 from Fort George to newly constructed Fort Vancouver (modern day Vancouver, Washington), 100 miles up the Columbia on the north bank. In addition to being in a location expected to become British territory, the climate, soil, and available tillage at Fort Vancouver were far better suited to agriculture than the Fort George locale. Sailing ships also could ply the river's deep water to the fort.

Initially, Simpson had hoped to establish the department headquarters at the mouth of British Columbia's Fraser River, which would have provided for more direct and safer access for ocean-going vessels than the

Columbia, with its treacherous sandbars at the mouth. However, the intended route to the interior—the rugged Fraser River canyon—proved too dangerous even for the company's most expert Iroquois and French Canadian boatmen. (On a second Northwest tour in 1828, Simpson took what turned out to be a hair-raising voyage down the Fraser. Barely cheating the grim reaper on this occasion, he thereafter proclaimed "the passage down . . . to be Certain death, in nine attempts out of Ten.")[5] Consequently, the focal point of the fur trade remained at Fort Vancouver, despite the navigational hazards of the Columbia's mouth.

Simpson was fully aware of the expansion of American fur hunters into the central Rockies, which had begun in the early 1820s. In an attempt to keep the Americans from pushing further westward into the Pacific Northwest, the governor ordered the creation of a "desert fur barrier" in the Snake River country—entailing southern Idaho and the adjoining parts of Montana, Wyoming, Nevada, and Utah. In this broad region, he recommended a policy of completely hunting out beaver. Consequently, this would serve as an obstacle to American encroachment, and incoming profits from the Snake River country would help carry the cost of developing the Department of the Columbia until it was self supporting. However, hostile tribesmen—particularly the region's nomadic Bannack, as well as raiding Blackfeet war parties coming from the Plains—made duty in the Snake River country hazardous, as the Astorians and Nor'Westers earlier had discovered when sending well-armed parties into the region in the 1810s.

When this policy was put into action, the HBC's Snake River expeditions by necessity were large and well-organized when setting out from Fort Nez Perces. These brigades exhibited a truly multicultural composition—in charge were Scottish, Irish, or English brigade leaders and other HBC officials. The rank-and-file hunters, camp keepers, and horse herders, often with their families, consisted of French Canadians and half-breeds, Iroquois and other eastern tribesmen, Plateau and Northwest Coast Indians, Hawaiians, and an occasional American or two. In the long run, Simpson's "desert fur barrier" proved largely effective, since relatively few American hunters from St. Louis penetrated the Columbia Plateau. (In the early 1840s, however, large numbers of American settlers, seeking farms rather than beaver pelts in the Willamette valley, would tip the region's population balance in favor of the United States.)

Another of Simpson's momentous decisions was the selection of Dr. John McLoughlin, a tall (6' 4") white-haired man, to serve as chief factor in charge of all HBC operations west of the Rockies. On Simpson's initial inspection tour, Simpson had met McLoughlin out on the Canadian Plains on September 26, 1824, and brought him along to the Columbia country. At the time of their meeting, McLoughlin had already spent many days of hard traveling in the wilderness. Simpson's typically caustic (and often unfair) pen recorded this description of the apparently disheveled McLoughlin:

> he was such a figure as I should not like to meet in a dark Night in one of the bye lanes in the neighbourhood of London, dressed in Clothes that had once been fashionable, but now covered with a thousand patches of different Colors, his beard would do honor to the chin of a Grizzly Bear, his face and hands evidently Shewing that he had not lost much time at his Toilette, loaded with Arms and his own herculean dimensions forming a tout ensemble that would convey a good idea of the high way men of former Days.[6]

Thirty-nine-year-old McLoughlin, born at Riviére-du-Loup, Canada, on October 19, 1784, had studied medicine as a young man, but soon took up the life of a trader. He already had worked 18 years in the fur trade before his appointment as head of the Columbia Department. Originally a partner in the North West Company, he participated in the hostilities with the Hudson's Bay Company in the Red River country, and served as one of the Nor'Westers' representatives when the union of the two fur-trading firms was arranged in London in 1821.

Reportedly not reconciled to the new order, it was thought by some that he was exiled to the Columbia for his earlier partisanship. If exile it was, destiny would make him the primary figure in Northwest history for more than two decades to come. From 1824 to 1846, the "White-Headed Eagle" directed the vast HBC operations west of the Rockies; and Fort Vancouver, McLoughlin's headquarters after 1825, was the largest HBC post in the region. Its complement of traders, voyageurs, clerks, interpreters, mechanics, laborers, and their families made it one of the first true commercial and agricultural communities on the Pacific Coast.

As with the founding of Fort Vancouver, Simpson likewise selected the site for Fort Colvile at Kettle Falls on the upper Columbia. On his return east upriver in the spring of 1825, Simpson investigated the Kettle Falls locality, personally negotiating with the local Indians when selecting ground for the new post. Like Fort Vancouver, the area's agricultural prospects were excellent. Furthermore, a post at this location would eliminate the cost and time of moving furs and supplies 60 miles between Spokane House and the Columbia.

While still formulating plans for the site, Simpson lost no time in proceeding on his journey east. Two days later on April 16, 1825, at Columbia Lake (British Columbia), Simpson addressed a letter to John Work in charge at Spokane House directing him to begin construction of the new fort at Kettle Falls:

> I have lined out the site of a new establishment at the Kettle Falls and wish you to commence building and transporting the property from Spokane as early as possible. Mr. [James] Birnie[7] has been directed to plant about 5 kegs of potatoes—You will be so good as (to) take great care of them[,] the produce to be reserved for seed, not eat[ing], as next spring I expect that from 30 to 40 Bushels will be planted.—Pray let every possible exertion be used to buy up an abundant stock of Fish and other Provisions [and] country Produce, as no imported provisions can in future be forwarded from the coast.[8]

Work and his men undertook this task in the autumn and winter of 1825-26, while abandoning Spokane House. (John Work, born in Ireland about 1792, had joined the Hudson's Bay Company in 1814. At 5' 7" tall with fair hair and complexion, he was described by a contemporary in 1821 as "a most excellent young man in every respect." He remained in charge at Fort Colvile from 1826 to 1829 and was an important downriver brigade leader, as will be described in detail shortly.)[9]

Simpson named Fort Colvile for his early mentor, Andrew Colvile, a director and later a governor of the HBC in London. (Years later in 1859, the U. S. Army's Fort Colville was established approximately 14 miles to the southeast near present day Colville, Washington; the spelling of the name of the military post differs in that it has a double "l" in the second syllable.) As an administrative and financial unit, the HBC's Colvile District supplanted the earlier Spokane District. In 1826, the new district's territory encompassed the northeastern quarter of Washington, northern Idaho, Montana west of the continental divide, and those parts of British Columbia drained by the Columbia River.

Fort Colvile, the largest post between the Cascades and the Rockies, occupied a key point in the line of communication on the Columbia between Hudson Bay, Montreal, and the Pacific Coast. Furthermore, it also served as a main provider of foodstuffs and horses for HBC brigades operating in the Columbia Plateau and interior British Columbia, as well as in the Snake River country.

At this time, New Caledonia remained linked to Montreal by the east-west routes across the Canadian Rockies pioneered by North West

Company explorers early in the century. Beginning in the mid 1810s, New Caledonia posts also had received supplies from North West Company supply ships arriving at the mouth of the Columbia River. The trade goods and supplies, of course, were hauled into the interior by boat and pack string. The HBC, taking control in 1821, continued this practice for a time, but then reinstituted receiving supplies packed over the lakes, rivers, and portages from the east.

Soon, however, Simpson concluded that this cross-continent travel was proving to be overly long, and thus too costly. As his hope of using British Columbia's Fraser River as a direct access to the Pacific Ocean proved fruitless, Simpson turned his attention to utilizing the Okanogan valley route.

Consequently, in the spring of 1826 he ordered the New Caledonia posts to again transport furs south to the Columbia by way of Fort Okanogan, and from there downriver to Fort Vancouver, in an annual brigade. The Astorians and Nor'Westers, of course, had pioneered this route. Simpson's directive instituted the major utilization of what came to be called the Hudson's Bay brigade trail in the Okanogan valley—a route regularly used by the HBC for the next two decades.

"Each winter the furs traded at the posts in the northern interior were brought to Fort St. James, the headquarters of New Caledonia, with dog sledges. As soon as the ice broke up, generally about April 20, boats loaded with cargoes of furs started from Stuart Lake to pick up" other furs at subsidiary posts along the way. "At Alexandria, the horse brigade started out for Fort Okanogan, sometimes accompanying and sometimes following the Thompson's river brigade, which was taking out the furs of the Kamloops District."[10]

Meanwhile, in the Colvile District, similar collections and arrangements were being made to pack furs at subsidiary posts in western Montana for shipment to Fort Colvile as soon as the ice broke up in the rivers and snow melted on the trails. Sometime in April, the winter proceeds from the Kootenai area likewise were brought south, in this case via present day Bonners Ferry, Idaho. From there, the furs were taken overland to the Pend Oreille River, then across the mountains of northeast Washington, and down the Colville valley to Fort Colvile.

In the meantime, men at Fort Colvile made preparations for launching the downriver flotilla to Fort Okanogan, Fort Nez Perces, and, ultimately, Fort Vancouver. In May, after the incoming parties brought in their furs and, sometimes, after being joined by an overland express from eastern Canada crossing the northern Plains and Rockies to Fort Colvile,

York Boat

the combined outbound brigade timed its departure from Fort Colvile to meet the New Caledonia cavalcade coming down the Okanogan valley at Fort Okanogan.[11]

The HBC men paddled bateaux: long, sturdy, cedar-plank boats, normally manned by a crew of six or eight, which hauled several thousand pounds of furs and provisions. The HBC bateau—especially a standardized type called a York boat—was used extensively by the Hudson's Bay Company throughout its northern realm as well as in the vast Columbia watershed. Earlier, fur traders on the Columbia had experimented with other types of watercraft; the North West Company, for instance, brought birch-bark canoes from Canada in the holds of seagoing vessels, but these eastern-woodlands canoes proved impractical in the Columbia system's rocky waterways and often treeless country. Furthermore, regional forests did not always provide the proper type of materials for canoe building or repairs. The Pacific Fur Company tried Chinook dugout canoes, which, despite being admirably seaworthy in coastal waters, proved impractical in the interior.

With the merger of the HBC and the North West Company in 1821, the HBC bateau supplanted the Nor'Wester canoe for heavy, long-range hauling. Under Simpson's orders in 1823, new bateaux built by the company were standardized at a minimum keel length of 24 feet. This directive was reenacted annually from 1825 until 1828, before becoming a permanent regulation. In the 1820s, Simpson reckoned that 1,000 pieces of 90 pounds weight each—or 3 tons for each boat—was a reasonable cargo for 14 boats to carry.

York boats had short lives, lasting "only about three years, having to undergo such severe strains and hard usage in the rapids and portages on the routes followed."[12] This was particularly true in the West where only soft woods were available for construction. The crews carried extra planks, nails, and pitch to make repairs as needed. Because of the bateau's short life, skilled boat builders were among the company's most valued employees.

Being low amidships, high and peaked at the bow and stern, and having a very shallow draft for hauling over rapids, these boats obviously were not designed for relying on sails. But since western rivers normally were shallow, the HBC did not need the luxury of deep-keeled sailing boats anyway. When traveling on the rare, open expanses of lakes or broad rivers in the west, the wind pushed these shallow-bottomed craft leeward. Despite this drawback, York boats were fitted with a central mast for a sail, with cables passing from the peak to both ends and the gunwales. Though the boat's great square sail often proved useless, with experienced crews and good conditions they could be sailed surprisingly close to the wind.

On the Columbia from Fort Vancouver to the mouth of the Snake, sails greatly reduced the labor of the upriver journey. Beyond Fort Nez Perces along the Columbia's Big Bend, however, the deep canyon walls and the change to a northerly course largely ruled out any steady reliance on the prevailing southwesterly breezes; more often than not sails proved useless here. Consequently, near the Snake River, crews often hid masts in the sagebrush to be picked up again during the downriver run the following year.

With one man to each oar, rowers sat on opposite sides of the boat to that to which their blades dipped into the water; thus, the men were spaced alternately left and right with their backs to the bow. When rowing, each man stood up, lifting his oar blade above the water at the start of each stroke, then he dropped to a sitting position while pulling back as the blade bit into the river.

John Work and the 1828 Columbia River Brigade

To understand the difficulties in moving furs, cargo, and men in flotillas down the Columbia from Fort Colvile to Fort Vancouver and then returning upstream with supplies and trading goods for the interior posts, it would be helpful to follow a typical brigade in its travels. Setting out on the Columbia from Fort Colvile in late spring or early summer, the river brigade first stopped at Fort Okanogan to connect with the New Caledonia brigade coming down from the north via the waterways and trails of British

Columbia. With the brigades now consolidated, the flotilla took on additional fur packs, cargo, boats, and men, and paddled on down to Fort Nez Perces, and then continued to Fort Vancouver, normally arriving during the first part of June.

The following account of a typical brigade's trip from Fort Colvile to Fort Vancouver, and back again, is from one of John Work's journals, a copy of which is in the holdings of the Bancroft Library at Berkeley, California.[13] Work, who was in charge at Fort Colvile at the time, directed the downriver brigade on its first leg, to Fort Okanogan.

His journal begins Tuesday, May 20, 1828, as the flotilla of 6 boats, 21 men, and the Indian wife and 2 children of one of the voyageurs, casts off into the Columbia at Fort Colvile between "3 or 4 oclock in the afternoon." Their cargo consisted of 70 packs of furs, 2 kegs of castoreum (collected from the glands of beaver; utilized by hunters for baiting beaver traps, and by manufacturers in the East and Europe for making perfume), 12 bales of leather, 8 bales of barley meal and 2 bales of corn meal (from Fort Colvile's 1827 crop), 10 saddles, a cage of 3 young pigs for sending to New Caledonia, a similar cage for Fort Nez Perces, 6 Indian lodges, and provisions for the voyage.

On the first day, they proceeded about a dozen or so miles to a point below Thompson's Rapid, later known as Grand or Rickey Rapids (now submerged by the Grand Coulee Dam reservoir). Two boats in the lead suffered damage, however, when shooting the white water, as Work relates:

> We were detained some time at the rapid, repairing two of the boats that were broken. The cargo got wet; all the other boats were lightened and half the cargo carried, and the boats ran down at two trips.
>
> We have only twenty men for the six boats, four men each for two of the boats, and three each for the other four, which certainly [are]weak crews for such a dangerous part of the river . . . Cloudy mild weather.
>
> *May 21.* Embarked at daylight this morning, and continued our route without any delay whatever, except . . . for breakfast, till a little before sunset, when we encamped . . . a little above the little Dalls [Mahkin Rapids], which is a days work for so few men. The current is very strong, and sent us along at a rapid rate, but the water is not so high as last year; it is now in a good state, and none of the rapids dangerous. Notwithstanding the time . . . taken gumming the boats, some of them are leaky, and two of them had to be gummed. Yesterday evening some of the people were employ[ed at that].

At this camp, the brigade had 33 miles to go to reach Fort Okanogan.

May 22nd. Cloudy cool weather in the morning, very warm afterwards. Resumed our route at daylight, and arrived at [Fort] Okanage[n] before breakfast, and found some of the people still not up. The Dalls [Mahkin Rapids] were found good, and the boats shot down them without stopping. [Upon arrival at Okanogan] Received and examined the cargo, all in good order . . . as the men had worked hard, gave them the remainder of the day, to rest, previous to commencing gumming the boats.

No news as yet of Mr. Conolly [Chief Trader William Connolly stationed at Fort St. James in New Caledonia] and his people . . . [We] had appointed the 24th as the date on which he was to reach Okanage. We expected that being so weakly [manned] it would have taken us also to that date to reach this [point]—where as, we were only a day & a half [in coming from Fort Colvile] . . . Finding some salmon in store, it was served out to the people, and the barley and corn used . . .

May 23rd.—Very warm in the middle of the day, stormy in the afternoon. Had three of the men employed making oars; all the others gumming their boats . . . One of the boats was in the water, and does not want much repairs, but . . . two, being [beached and] exposed to the sun, the gum was melted off them. The seams opened, so that it takes a considerable deal of labor, to put them in order. There are two other boats, which are so old and out of order, and so much decayed that it is considered impossible to repair them so that they could be brought up the river again with any safety. Two of the men . . . are both bad with sore eyes.

May 24th. Stormy weather[,] warm in the middle of the day. The men finished gumming the boats, and had them in the water before breakfast.

About noon on this day, New Caledonian trader Francis Ermatinger came down the Okanogan River, announcing that Mr. Connolly and his main party would not arrive for another two days. Ermatinger was an experienced hand in the Columbia Department (he eventually became a chief trader in 1842).

May 25th. A storm of wind with a great deal of dust.
May 26th. Fine weather, some gusts of wind. Mr. Conolly arrived at noon, his people are close too.

The main brigade, however, arrived the next day, but let us take the opportunity here to break from Work's account while he was waiting at Fort Okanogan and describe the pack trains that traveled between central British Columbia and Fort Okanogan in the flush days of the Indian trade. In the words of a fur trader, "A beautiful sight was that horse brigade, with no broken hacks in the train, but every animal in his full beauty of form and color, and all so tractable!—more tractable than anything I know of in civilized life."[14] HBC records extensively document the annual brigade's use of the Okanogan route from 1826 until 1847, after which time the area became American territory.

The large overland brigades consisted of one to three hundred pack horses with each animal carrying two pieces, or bales, weighing 90 to 100 pounds each. Mounted men rode in among the caravan, shouting and prodding the horses to keep them moving, while their Indian wives and children trailed behind with kitchen equipment and bedding. At the front rode the chief trader, normally wearing a broadcloth suit, white shirt, collar, and a gentlemen's tall-brimmed beaver hat on his head to indicate his authority over the HBC's employees and to impress the Indians. Usually, cannon or rifle salutes rang out as the chief trader and his entourage set out from, or approached, a fort—be it either a New Caledonian post or Fort Okanogan. Another company official, or in later years a missionary, might ride alongside him, given safe passage by the brigade. Sometimes a bagpiper rode next in line, playing a Scottish air that echoed off the Okanogan's many rocky canyon walls.

Few of the large, cargo-laden, pack trains could proceed more than 18 or 20 miles a day. In the morning, fires had to be started, breakfasts cooked (frequently dried salmon), stock rounded up, and packs loaded. Most of the brigade set out after about 9 o'clock, and by 4 o'clock went into camp at some choice location with wood, water, and grass.

One of the Northwest's first Catholic missionaries, Father Modeste Demers, provided a firsthand description of a New Caledonia brigade in the summer of 1842, in this case while traveling northward on the Okanogan trail. Demers obviously was something of a "greenhorn," unaccustomed to the hardiness and fortitude needed on the trails. He was not adaptable to, nor inclined toward, wilderness living, as his account to the Bishop of Quebec clearly reveals:

> This type of caravan is composed of a numerous troop of men and of horses loaded with baggage and merchandise destined for the different posts in the north. All this grouping of men, horses and baggage naturally renders the march slow and wearisome. Each morning's preparations are not finished until nine or ten o'clock. Horses let out haphazard during the night and scattered in every direction must be hunted up. After long delays you at last find everything ready, and the neighing of horses, the shouts of the engagés, the oaths jerked out by impatience, the disputes, the orders of the leaders form a hullabaloo by which scrupulous ears are not always flattered. At last, after having

eaten on the grass a repast of dried salmon, the horses are loaded, and at ten o'clock you are on your way. The march is extremely slow and filled with incidents more or less disagreeable. There is a feverish atmosphere, an oppressive sun, a choking dust, a hill to climb, a ravine to cross. The first days, especially, one experiences general discomfort and numerous inconveniences through the irksome position when on horseback, having on the crupper ones church plate, bed, household equipment, and even kitchen. Good luck indeed if some untoward wind does not force us to breathe a thick dust which prevents us from seeing two rods ahead of us. A low buzz of conversation is heard with a monotony only broken when passing through a creek or a river. Then we draw closer together, horses hesitate, men shout, get angry, jostle each other, tumble; and often wrecks follow, exciting general hilarity and reviving conversations for the rest of the day. Halts are made only for camping, that is to say in the idiom of the country, one only hitches up once; and the day's travel ends in three or four hours. Then arrangements are made for camping; the horses are turned loose and sent to pasture as they can; the baggage is arranged in an orderly manner; men gather in groups to pass the night; they eat their meal of dried salmon, and the sun has banished from the horizon.

Buried in these immense deserts in the midst of a class of men uncultured and occupied solely in the search of terrestial goods to the profit of those who pay for them, a man whose soul and heart are shaped to higher feelings—a missionary in brief—would experience only distaste and unbearable boredom, if he was not revived by the comforts of faith.[15]

Now to continue with Work's account, as he waited on the Columbia for the arrival of the main New Caledonia pack train, closing in on Fort Okanogan. Finally, before noon on May 27, the overland brigade under the charge of Thomas Dears came into sight. Upon their arrival, all of the men quickly gathered up the New Caledonia furs and other items, incorporating the packs into the cargo of the downriver brigade's boats, now 9 in number.

With everything arranged to start the next day, the combined brigades now came under the command of William Connolly, while Thomas Dears, Francis Ermatinger, and John Work acted as subordinates. The cargoes consisted of 33 packages per boat, for a total of 228 packs of fur, 7 bales of leather, 6 kegs of castoreum, 8 saddles, 1 packet of pamphlets or books, 16 packages of gum, and 6 lodges with baggage. Thus, 156 packs of furs have been added, with each pack weighing 90 to 100 lbs, along with additional baggage and provisions. Meanwhile, a pig crate, 2 kegs of grain or meal, 5 bales of leather, and 4 saddles have been left at Fort Okanogan for the New Caledonia District.

> *May 28th.* Fine weather, blowing fresh part of the day. Some time was spent in the morning gumming two boats that were a little leaky; that detained us till between 7 & 8 oclock when the baggage started . . . The men used oars in preference to paddles, and had as many as could work in each boat. The wind some time detained us, and the current was very strong. In the evening we encamped a little above the [Priest] Rapids. The oars were far superior to paddles; the men do more work with greater ease.
>
> *May 29th.* Overcast in the morning, and raining afterwards. Resumed our route at daylight, or a little before it, and put ashore near the lower end of the [Priest] Rapids to wait for one of the boats . . . in the meantime breakfasted. After which . . . [Pierre Letange,] the guide, who was in Mr. Conolly's boat embarked with [Lewis] Prim[eau's boat], when all proceeded, and ran down the rest of the Rapid, and continued our course . . . [Primeau's boat] remained behind, as the place was not dangerous . . . [our] boats did not stop till they reached Nupims [Fort Nez Perces] in the afternoon, when [the furs, goods and provisions] received and distributed among the boats, and everything arranged to continue our journey tomorrow morning.

Upon arriving at Fort Nez Perces, however, the main party had no inkling that disaster had struck the trailing boat (containing Primeau, guide Letange, and several men) in the Priest Rapids. Late in the evening, guide Letange and another man arrived at the fort

> in an Indian canoe, with this unexpected intelligence, that when coming down the lower part of the Prists Rapids in the morning just after the other boats . . . they struck upon a stone, broke their boat, and three of the seven men that were in her [Primeau, foreman J. F. Laurent, and Joseph Plouff] . . . were drowned, and the others very narrowly escaped. Some of the Indians assisted the survivors in getting some of the packs ashore, but how many would be saved, cannot yet be ascertained . . . [Laurent, one of the drowned men] had been sick, and was very weak. The Guide [stated that] a gust of wind, and the people not pulling fast enough, is the cause of them not being able to clear the rock. Mr Cumatage [Ermatinger] and Mr Dear's were immediately sent off with two boats and 22 men to endeavor to move the bodies and to that may be saved from the water. I am to start early tomorrow morning on horse-back with two men, for the same purpose, by crossing to the [west] side of the river, and straight across the plains. It is expected we will arrive before the boats, and prevent the Indians from carrying off any of the packs, if they be so inclined.

May 30th. Blowing a storm the fore part of the day. The weather was so stormy, and the river so rough, that it was impossible to cross the horses without drowning them, and I could not start as was intended, for the Prist's Rapids where the accident happened.

Because of this delay, the traders realized that it was too late for Work to proceed overland through the Rattlesnake Hills or the Cold Creek valley to Priest Rapids, since the river party now would arrive first. All they could do was sit and wait. (Over the years, the Columbia regularly took a toll of drowned fur traders.)

Meanwhile, news from another locale was received. An Indian arrived from the old Spokane House site with information announcing the death of Jaco Finlay about 10 days before. Finlay, a former Nor'Wester and one of David Thompson's original founders of Spokane House, had continued to occupy the site after the HBC removed its operations to Fort Colvile. He was interred at the fort he helped build.

May 31st. Stormy in the morning, calm afterwards, a little rain in the evening. The furs all covered with oil cloth.

June 1st. Dark cloudy weather. Mr. Cumatinge & Dear arrived with the party at noon, they found all the furs, Oky [a keg] of customs, [castoreum, parflesh] a bale of leather, and 3e . . . [skins] of gum. Nothing was seen of the bodies of the three unfortunate men that were drowned. The old prist and his people behaved well. One of the old mans son came to the fort, and rceived in remuneration for his good conduct in the assistence given in saving the furs.

The after part of the day was employed drying the furs, repairing the boats, and getting everything ready to start early tomorrow morning. The . . . [beaver] skins seem not to be much injured, but the small furs will be a good deal the worse of this wetting; fortunately there were not many.

Monday 2nd. Cloudy most of the day. Left Walla Walla at sunrise, this brigade consists of 9 boats, provisions and baggage. We were nearly three hours ashore drying the wet furs, that were not sufficiently dry yesterday. Some time was also lost going ashore to trade provisions. The wind also considerably retarded our progress; nevertheless, we encamped in the evening, a little above [John] Day's River . . .

Tuesday 3rd. It was a little calm in the morning, and we embarked, but a little after sunrise, we had to put ashore at Day's River with the wind, where we remained all day. A few Indians encamped here, from whom a few salmon were got . . .

June 4th. Blowing a storm all day, so we could not stir.

June 5th. Blowing all night, but calm a little after sunrise—when we embarked, but were again stopped by the wind. We breakfasted;

after a little while it became calm, and we proceeded . . . to the Dall[e]s and made the portage to the rocks with boats. Here we encamped early . . . Traded enough salmon to serve the people for nearly two days. There are not many Indians about the Dalls now; the most of them are out on the plains collecting roots.

June 6th. Embarked early this morning, made the lower Portage of the Dalls, had to put ashore to gum one of the boats, afterwards proceeded down the river. Reached the Cascades in the afternoon, made the portage with all the goods, and got the boats halfway across. Part way they were towed, and part carried. When the men left the boats they pulled up on the beach. We could get few salmon from the Indians . . .

June 7th. Had the boats brought to the lower end of the portage, which detained the people a considerable part of the morning. In order to save time, we breakfasted before we started; we then proceeded, and reached Vancouver, where we arrived in the evening.

The arrival of the interior brigades at Fort Vancouver usually occurred in June when the river was high in spring flood. The landing of a downriver brigade was a momentous, even stirring occasion, which, unfortunately, Work failed to describe in any detail in his journal. However, Frances Fuller Victor, the Northwest's noted nineteenth-century female writer and historian, with her very lively pen provides the following excellent description of a typical brigade's arrival at the fort:

> there was much that was exciting, picturesque, and even brilliant; for these *couriers de bois*, or wood-rangers, and the *voyageurs*, or boatmen, were the most foppish of mortals when they came to rendezvous. Then, too, there was an exaltation of spirits on their safe arrival at headquarters, after their year's toil and danger in wildernesses, among Indians and wild beasts, exposed to famine and accident, that almost deprived them of what is called "common sense," and compelled them to the most fantastic excesses.
>
> Their well-understood peculiarities did not make them the less welcome at Vancouver. When the cry was given—"the Brigade! the Brigade!"—there was a general rush to the river's bank to witness the spectacle. In advance came the chief-trader's barge, with the company's flag at the bow, and the cross of St. George at the stern: the fleet as many abreast as the turnings of the river allowed. With strong and skillful strokes the boatmen governed their richly laden boats, keeping them in line, and at the same time singing in chorus a loud and not unmusical hunting or boating song. The gay ribbons and feathers with which the singers were bedecked took nothing from the picturesqueness of their appearance. The broad, full river, sparkling in the sunlight, gemmed with emerald islands, and bordered with a rich growth

of flowering shrubbery; the smiling plain surrounding the Fort; the distant mountains, where glittered the sentinel Mt. Hood, all came gracefully into the picture, and seemed to furnish a fitting back-ground and middle distance for the bright bit of coloring given by the moving life in the scene. As with a skillful sweep the brigade touched the bank, and the traders and men sprang on shore, the first cheer which had welcomed their appearance was heartily repeated, while a gay clamor of questions and answers followed.

After the business immediately incident to their arrival had been dispatched, then took place the regale of pork, flour, and spirits, which was sure to end in a carouse, during which blackened eyes and broken noses were not at all uncommon; but though blood was made to flow, life was never put seriously in peril, and the belligerent parties were the best of friends when the fracas was ended.

The business of exchange being completed in three of four weeks—the rich stores of peltries consigned to their places in the warehouse, and the boats reladen with goods for the next year's trade with the Indians in the upper country, a parting carouse took place, and with another parade of feathers, ribbons, and other finery, the brigade departed with songs and cheers as it had come, but with probably heavier hearts.[16]

Certainly, the arrival of the 1828 brigade was reason for a "regale," and we can assume that one did occur. After staying two weeks at Fort Vancouver to unload furs and take on new supplies and dispatches for the interior, Connolly's brigade left on the return trip to Fort Nez Perces on July 23, 1828, probably after another usual parting "carouse." After a good first day's journey to the Columbia River gorge, Work noted:

encamped a little below the Cascades. We had a sail wind a while in the afternoon.

The brigade consists of 9 boats 54 men including two Indians. These are passengers Mr. Conolly who commands the party, Messrs Cumtage, [James] Yale, Deace, and myself. The boats are heavily laden, besides provisions. The cargoes were delivered and the boats loaded and moved up to the upper end of the place yesterday evening, when the men got their provisions for the voyage, which consists of corn, fish, and grease.

July 24th. Cloudy weather, with fine breeze. Continued our route early in the morning, and were employed the whole day, getting to just a little above the Cascades. The water is very low, and it was very difficult dragging the boats. The line broke, and one of the rudders; so considerable time was lost fixing them. Part of the cargo had to be carried, both at the New Portage, and at another place below the Cascades. The Indians at the Cascades are taking plenty of salmon, but would give us none—a superstitious idea, that if our people, who had been at war, would eat of the salmon, they would catch no more. Had we been in want of provisions, we would have [helped] ourselves without caring; but that not being the case, we did not take any; though we told the Indians we would do so if we chose.

July 25th. Embarked at daylight, and had a fine sail wind all day, and early this evening reached the lower end of the Dalls, when we encamped, it being too late to reach the Portage. The Indians here are taking plenty of Salmon, and gave us a few for the people, making no objections about the men having been at war.

26th. The whole day was getting the goods across the portage, and the boats only part of the way. The weather part of the day was very warm. In the morning we were met by [Peter Skene Ogden of the Snake River expedition] . . . on his way to Fort Vancouver. The rest of his party are off with Mr. [Thomas] McKay for some furs that were hidden in the plains . . . [Ogden] remained with us all day, and stayed over night.

(Peter Skene Ogden, leader of a number of annual Snake River expeditions in the 1820s and 1830s, investigated and exploited a vast portion of the West including the upper Snake River drainage, eastern Oregon, the Great Basin, the Great Salt Lake valley, and northern California. Distance, weather, and the potential for Indian hostilities, however, made the arrival of the Snake River brigade at Fort Nez Perces or other Interior Northwest posts too unpredictable to normally allow a scheduled junction with the annual Columbia River brigade. Consequently, these furs, usually arriving in midsummer, were dispatched separately to Fort Vancouver. Often, however, the Fort Colville brigade would leave boats at Fort Nez Perces for use by the incoming Snake River expedition.)

Now, to return to Work's journal on July 26, 1828:

Three of our men are sick, disabled, and unfit for duty. Got plenty of salmon in the evening for the people.

July 27th. It employed the men before breakfast carrying the boats across the portage; we got them loaded, and after breakfast took our leave of Mr. Ogden, and proceeded under sail to the Chutes, when boats and cargo had to be carried. We got to the upper end of the Portage late in the evening; loaded the boats, and encamped for the night. It was very warm during the day, though it blew a storm, and the people were nearly blinded with driving sand. The Indians here had a few fresh salmon, but we got some dried ones from them. One Indian lodge took afire and was burnt; and though it was on an island, and apart from where we were working, they came and demanded payment for the property destroyed, and in case of refusal, they would take it by force. We threatened them with severe punishment for their conduct, when they became quiet. However, as a boat had to return from above, it was deemed advisable to give them a little tobacco.

28th. Clear warm weather. Embarked at daylight, and were employed all day with the poles. In the evening we encamped a little above Day's River. Two Indians, which were employed at the Dalls to work in place of the disabled men, left us this morning; they were not worth taking with us. Traded a few fish, and some dried salmon, from some Indians, where we stopped for breakfast. An Indian was dispatched to Fort Nespus [Nez Perces] with a letter.

29th. Continued our journey with the poles. Had a light wind, and got up the sail a short time in the evening; but the wind was too weak to be of much servise. We encamped in the evening a good way below the island. Passed some camps of Indians during the day they had very few fish, and report that Salmon are scarce above.

30th. Embarked at daylight. After breakfast a fine breeze sprung up, when the sails were hoisted, and we had a splendid run the remainder of the day. Encamped late in the evening a good piece above Grand Rapid. One of the sick men is again better, and able to do his duty, but the other two are still unable to work. Some other men are bad with severe colds, while some of them have sore hands from poling.

July 31st. A fine wind again, we proceeded under sail, and arrived at Nespuses at 8 oclock. The Nespuses outfit was delivered, and the remainder of the property distributed among 8 boats, as one is to be left. Mr McKay has arrived, he left his men yesterday. I found P[ambrum's] boys here, they are going off to Colville in two days; by them I wrote to Mr Kitter [William Kittson] and sent six sickels so that he may be able to get on with the harvest . . . From his letter I understand that provisions are scarce—few salmon to be got, but the crops have a fine appearance . . .

Aug. 1st. Left Nespurs at 7 o'clock, and encamped in the evening above the Yakaman River. The men worked with the poles all day, the weather very calm and warm. The river is unusually low for this season of the year. We have 8 boats, as deeply laden, as when we left Vancouver, but . . . two more of the men are disabled . . .

2nd. The weather very warm and sultry. Proceeded on our journey, and encamped in the evening at White banks. From an Indians' information, part of the bones of one of our unfortunate men that were drowned in the Spring was found. We had them collected and buried. Mr. Conolly read the funeral service. There are few Indians on the river, and these are starving; they are taking no salmon.

3rd. Continued our journey at an early hour, and encamped in the evening at the lower end of the Prist's Rapids. The current during the day was strong. The water is very low. We found a lodge of Indians, from whom a few dried Salmon were obtained, they seem very scarce in the river.

4th. Cool pleasant weather in the morning, but very warm afterwards. It took a considerable portion of the day to get up the Prist Rapid. Some time was spent gumming the boats, when we again proceeded, and encamped in the evening a little above the Rapid.

Here, on the opposite side of the river, Work sighted the encampment of another HBC party led by Francis Ermatinger and Thomas Dears. As was fairly common in these years, they were driving horses north from Fort Nez Perces across the Big Bend country to Fort Okanogan. The next day, Work's men gave them some assistance.

It is interesting to note that the Indians were taking few salmon out of the river during this summer of 1828. This is evidence of the fact that, even before the building of modern dams on the river, Salmon were scarce in some years.

Aug. 5th. Very warm weather, it is really hot passing over the burning sands . . . encamped in the evening, a little below Roscal [Qualque] Rapid.

Aug. 6th. Continued our journey, and encamped early, and got the boats just above Stony Island, the boats are lighted, and the cargoes carried, to Rend [Cabinet] Rapids. The weather very warm, though occasionally blowing a little. Very few Indians in the River, and salmon very scarce. Another man left work with a sore hand.

Aug. 7th. Warm sultry weather. Passed Pirtanhause [Wenatchee] River in the afternoon. We were detained some time mending one of the boats . . . had sail wind a little in the evening. Traded some Salmon from the Indians.

Aug. 8th. Had a good breeze, and sailed most of the day. The wind though warm was a great relief from the scorching heat we experienced three days past. Encamped in the evening a little above Clear Water [Chelan] River. A man from Okanagan met us in the evening, with two horses from there.

Aug. 9th. Cloudy, but very warm weather. In the morning, Mr. Conolly and I left the boats, and proceeded on horseback to Okanagan, where we arrived about nine oclock in the morning. Four of the boats arrived late in the evening, the others are a little behind.

Aug. 10th. Arrived early in the morning, when the boats were unloaded, and the different outfits separated . . .

Aug. 11th. Went to the boats early this morning, but it was near 8 oclock before they got through gumming, when we proceeded up the river, and encamped for the night a little about the Dalls [Mahkin Rapids]. The current is very strong, nevertheless we got on well.

Aug. 12th. Continued our route, this morning passed the Dalls, and encamped in the evening a little below the Big Stone [Equilibrium Rock]. We lost some time gumming Charlie's boat. The boat had to be lighted at a place near the Dalls.

Aug. 13th. Continued our route early, and encamped a little above Spellium [Nespelem] River. Some more time was lost gumming. Met a family of Indians going down the river, but they had no Salmon worth mentioning.

Aug. 14th. Continued of journey early, and encamped a little below Semapoilish [Sanpoil] River. One of the men not able to work with a sore hand. Chatfaux is also complaining of his hand, but does not give up working yet.

Embarking early on August 15, Work wryly noted that the above mentioned boatman, Chatfaux, could not work due to a sore hand, and now was walking along the shore "like a gentleman" of the HBC. By prior arrangement, Work met the Fort Colvile horse keeper near the mouth of the Spokane River. Leaving the boats, Work set off by horseback for the fort. Thus, on the 18th day of the upriver journey, Work ended his journal.[17] The main brigade arrived later at the fort, where supplies and Indian goods soon were transferred to pack strings and carried to the scattered posts of the inland Northwest, the northern Rockies, and southeast British Columbia.

This then, was the HBC's brigade system. It was an integral part of the seasonal trading pattern practiced for two decades by the company, as the HBC adopted long-range policies to sustain the region's fur and other wilderness resources. It also was in the HBC's interest to encourage maintenance of the indigenous peoples' traditional lifeways, as the Indians inevitably, for better and worse, became economically dependent on the trading posts for goods, equipment, and supplies in their daily lives.

Endnotes

1. "*Simpson*, George: Probably born about 1786-87 an illegitimate son of George Simpson . . . He was brought up as a child by his aunt, Mary Simpson, till she married in 1807 and the boy was sent to London. Here he entered the sugar brokerage house of his uncle, Geddes MacKenzie Simpson, whose daughter he later married. The firm was then Graham and Simpson; later it was Graham, Simpson and Wedderburn. One member was Andrew Wedderburn who in 1814 changed his name to Andrew Colvile. He became a member of the Committee of the Hudson's Bay Company in 1810. He took an interest in young George Simpson and placed him in the Hudson's Bay Company. In 1820 he was sent to Canada directly to the then Governor Williams at Norway House. Governor Williams sent him to Athabasca to take the place of Colin Robertson. He conducted a bitter fight throughout 1820 with the North West Company which became so bitter that in 1821 the Hudson's Bay Company and the North West Company entered into a coalition resulting finally in Simpson taking the place of Governor Williams." Burt Brown Barker, ed., *Letters of Dr. John McLoughlin: Written at Fort Vancouver, 1829-1832* (Portland, Oregon: Binfords and Mort, 1948), 325.

2. J. Orin Oliphant, *On the Cattle Ranges of the Oregon Country* (Seattle: University of Washington Press, 1968), 7. See also, Dorothy O. Johansen and Charles M. Gates, *Empire of the Columbia: A History of the Pacific Northwest*, 2nd Ed. (New York: Harper and Row, 1967), 123-24.

3. Frederick Merk, ed., *Fur Trade and Empire: George Simpson's Journal . . . 1824-25*, revised ed. (Cambridge, Massachusetts: Harvard University Press, 1968), 47-48, 50-53, 58, 65, and 128.

4. Oliphant, *On the Cattle Ranges of the Oregon Country*, 8.

5. Governor George Simpson, on his 1828 inspection tour, quoted in Willard E. Ireland, "Simpson's 1828 Journey," *The Beaver*, September 1948, 45. For a complete account of Simpson's 1828 travels see, E.E. Rich, ed., *Part of Dispatch from George Simpson . . . to the Governor and Committee of the Hudson's Bay Company, London, March 1, 1829* (Toronto: Champlain Society, 1947). Simpson also journeyed a third time to the Pacific Northwest in 1841-42; see, George Simpson, *Narrative of a Journey Round the World, during the Years 1841 and 1842* (London, 1847).

6. Merk, *Fur Trade and Empire*, 23. See also, Johansen and Gates, *Empire of the Columbia*, 127-28.

7. "*Birnie*, James: A native of Aberdeen, Scotland, was born about 1799, and entered the employ of [the] North West Company as an apprentice clerk in 1818. He was stationed at Fort George, Columbia District in 1820-21, a 'promising young man.' After the coalition in 1821 he continued with the Hudson's Bay Company. He kept the Spokane House *Journal* in 1822-23; was in charge at Okanagan 1824-25, and established a post at The Dalles in 1829; from 1834-37 he was at Fort Simpson, New Caledonia. Birnie Island was named for him. In 1839 he was given charge of Fort George, Columbia River, where he remained until he retired to Cathlamet, Washington Territory in 1846. He died there in 1864." Barker, *Letters of Dr. John McLoughlin*, 298.

8. T.C. Elliott, ed., "Journal of John Work, June-October, 1825," *Washington Historical Quarterly* 5 (April 1914): 98; and J. Orin Oliphant, "Old Fort Colvile," *Washington Historical Quarterly* 16 (April 1920): 29-31. See also, Merk, *Fur Trade and Empire*, 139-40. For an overview of the interaction between Native Americans and the HBC, see David H. Chance, "Influences of the Hudson's Bay Company on the Native Cultures of the Colvile District," *Northwest Anthropological Research Notes Memoir No. 2*, 1973.

9. Barker, *Letters of Dr. John McLoughlin*, 326-27.

10. Margaret A. Ormsby, "The Significance of the Hudson's Bay Brigade Trail," *Okanagan Historical Society—1949*, 33-34, quoted in Bruce A. Wilson, "Hudson's Bay Brigade Trail," *Okanogan County Heritage* 4 (September 1966), 4-5. For an historical overview of the Okanogan country see, Bruce A. Wilson, *Late Frontier: A History of Okanogan County, Washington, 1800-1941* (Okanogan: Okanogan County Historical Society, 1990).

11. Meinig, *The Great Columbia Plain*, 76-81. For an excellent firsthand account of an official party carrying dispatches along the streams and trails of the HBC's transcontinental express route, see, C.O. Ermatinger, ed., "Edward Ermatinger's York Factory Express Journal, Being a Record of Journeys Made Between Fort Vancouver and Hudson Bay in the Years 1827-1828," in *Royal Society of Canada Proceedings and Transcriptions*, Vol. VI, Sec. 2 (Ottawa, 1912), 67-127, and map.

12. H.Y. Hind (1860), quoted in R. Glover, "York Boats," *The Beaver*, March 1949, 22.

13. Northwest historians William S. Lewis and Jacob A. Meyers transcribed Work's journal, publishing it in 1920; William S. Lewis and Jacob A. Meyers, eds., "John Work's Journal of a Trip from Fort Colvile to Fort Vancouver and Return in 1828," *Washington Historical Quarterly* 11 (April 1920), 104-14. Bruce A. Wilson presented a brief synopsis of Work's journal in "University Library: Okanogan County in California," *Okanogan County Heritage* 2 (June 1964): 25-27. Most of Work's 1828 journal is reproduced in this chapter of *Forgotten Trails*.

14. Archibald McDonald, *Peace River. A Canoe Voyage from Hudson's Bay to Pacific by the Late Sir George Simpson, (Governor, Hon. Hudson's Bay Company.) in 1828. Journal of the Late Chief Factor, Archibald McDonald, (Hon. Hudson's Bay Company), Who Accompanied Him* (Ottawa, Montreal, and Toronto, 1872), 114. Also see, Wilson, "Hudson's Bay Brigade Trail," 3-8.

15. *Notices and Voyages of the Famed Quebec Mission to the Pacific Northwest* (Portland: Oregon Historical Society, 1956), 152-53. For further information about the brigade trail see, F.M. Buckland, "The Hudson's Bay Brigade Trail," *Sixth Report of the Okanagan Historical Society* [British Columbia], 1935, 11-22.

16. Frances Fuller Victor, *The River of the West* (Hartford, Connecticut, 1870), 27-28. Victor's account primarily focuses on the adventures of the American mountain man, Joe Meek, in the Rocky Mountains and the Pacific Northwest. However, her very readable and entertaining book, published in 1870, also presents much valuable information about the early history of the British fur trade and American settlement in the Pacific Northwest.

17. "John Work's Journal of a Trip from Fort Colvile to Fort Vancouver and Return in 1828," *passim*.

The "Grand Coulee," by artist John Mix Stanley. Stanley was a member of Lt. Arnold's U.S. Army survey party, which explored the Grand Coulee in the autumn of 1853. *Pacific Railroad Explorations and Surveys, Vol. 12*

VI
To the Grand Coulee

HISTORIC MAPS LEFT TO posterity indicate the existence of important fur trader trails extending north/south and east/west through the Big Bend country via the Upper Grand Coulee. Included among these maps are two attributed to Alexander Caulfield Anderson, a former HBC chief trader. Anderson worked for the HBC from 1832 to 1851, and was in charge of Fort Okanogan for a time in the 1840s. From his experience as a wide-ranging HBC official, Anderson was thoroughly familiar with all of the company's trails in the region. The maps he later prepared in retirement show routes utilized during the HBC's heyday, from the 1820s to the 1840s.[1]

The modern historian has access to extensive HBC archival and other written sources recording the New Caledonia brigades' annual use of the Okanogan valley route (which Anderson labeled on his map as the "Old Brigade Trail H.B.C. to Alexandria"). This is not the case, however, in regard to the trails actually crossing the Big Bend. Though considerable documentation about them exists, there are gaps in the historical information that make it difficult to ascertain the frequency of the fur traders' overland travel. But it is known they traveled here, and apparently sometimes often.

Traders probably first traveled over the Big Bend trails between the mouth of the Snake and Fort Okanogan or Spokane House in the mid to late 1810s, particularly after the North West Company established Fort Nez Perces at the mouth of the Walla Walla. At any rate, these routes definitely were in use by the mid 1820s. By that time, an annual supply of about 250 horses was traded from the Indians at Fort Nez Perces and sent northward to replenish the herds of the northern brigades. At times, these animals were driven up the Grand Coulee trail to the Okanogan or Spokane. Frequently, HBC men traveled on these routes along with Plateau peoples, and in many instances Indians served as couriers for the traders.

The fur company men did not seem to have definite names for routes in the Big Bend. They simply referred to a trail as going "to Walla Walla," "to Okanogan," or "to Colvile." All indications are that the overland trip between Fort Nez Perces and Fort Okanogan via the Moses Lake/Grand Coulee route took four or five days, whereas going up the Columbia by bateaux required up to 10 days.

HBC Trails through the Big Bend

Perhaps the earliest actually recorded reference to white men crossing overland through the Big Bend country between Fort Okanogan and Fort Nez Perces occurs in George Simpson's journal, written on his return trip in 1825 by boat up the Columbia en route to Hudson Bay. Arriving at Fort Okanogan on April 4, 1825, Simpson noted that Fort Nez Perces (which he had visited a few days previously) had an insufficient number of horses to equip that year's Snake River expedition. Consequently, he was determined to send 15 HBC horses at Fort Okanogan, along with 11 belonging to the post's employees, to Fort Nez Perces.

Continuing in his diary: "Had much difficulty in prevailing on Mr M. . . . to conduct the party required to take those Horses to Walla Walla, he pleaded indisposition, the unfortunate state in which his Woman was and a variety of other excuses but all would not do."

Simpson proved true to his word that no "excuse" would "do," because on the next day, April 5, 1825, he noted: "dispatched Mr M. . . . with his band of Horses for Walla Walla."[2] No other details are known about this overland trip south to Fort Nez Perces.

Messengers and smaller parties, of course, likewise soon utilized the route between the trading posts. John Work, for example, with a brigade at Fort Okanogan a few months later, desperately needed to send dispatches down to Fort Vancouver. On July 26, 1825, he wrote in his journal:

> It is indispensably necessary that these despatches should be sent to Fort Vancouver as soon as possible, they must be sent either direct to Fort Nezperces from this place or around by Spokane, by the former route [south from the Grand Coulee] they will reach Nezperces in four days, by the latter [via the Palouse River] they will require six . . .

Work noted that a man at Fort Okanogan named La Prade was familiar with the Fort Okanogan-Fort Nez Perces route, having been over it the previous spring (perhaps in the above mentioned horse party that Simpson ordered to Fort Nez Perces). La Prade, however, proved to be indispensable for other tasks and could not be spared to guide Work's messenger, clerk Thomas Dears, to Fort Nez Perces. (The mixed-blood La Prade—also La Pratt or other spellings—served many years at Fort Okanogan.)[3]

Arrangements finally were worked out three days later, on Friday, July 29, 1825, as Work explained:

> Sultry warm weather.
>
> This day was employed preparing dispatches for the sea which are to accompany Mr. Ogdens letters which are to be sent off tomorrow. I expected that Mr McLeod would have spared a man [La Prade] to accompany Mr Dears [the messenger] to Wallawalla, but he cannot . . . on consulting Robbie Doo [Robideaux] the Indian who came with me, he engages to take him [Dears] from here to Wallawalla though he never was [on] that road, this will save the horses, and two or three days time. Mr Dears is to return straight to Spokane . . .
>
> [On July 30, 1825] Mr Dears & the Indian . . . set out in the morning for Wallawalla.[4]

During the following week, while Dears and Robideaux made their way to Fort Nez Perces through the Big Bend, Work and his party left Fort Okanogan and proceeded east to Spokane House. Work expected to meet Dears there, since Dears had orders to return to Spokane House after completing his journey to Fort Nez Perces. Work, however, after arriving at Spokane House, apprehensively wrote in his journal on August 7, 1825:

> Mr. Dears contrary to my expectations is not yet arrived, 9 days are now elapsed since he left Okanagan for Wallawalla, which is a day later than I had calculated on his being able to reach this place. Probably something may have occurred to prevent him from arriving on the day expected.

But on the following day, to Work's relief:

> Mr. Dears and the Indians arrived at noon from Wallawalla with despatches from that place, they were five days coming and had been four days going from Okanogan to Wallawalla. however he got through safe.[5]

It is certain that Dears took the Big Bend trail south to Fort Nez Perces. However, it is not clear in Work's account whether Dears traveled north to Spokane House via the Big Bend (see below) or by the Snake-Palouse route farther east.

Description of the Route

The trail system followed by the fur traders in the Big Bend between Fort Nez Perces and Fort Okanogan, and Fort Colvile as well, was hardly a new one. Indians, of course, had been passing this way for centuries. There were variations in the actual trek of the routes, of course, but one of the important, standard HBC trails appears to have been as follows (see map, opposite page 1). Leaving Fort Nez Perces and heading northward, travelers proceeded up the east side of the Columbia, fording the Snake River at its mouth. The route continued along the Columbia's east bank to approximately Ringold where the State of Washington fish hatchery is now located. The trail then left the river, extending in a northerly direction generally along what is now wasteway DP 216.

It continued into the Othello Channels to Eagle Lake or, as it was known historically, Skooteney Spring (in the historical record there are several spellings for the spring's name). Eagle Lake was always a crossroads for trails in this part of the Big Bend. Leaving Eagle Lake, the trail skirted around the eastern end of the Saddle Mountains, continuing to where Deadman Lake is today, six miles northwest of Othello. The route then followed up the lower Crab Creek drainage into the U.S. Fish and Wildlife Service's Marsh Unit I.

Early maps clearly indicate the peculiar basaltic channel of lower Crab Creek through which the trail passed. This was the most direct path through the scablands. After leaving the Crab Creek channel, the route skirted east around the extensive sand dunes south of Moses Lake to tie in again with Crab Creek at Parker Horn on the east side of Moses Lake. From there, it followed Crab Creek north to Adrian (where the Northern Pacific railroad later established a siding). Here, the prominent nearby rock formation known as Black Butte (or "Rocky Mound") is shown on early maps.

At Black Butte the trail divided. The route to Fort Colvile (or before 1825-26 to Spokane House, with some variations in the route) continued easterly up Crab Creek to its junction with Lake Creek. At Lake Creek, the fur men then turned north, crossing the Spokane River at about its mouth, and following up the east side of the Columbia to the fort.

The other fork in the trail at Black Butte continued to Fort Okanogan. From Adrian, the Okanogan route went almost due north into Dry Coulee, from there to Deadman Springs, and on to McEntee Springs, now the town of Coulee City. Entering the mouth of the Upper Grand Coulee, the trail extended about 20 miles up the Grand Coulee to Steamboat Rock

Fur traders explored the Big Bend's Indian trails as early as the 1810s, and soon established a network of routes between the fur posts. By mid century, government survey parties and other visitors followed in their footsteps. On this map prepared by the 1853 Stevens scientific expedition, solid lines indicate proposed railroad routes. *Pacific Railroad Explorations and Surveys, Vol. 12*

before turning west into Barker Canyon and over to Foster Creek; a spur also extended eastward up Northrup Canyon toward Spokane House or Fort Colvile. (At McEntee Springs, a variation, i.e., the Cariboo trail, eventually was developed that crossed the Grand Coulee here, and extended northwest across the Mansfield-area plateau, thus bypassing the Upper Grand Coulee.) Travelers continued on down Foster Creek to where it flows into the Columbia River near present day Bridgeport. Crossing the river here, the trail followed the Columbia's north bank down to Fort Okanogan.

This then, was the primary Big Bend trail used in the HBC era. The fur men, of course, occasionally utilized variants of these routes or other secondary Indian trails as needed. (For instance, there appear to have been alternate paths in the east-west trail system between Okanogan and the Colvile-Spokane area.) The lengthy north-south route from Fort Nez Perces to Fort Okanogan, and on up the Okanogan valley into New Caledonia, basically was a good trail, usually with ample water and unlimited bunch-grass, and provided good footing in most sections for travelers on horse-back or foot.

The brigade trail north from Fort Okanogan up the Okanogan Valley extended 491 miles to Fort Alexandria (founded by the Nor'Westers in 1821). From there, travelers took to canoes on the Fraser, Nechako, and Stuart rivers, proceeding another 236 miles to Fort St. James (also founded by the Canadians in 1806). Thus, the total distance from Fort Okanogan to Fort St. James, the headquarters of fur-rich New Caledonia, was 727 miles. The Astorians, of course, pioneered the southern section of the brigade route (i.e., the Okanogan Valley) in 1811, whereas British fur hunters worked out the northerly segments.[6]

From Fort Okanogan, brigades proceeded along the east shore of the Okanogan River, staying reasonably close to the stream except where it meandered away. Approximately 25 miles out, travelers most likely passed through what is today east Omak. About a dozen miles farther on, rugged terrain north of Riverside forced the route to turn away from the Okanogan River to pass through McLoughlin Canyon (later the site of a large battle between Indians and miners in 1858). The trail then returned to the river a short distance below Bonaparte Creek near modern-day Tonasket.

From here, the brigades continued on up the east side of the river to Osoyoos Lake, where the trail lay through the hills on the west and crossed over the 49th parallel. Continuing northward, the route likewise skirted the west side of Okanagan Lake, though sometimes brigades passed along the east side as well. Once past Okanagan Lake, brigades turned in a somewhat westerly direction to the Kamloops post, where packs were reloaded on fresh horses for the long northwesterly trek to Fort Alexandria. At Alexandria, trade goods and supplies were transferred to boats and paddled up the Fraser River to the New Caledonia forts.

"Except where geographic features offered only narrow passageways, as at McLoughlin Canyon, the trail was more of a route than a roadway and the brigades at one time or another might deviate considerably from the medium of their courses."[7] This apparently also was true for travelers on Big Bend routes as well.

The Grand Coulee

The Grand Coulee along the route to and from Fort Okanogan greatly impressed the fur traders and other early visitors passing through the Big Bend country. The part of the Grand Coulee generally seen by these men, was, in fact, the Upper Grand Coulee—an obstacle they could not detour around while en route between Okanogan and Walla Walla or Colvile.

A surprising number of keen and very-literate early travelers, especially when considering that this region was one of the continent's most distant frontiers at the time, left excellent written descriptions of the Grand Coulee. Following here are their accounts.

Alexander Ross, Fur Trader, 1814

The first fur trader to "record" visiting this great natural feature was Alexander Ross, whose party drove horses from Fort Okanogan to Spokane House in the spring or early summer of 1814. In his account of this journey to and from the Spokane country, Ross states:

> set off with all haste to Fort Spokane, distant 160 miles southeast from Oakinacken, with 55 of our horses: and on our way both going and coming, made a short stay at a place called the Grand Coulé, one of the most romantic picturesque marvellously formed chasms west of the Rocky Mountains. If you glance at the map of Columbia you will see some distance above the great forks [or Snake-Columbia junction] a barren plain . . . there in the direction of mainly south and north is the Grand Coulé, some 80 or 100 miles in length. No one travelling

in these parts ought to resist paying a visit to the wonder of the West . . . [No one is] able to account for the cause of its formation . . .

The sides or banks of the Grand Coulé was for the most part formed of basalt rocks and in some places as high as 150 feet, with shelving steps formed like stairs to ascend and descend and not infrequently vaults or excavated tombs, as if cut through the solid rocks like the dark and porous catacombs of Kiev. The bottom or bed, deep and broad, consists of a conglomerate of sand and clay paved and smooth when not interrupted by rocks; the whole form is in every respect the appearance of a deep bed of a great river or lake, and now dry and scooped out of the level and barren plain. The sight in many places is truly magnificent. But perils and pleasures succeed each other: for while in one place the solemn gloom forbids the wanderer to advance, in another the prospect is lively and inviting and almost everywhere studded with ranges of columns, pillars, battlements, turrets, and steps above steps, in every variety of shade and colour. Here and there, endless vistas and subterraneous labyrinths add to the beauty of the scene, and what is still more singular in this arid and sandy region, cold springs are frequent; yet there is never any water in the chasm, unless after recent rains. Thunder and lightening is known to be more frequent here than in other parts, and a rumbling in the earth is sometimes heard. According to Indian tradition, it is the abode of evil spirits. In the neighbourhood there is neither hill nor dale, lake nor mountain, creek or rivulet to give variety to the surrounding aspect. Altogether it is a charming assemblage of picturesque objects to the admirer of nature.[8]

Ross's statement that the Grand Coulee's cliffs were no higher than "150 feet" obviously is a gross underestimation. No doubt it is attributable to the fact that Ross wrote his account several decades afterward, and his memory had not served him well in this regard. Other early visitors frequently misjudged heights and distances in the coulees too.

David Douglas, Naturalist, 1826

The noted English naturalist, David Douglas, was another early traveler to record an eyewitness account of the Grand Coulee. In two lengthy tours of the Northwest (1825-27 and 1830-32), Douglas identified hundreds of new botanical specimens, introducing them for the first time to scientists in the East and Europe. The Pacific Northwest's native pine, mistakenly referred to as the Douglas fir, is named in his honor.

In 1826, while coming up the Columbia River with HBC supply boats, he moved along daily on shore by horseback to collect specimens while the boats made slow progress upstream. On April 9, 1826, Douglas passed near the head of the Grand Coulee. At this time, however, he did not record his impressions of the Grand Coulee, since he perhaps was too close to the Columbia to have a good view of the chasm. Interestingly enough, in his botanical observations this day he noted "a very beautiful yellow lichen over the dead brushwood," which "affords a very durable yellow colour . . . used by the natives in dyeing."

Later that summer, he returned to the same locality principally to obtain the fruit and seeds of plants collected in the spring. Traveling westward by horseback with an Indian guide and an extra pack animal, his diary for Monday, August 21, 1826, relates a description of the north end of the Upper Grand Coulee:

> To-day I overslept myself; started at four o'clock . . . at eight passed what is called by the voyageurs the Grand Coulee, a most singular channel and at one time must have been the channel of the Columbia. Some places from eight to nine miles broad; parts perfectly level and places with all the appearances of falls of very extraordinary height and cascades. The perpendicular rocks in the middle [i.e., Steamboat Rock locality], which bear evident vestiges of islands, and those on the sides in many places are 1500 to 1800 feet high. The rock is volcanic and in some places small fragments of vitrified lava are to be seen. As I am situated, I can carry only pieces the size of nuts. The whole chain of this wonderful specimen of Nature is about 200 miles, communicating with the present bed of the Columbia at the Stony Islands [Rock Island/Cabinet rapids vicinity] . . . The same plants peculiar to the rocky shores of the Columbia are to be seen here, and in an intermediate spot near the north side a very large spring is to be seen which forms a small lake. I stayed to refresh the horses, there being a fine thick sward of grass on its banks. The water was very cold, of a bitterish disagreeable taste like sulphur. My horses would not drink it, although they had had no water since last night. At noon continued my route and all along till dusk. The whole country covered with shattered stones, and I would advise those who derive pleasure from macadamised roads to come here, and I pledge myself they will find it done by Nature.

By this time, Douglas had left the Grand Coulee, continuing on the trail westward over the high prairie. Douglas's statement that the Grand Coulee extended "200 miles" is, of course, far too long of an estimate.

Douglas records the following interesting incident on the path toward Fort Okanogan:

Coming to a low gravelly point where there were some small pools of water with its surfaces covered with *Lemna*, or duck weed, and shaded by long grass, one of the horses, eager to obtain water, fell in head foremost. My guide and myself made every effort to extricate it, but were too weak. As I was just putting some powder in the pan of my pistol to put an end to the poor animal's misery, the Indian, having had some skin pulled off his right hand by the cord, through a fit of ill-nature struck the poor creature on the nose a tremendous blow with his foot, on which the horse reared up to defend himself and placed his fore-feet on the bank, which was steep, when the Indian immediately caught him by the bridle and I pricked him in the flank with my pen-knife, and not being accustomed to such treatment, with much exertion he wrestled himself from his supposed grave. The water was so bad that it was impossible for me to use it, and as I was more thirsty than hungry I passed the night without anything whatever.[9]

Samuel Parker, American Missionary, 1835

Certainly by the late 1820s and in the 1830s, the HBC men had become quite familiar with the Grand Coulee and its environs, passing this way many times. Perhaps, a few wide-ranging American fur seekers—either an occasional American employed by the HBC, or, possibly, hunters venturing on their own into the area—likewise may have seen the Grand Coulee in this period. However, if written records of such visits were recorded, they remain obscure or have yet to surface. Thus, it is the missionary-traveler Samuel Parker, investigating the region for the American Board of Commissioners for Foreign Missions, who apparently became the first American to report seeing the Grand Coulee.

In 1835, Parker and Marcus Whitman had crossed the Great Plains to the American fur hunter's annual Rocky Mountain rendezvous in what is now Wyoming, where the newcomers were favorably received by the Nez Perce encamped with the mountain men. While Whitman returned back east to make preparations for establishing the first missions in the Columbia Plateau, Parker continued westward with a band of Nez Perce through the Bitterroots to the Snake-Clearwater junction, and, from there, overland along the Indian trail south of the lower Snake to Fort Nez Perces. Embarking in a canoe with three Indians for a nerve-wracking voyage down the Columbia, Parker was cordially received by John McLoughlin at Fort Vancouver as he was at all the HBC posts he visited. Parker spent the winter there as a guest of the Hudson's Bay Company.

Wishing to learn more about the interior, he returned to the Nez Perce country in April 1836, and then proceeded northward to the Spokane area. Arriving at Fort Colvile late in the afternoon of May 28, 1836, he was disappointed to find that "Mr. McDonald," in charge at the fort, had set out several days before with the annual brigade to Fort Vancouver. Parker had hoped to travel with the flotilla. At any rate, on Monday, May 30, 1836, he commenced his journey down the Columbia. In his book *Journal of an Exploring Tour beyond the Rocky Mountains*, first published in 1838 and widely read in the East, Parker reported:

> The brigade having taken all the boats from this place on their late passage to Fort Vancouver, we were compelled to take horses for Okanagan. I changed my guides for two others; one a Spokein, and the other a Paloose; retaining my two *voyageurs*. As we left Fort Colvile we had a fine view of Kettle falls . . .
>
> After a few hours ride, on the morning of the 31st, we re-crossed the Spokein River just above its entrance into the Columbia . . .
>
> At this place we left the river, to save traversing a great bend, and took a westerly course, expecting to reach it again before night. We pursued our way over an elevated prairie, destitute of wood and water. It became evident that night would overtake us before we could reach the river, unless we should urge forward with all the speed that humanity for our horses would permit. Before five o'clock we came near the great gulf walled up with basalt, which as we supposed, embosomed the deep-flowing Columbia. Our next object was to find a place where we could descend to its shores. After ranging along two or three miles, we found a descent by a ravine [Northrup Canyon]; but to our disappointment discovered that it was the Grand Coulé, which was undoubtedly the former channel of the river. With considerable difficulty we wound our way into it, and found it well covered with grass, and by searching, obtained a small supply of water. This quondam channel of the river is nearly a mile wide, with a level bottom, and studded with islands. It sides are lined, as the river itself is in many places, with basaltic rocks, two and three hundred feet perpendicular. This Coulé separates to the left from the present channel of the Columbia, about one hundred miles below Colvile, and is about one hundred miles in length, when it again unites with the river. The basaltic appearances are exhibited here as in other places, furnishing evidences of eruptions at different periods of time. A peculiarity in this instance was a stratum of yellow earth, eight or ten feet in thickness between the strata of basalt. Those who have traveled through the whole length of the Coulé, represent it as having the same general features throughout, while the whole distance of the river around to the place where it again unites,

as I know from personal observation, has not the peculiarity of a deep channel, cut through the rocks.

We left the Grand Coulé early on the morning of the 1st of June, and with difficulty ascended the western bank [Barker Canyon]. Before noon my guides lost the way to Okanagan, and wandered far out upon the wide prairie where there was no water. Losing my confidence in their knowledge of the country, except on some frequented routes, I directed my course for the river; and perceiving a snow-topped mountain [apparently one of the Cascade peaks to the west] in the distance, I concluded the river must lie between it and ourselves, and accordingly made it my landmark. Pursuing this direction a few hours with rapid speed, we came to a slope which gradually narrowed into a ravine [probably Foster Creek Canyon], and introduced us at length to a spring of water. Our thirsty horses rushed into it, and it was with difficulty we could control their excess in drinking. We followed this ravine, the water of which continually gained accessions until it became a large stream, with a rich valley of alluvial bottom, and united its waters with the Columbia, a few miles above Fort Okanagan, the place of our destination . . . At this place I had an opportunity to see some of the Okanagan tribe. Their personal appearance is less noble than the Spokeins, but they are not less peaceable and honest in their dispositions . . . They are much employed in the salmon industry, and large quantities are prepared by drying for the winter's use. Their country does not abound in game, and hunting occupies but little of their time. The climate here, as in other parts of the Oregon Territory, is very mild and salubrious.

Wishing to pursue my way down the river [on June 2, 1836], I hired two Indians to assist my two Frenchmen in navigating a bateau which we obtained at this place; and committed our horses to my Indian guides to take them across the country to Walla Walla. My confidence in the honesty of these men was without any suspicion, and I could trust them with our six horses, saddles and bridles, to go on any enterprise within their capacity to accomplish [a few days later, these Indians and Parker's party met up again at Fort Nez Perces].[10]

Modeste Demers, Catholic Missionary, 1839

Catholic missionary Modeste Demers was another person to leave a record of having traveled overland through the Big Bend country a few years later. In the summer of 1839, Demers had left Fort Vancouver with an upriver HBC brigade to make an initial investigation of missionary prospects at the interior posts. Demers stopped at Fort Nez Perces, and then proceeded by horseback overland to Fort Colvile. After a lengthy visit at Fort Colvile, Demers continued on to Fort Okanogan, traveling six days to get there.

Though it is almost certain that Demers, on his way to Okanogan, passed through at least the Grand Coulee's Steamboat Rock vicinity, he did not actually describe the great chasm. However, he did report some interesting comments about traveling conditions:

> The heat of day was stifling, and there was no wind at all. Fire having passed over the plains, the ground presented only a scorched surface and without verdure. One could hardly find here and there a few untouched spots where there was grass for the horses. We were often without water, and more than once we were reduced to lessen our thirst with half-tainted water.[11]

Demers stayed at Fort Okanogan for nine days before taking the Big Bend trail south to Fort Nez Perces, arriving September 11, 1839—a trip that took five days. From there, he continued on to Fort Vancouver. Regrettably, Demers did not write down any other details.[12]

U.S. Exploring Expedition, 1841

In 1841, a small group of American scientists and soldiers likewise traversed the Big Bend country. In May of that year, the United States Exploring Expedition under the command of Captain Charles Wilkes, U.S.N., sailed into Puget Sound to investigate the region's geography and natural resources. Since 1838, Wilkes had guided the squadron on a voyage of discovery and scientific exploration to South America, Antarctica, the South Pacific, Hawaii, and, finally, the Northwest Coast. While plying the inland waterways of Puget Sound, Captain Wilkes made plans for sending out detachments by land for a closer inspection of the region.

Consequently, on May 20, 1841, a party designated for exploring the Columbia interior set out on horseback from the HBC's Fort Nisqually on southern Puget Sound, where Wilkes had dropped anchor. Led by Lieutenant Robert E. Johnson, this small group of scientists, marines, and other aides, with French Canadian and Indian guides, interpreters, and packers, crossed the Cascades north of Mt. Rainier. Traversing eastward through the Yakima watershed, they forded the Columbia above the Entiat, while proceeding on to Fort Okanogan and their ultimate objective, Fort Colvile.

Several members of the detachment prepared written accounts of the journey. Botanist W.D. Brackenridge, in particular, kept an especially detailed diary clearly identifying their route, particularly where the HBC trail crossed the Grand Coulee. We take up Brackenridge's journal on June

8, 1841, just after the detachment had crossed the Columbia on their way to Fort Okanogan, and a few days before reaching the Grand Coulee:

8th. Expecting to reach Okanagan Fort today, in the early part of the forenoon Mr. J[ohnson] and three indians left us and went on towards it. After a pretty smart ride our party reached the banks of the Columbia right opposite the Fort at one P.M. when we saw a canoe setting towards us to carry the party over, Mr. J[ohnson]. having arrived about an hour before us.

The fort we found under the Charge of a Canadian Frenchman [by] the name of La Pratt, who rendered us all the assistance in his power . . .

9th. The Collection of Plants made, by being carried in a bag on horseback, were moist and a good deal bruized, so that this day was pretty much occupied in overhauling them—towards sundown walked down to the junction of the Okanagan with the Columbia . . . the Fort [is] . . . a solitary Palisaded square, destitute of Basteons, about 60 yards removed back from the Columbia, on a poor flat Sandy neck or Peninsula formed by the approach of the two rivers.

Inside of said Fort is a large House for the reception of the Companys Officers, consisting of several appartments; from the end of this house runs two rows of low mud ones towards the entrance, which serves as Offices, & dwellings for the trappers & Families, leaving the centre an open oblong square.

This Station or Fort is more for the convenience of the Companies Fur business in New Caledonia, used as it is as a kind of depot, than for any Furs which are found in its vicinity. While we were there a troop of horses arrived with Flour from Colvile for the N. Caledonia Station. Out of which we recd. a supply along with several necessaries. The soil is to[o] poor to admit of anything being done in the Farming Way at Okanagan, but I must say that I never beheld finer Cattle in my life than I did there.

10th. We did not procure any fresh horses here, but Mr. Maxwell, one of the H.B. Co's. Clerks about to return to Colvile with horses promised to overtake us tomorrow so getting all our luggage ferried accross to the opposite shore, by 2 o'clock P.M. we were on the road, retracing part of what we had arrived by.

Mr. Johnson rode ahead of the party so far that we lost sight of him, till rounding the point of a hill his Horse came towards us at full gallop: by this we all suppos'd he had come to a good camping place, had unsaddled his horse & laid himself down to rest. So we kept onwards till sundown where we encamped at a fine little stream; had supper—still no signs of Mr. J. When Sergt. Stearns & Pier[r]e [Charles] went back in search, while I kept firing signal guns till 11 P.M. when they returned without him, so we all went to rest. Our camp was about 1½ miles up from Columbia & we had traveled this day from fort about 8 miles along its banks—

June 11th. At 5 A.M. Pier[r]e, Peter, S. Stearns, & myself went in search of Mr. J. and about 9 Peter came upon him fast asleep behind a bluff about 3 miles back, so that this frolick of his kept the party 2/3 of a day back. As I observed before we had left the river and were on the way for the Grand Coule[e]—the land was truly prairie with here and there pools of water, amid a salt marsh which gave birth to some singular plants—the crusted Saltpetre or salt on the surface had very much the appearance of hoare frost. We put our tents down for the night in an open place.

12th. At 10 A.M. made the grand Coule[e]. The pass that led us into it was down a bank of loose rock about 500 feet high. Its breadth where we crossed it was about 5 miles. About the centre are several deep lakes bounded on the upper end b[y] precipitous rocks. Here we found an abundance of Ducks. I could observe no feature whatever that could lead one to suppose confidently that the valley had ever been the course of the Columbia, as it bears no traces of a sweeping current having passed through it at any time. On the contrary it presents in many places a rolling surface, with several rotund bluffs to the height of 700 feet. At the upper end of one of the lakes is a deep gap or hollow so that had water ever flowed through the Coule[e] this must have been the principal channel, and yet these rocks in place of being water worn or rounded of[f] are angular and show their natural disposition. The Coule[e] appeared to me to be like the seat of a former *Lake* or *Sea*, which by some convulsion or another had a gap formed in its banks by which its waters forced their way into the Columbia. There is a large tract of flat land in its bottom, but to[o] much impregnated with salt to raise crops or Grain on, but I should think admirably adapted for the raising of Sheep & Cattle, there being plenty of water and abundance of Good grass, both in the Coule[e] and within 20 miles of it on both sides. In the afternoon Mr. Maxwell came up with us—he loaned us several of the Companies Horses to help us along. The general course of the Coule[e] where we made it tends N & South. On leaving it we made a few miles on the opposite side & Camp'd on the prairie.[13]

In the official report of the United States Exploring Expedition, prepared by Charles Wilkes from information provided by Lt. Johnson and other members of the party, these further details regarding the Grand Coulee were recorded. Wilkes denied the notion that the Grand Coulee had been "a former *Lake* or *Sea*." Rather, Wilkes noted that the "common supposition," no doubt derived from comments by HBC officials,

relative to this remarkable geological phenomenon is that it once had been the bed of the Columbia, and this is what would strike every one at its first view; but, on consideration, it is seen that it is much too wide, and that its entrance is nearly choked up by the granite hills that do not leave sufficient space for the river to flow through. The walls of the Coulée consist of basaltic cliffs, similar to those of the Palisades of the Hudson, seven hundred and ninety-eight feet high; and where it was crossed by the party, it was three miles wide; but, a few miles farther to the south, it narrowed to two miles. Its direction was nearly north and south for a distance of at least fifteen miles. In places, the cliffs were broken and appeared as though tributary valleys had been formed in like manner, with perpendicular walls, though but of short extent. In the northern portion of it were several granite knolls resembling islands capped with basalt and called Isles des Pierres. The bottom of the Coulée is a plain having some irregularities, but in places, for two miles together, to appearance it was perfectly level. There are in it three lakes: one on the top of the west border, another after descending, and a third between two of the granite islands. The last of these was the largest, being about a mile long, but is not more than three hundred feet broad; these lakes have no visible outlets. Although the soil abounded in the same saline efflorescence that had been remarked on the high prairie, yet the lakes were found to be fresh, and wild ducks were seen in great numbers. In other spots, the earth was damp and overgrown with a rank grass of the same kind as that growing on the prairie. Next to this the wormwood predominated.

In the level places the earth was much cracked: incrustations were abundant, which, sparkling brilliantly in the sun, gave the plain somewhat the appearance of being covered with water. Specimens of these were procured, the analysis of which will be found in the Geological Report.

The granite islands, above spoken of, were found to be seven hundred and fourteen feet high. Mr. Johnson named the southern one Ram's Head. Dr. [Charles] Pickering [a physician and naturalist], who visited the north part, found no regularity of structure. All were satisfied, after leaving the Coulée, that it has been the seat of a lake, in the northern branch of which some convulsion had caused a breach, through which it had discharged itself into the Columbia . . . yet it seems remarkable that the Coulée had extended from one point of the river to another and, with the exception of its breadth, forming very much the same kind of trench as the Columbia would leave if it forsook its present channel.

From the observations subsequently made at the lower end of the Grand Coulée, there is, however, reason to believe that it was at one period the bed of the Columbia. The fact of there being large boulders of granite at its lower or south end while there is no rock of similar kind except at its north end would warrant the conclusion that they had been brought from the upper part of it. There were a great number of stones, having the appearance of being water-worn, lying in its bed at the south end as if they had been brought down by the current of a rapid stream . . .

>They left the Grande Coulée by passing up the east cliff or bank
>at a place where it was accessible for horses and which was much stained
>with sulphur. Soon afterwards they were overtaken by Mr. Maxwell
>from Okanogan, which place, although twenty-five miles distant, he
>had left in the morning.[14]

It is interesting to note that the cliff "much stained with sulphur" is the
same feature described by Parker as "a stratum of yellow earth" in 1836.

Theo. H. Scheffer, retracing the Johnson party's route a century later,
determined that their camp on the night of June 11, before they reached
the Grand Coulee, was "at a spring or lakelet three miles short of the rim of
the coulee on the Okanogan trail just above" Barker Canyon.

The next day, June 12, their route into the coulee led "down a bank
of loose rock about 500 feet high." The trail came out on the coulee bottom at the mouth of Barker Canyon, and crossed the floor of the "chasm
by rounding Steamboat rock" on its north side. Scheffer felt certain that
the 700-feet-high granite island, named Ram's Head by Johnson, was the
granite knoll or pinnacle between the old and new highway just off
Northrup Creek.

Other details of Lt. Johnson's report fit well with the early maps and
other travel accounts of that era, including their passage eastward up
Northrup Canyon when leaving the Grand Coulee. The three lakes that
Johnson mentions also fit into the known topography: these included "one
on the top of the west border, another after descending, and a third between two of the granite islands." Respectively, these were a small, apparently unnamed lake above Barker Canyon, Tule Lake in the coulee, and
Devils Lake located not far above.[15]

After spending time at Fort Colvile, the Spokane River, and Coeur
d'Alene Lake, Johnson's detachment proceeded through the Palouse Hills
to the Clearwater River country, and from there to Fort Nez Perces and on
up the Yakima River, crossing the Cascades by the same route they had
come.

Paul Kane, Artist, 1847

The Canadian artist Paul Kane visited the Grand Coulee in 1847, leaving
to history one of the region's most complete early travel accounts, as well as
the first artistic depictions of the Big Bend country. Kane, trained in Canada
and Europe, had made a reputation as a portrait painter in the United
States at Mobile, Alabama, before his western adventure.

In 1845, gaining the support of Governor Simpson, Kane set out with HBC brigades from eastern Canada to visit the western wilderness and sketch its scenery and indigenous peoples. Kane's inspiration for doing this had come two years earlier from his meeting with artist George Catlin in England. Catlin's special "Indian Gallery" exhibit, depicting the natives of the western American Plains, was extremely popular at the time. Kane decided to attempt to do the same for Canada's Indians, and, as it turned out, those of the Oregon Country as well. Crossing the Rockies in the fall of 1846, he arrived at Fort Vancouver on December 8.

In the summer of 1847, Kane had returned upriver and was at Fort Walla Walla (the name "Fort Nez Perces" had generally fallen out of fashion by this time). What follows is his account of a trip made from Fort Walla Walla north to Fort Colvile by way of the Grand Coulee in late July 1847. Kane was something of a greenhorn, as will become evident to the reader from the misadventures recorded in his journal, not the least of which was his decision to visit the Grand Coulee at the hottest time of the year. Furthermore, he had a tendency to somewhat exaggerate events and facts for dramatic effect (e.g., his apprehensions about potential Indian hostility at this time), and his descriptive accounts and his timetable are sometimes confusing and inconsistent. Regardless, his narrative is extremely detailed, and it is invaluable for Big Bend history.

On July 29, 1847, he set out on the parched trail from Fort Walla Walla, traveling under the blazing, mid-summer sun toward the Grand Coulee, and eventually Fort Colvile:

> I had determined to go to Colville by the Grand Coulet; this, from the appearance of the two extremities, seemed to have been a former bed of the Columbia River . . . the place was . . . so much talked of as the abode of evil spirits and other strange things, that I could not resist the desire of trying to explore it. I accordingly sent on everything by the boats, except what I usually carried about my own person, but I could not get an Indian guide, as none of them would venture an encounter with the evil spirits.
>
> At last a half-breed, called Donny, although ignorant of the route, agreed to accompany me. We procured two riding horses, and one to carry our provisions, consisting of two fine hams, which had been sent to me from Fort Vancouver, and a stock of dried salmon, cured by the Indians. About ten miles from the fort, we swam our horses across the Nezperees [Snake] River, where it enters the Columbia, and then proceeded along the banks of the Columbia, about ten miles further, where we encamped for the night. [Kane's camp would be approximately opposite to the mouth of the Yakima River.]

The Ringold formation (White Bluffs) on the east side of the Columbia River. *Ron Anglin photograph, 1984*

Historic maps depicting the route of the HBC/Cariboo trail frequently indicated the prominent rock formations on either side of Crab Creek. O'Sullivan Dam now blocks this channel in T17N, R28E, Sec. 11. *U.S. Bureau of Reclamation photograph, 1945*

A view from the west wall of the Grand Coulee looking northeast toward Steamboat Rock and showing playa lakes along the south central part of the Upper Grand Coulee. A few years after this picture was taken, pumps at Grand Coulee Dam filled the coulee to create Banks Lake for distribution of irrigation water to the Columbia Basin Project. *U.S. Bureau of Reclamation photograph, March 24, 1942*

A view of Banks Lake from the west side, looking north to Steamboat Rock in the far distance.
U.S. Bureau of Reclamation photograph, May 20, 1976

Paul Kane (1810-1871) and his Indian companion struggled through the sand dunes south of Moses Lake in 1847. Crab Creek can be seen in the upper left hand corner. The area now is part of the Potholes Reservoir. *U.S. Bureau of Reclamation photograph, March 17, 1944*

Paul Kane's watercolor of the Grand Coulee. The location is near to where the trail left the Grand Coulee and headed west up Barker Canyon toward the Okanogan country. *Courtesy Stark Museum of Art, Orange, Texas*

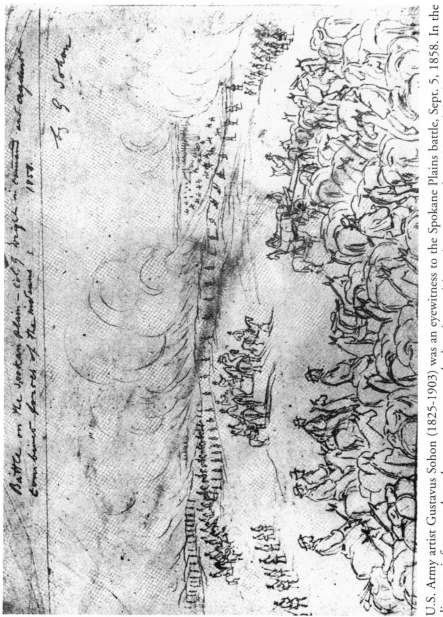

Battle on the spokan plain — Col. G. Wright and against
combined forces of the indians. 1858.

G. Sohon

U.S. Army artist Gustavus Sohon (1825-1903) was an eyewitness to the Spokane Plains battle, Sept. 5, 1858. In the distance, infantry and cavalry maneuver over the burning prairie against mounted warriors, while the commanding officer's group watches from a little promontory. Note the large pack train in the foreground; later, many of the civilian packers participated in the mining rush over Big Bend trails to Canada. *Smithsonian Institution*

Camp i Moses Coulé   Feby 21 1880

While encamped in Moses Coulee on July 21, 1880, topographical assistant Alfred Downing sketched this view of Lt. Thomas Symons's survey pary. *Washington State Historical Society*

View of Steamboat Rock in the Upper Grand Coulee before the establishment of Banks Lake. *National Archives photograph, August 15, 1944*

During the day we passed a large encampment of Nezperees . . .

July 30th—Proceeded along the shore for eight or ten miles, when I discovered that I had left my pistols and some other articles at our last night's encampment. I had, therefore, to send my man back for them, whilst I sat by the river, with the horses and baggage, under a burning sun, without the slightest shelter. Whilst sitting there, a canoe approached with four Indians, streaked all over with white mud (the ordinary pipe clay). On landing, they showed much surprise, and watched very cautiously at a distance, some creeping close to me, and then retreating. This continued for about three hours, during which not a sound broke through the surrounding stillness. I had commenced travelling very early, and this, combined with the heat and silence, made me intensely drowsy. Even the danger I was in scarcely sufficed to keep my eyes open, but the Indians were evidently at fault as to what to make of me . . .

At length my man returned with the missing articles, and the Indians hastily took to their canoe and crossed the river. We now continued our course along the river until evening, when we encamped, and as we were very hungry, and expected a hard journey next day, we determined upon attacking one of our hams . . . when, alas . . . [it was] a living mass of maggots, into which the heat had turned the flesh . . . we found the other in the same state, and had to satisfy our hunger on the salmon, which, as usual, was full of sand. [This camp site was about where Ringold is today.]

July 31st—Owing to the great bend which the Columbia takes to the northward, I thought I should save a considerable distance by striking across the country, and intersecting the Grand Coulet at some distance from its mouth. [Here, however, Kane appears to be on the HBC's standard route northward.] We accordingly left the river early in the morning, and traveled all day through a barren, sandy desert, without a drop of water to drink, a tree to rest under, or a spot of grass to sit upon. Towards evening, we saw in the distance a small lake, and to this we accordingly pushed forward: as soon as our horses perceived it, wearied and exhausted as they were, they rushed forward and plunged bodily into the water. No sooner, however, had they tasted it, than they drew their heads back, refusing to drink. On alighting, I found the water was intensely salt, and never shall I forget the painful emotion which came over me, as it became certain to my mind that I could not satisfy my thirst. Our horses were too weary, after our long and rapid ride, to proceed further; and though it was tantalizing to look at the water which we could not drink, the vegetation which surrounded it was refreshing to the horses, and we remained here all night, though we enjoyed scarcely any sleep owing to our thirst.

August 1st—We started at 4 o'clock this morning, and travelled steadily on without getting water, until about noon, when we fell in with a narrow lake, about a mile long, very shallow, [probably a seep lake about where the Potholes Reservoir is today], and swarming with pelicans, [these birds once nested in great numbers in the Big Bend, but today relatively few are seen] whose dung had made the water green and thick. Bad as this was, added to its being also rather salt, yet our thirst was so great, that we strained some through a cloth and drank it. Leaving this Lake of Pelicans, we now entered upon a still more discouraging route: the country, as far as the eye could reach, was covered with loose fine sand, which the violent winds of this region had drifted into immense mounds, varying from 80 to 120 feet in height.

Here, Kane and his Indian guide have entered the large sand dune area south of Moses Lake, and this is where he made his first sketch. The drawing is not particularly descriptive and thus is not reproduced in *Forgotten Trails*.

This was very toilsome to us, as our horses had become so exhausted that we were obliged to lead them, and we sank deep at every step in the hot sand. Had the wind risen while we were crossing this place, we must have been immediately buried in the sand. Towards evening we arrived at a rock, and in a small cleft we discovered three or four gallons of water almost as black as ink, and abounding in disgusting animalcula. The horses no sooner saw it, than they made a spring towards it, and it was with the greatest difficulty we drove them back, fearing that they would drink all, and leave us to our misery. After satisfying our drink, we strained a kettleful for our supper, and allowed the horses to drink up the remainder, which they did to the last drop, showing how necessary was the precaution we had taken. Here we passed the night.

Kane now was near Moses Lake, but made no mention of seeing it. This may be because he passed too far to the west to see it, or the fluctuating lake was much reduced in size or even dry due to variabilities in sand dune activity and annual precipitation.

August 2nd . . . We proceeded on, and about noon emerged from these mountains of sand; the country was still sandy and barren, but here and there we found tufts of grass sufficient to support our horses. The country was intersected with immense walls of basaltic rock, which continually threw us out of our direct course, or rather the course I had determined on, for of the actual route I had no information. These interruptions added considerably to our difficulties, as I had no compass, and it was only by noticing the sun at mid-day by my watch, and fixing on some distant hill, that I guided my course. We still suffered from the want of water, and my man was getting disheartened at our wandering thus almost at random through this trackless desert.

In approaching the Dry Coulee area, Kane and his companion appear to have been off the primary trail, and shortly would suffer many difficulties. His exact route through this basaltic labyrinth from Dry Coulee to the Coulee City vicinity probably never will be known with certainty, though he seems to generally have been proceeding a mile or more west of the main trail. Some of the features he describes, however, appear to be identifiable (see endnote 16).

August 3rd—After riding a few hours, we came to an immense gully of dried-up water-courses crossing our route [Kane appears to have reached Dry Coulee too far down its course; the main trail already had left the coulee about 2 miles to the southeast]. The banks rose seven or eight hundred feet high from the bottom on each side, and its width was nearly half a mile. At first it seemed impossible to pass it; however, after many difficulties, we succeeded in leading our horses to the bottom, which we crossed, and clambered up the rocks on the opposite side for about 200 feet, when we came to one of the most beautiful spots that can well be conceived: at least, it appeared to us all that was beautiful, amongst the surrounding desolation.

It was a piece of table land, about half a mile in circumference, covered with luxuriant grass, and having in its centre a small lake of exquisitely cool fresh water. The basaltic rock rose like an amphitheatre,[16] from about three-quarters of its circuit to the height of about 500 feet, while the precipice up which we had toiled sank down at the other side. We remained here three hours, luxuriating in the delicious water, so sweet to us after suffering the torments of thirst for so long. My man seemed as if he never could have enough of it, for when he could swallow no more, he walked in, clothes and all, and actually wallowed in it, the horses following his example. How much longer we might have been tempted to stay here, it is impossible to say, but we accidentally set fire to the grass [probably when lighting a pipe] and were obliged to decamp; this was accomplished with considerable difficulty, and in getting up the precipitous rocks, the pack-horse lost his footing and fell to the bottom, but pitching, fortunately, on his back with the packs under him, he escaped with a few cuts on his legs only. Had he been anything but an Indian horse, he would doubtless have paid the forfeit of his life for the insecurity of his feet.

As soon as I arrived at the level of the country once more, I saw in the distance another vast wall of rock, and leaving my man to bring up the unfortunate pack-horse, I rode briskly forward to endeavour to find a passage over this formidable barrier, considering it to be like many others that we had already passed, an isolated wall of basalt. I therefore rode backwards and forwards along its front, exploring every part that presented any opening, but without finding one that our horses could traverse. At last I came to the conclusion that we must go round it, but my man not having come up, it was necessary for me to return and seek him, which proved for several hours unavailing, and I began to fear that he and my provisions were inevitably lost; however, after riding a long way back, I fell upon his track, which I followed up with care.

I soon perceived that he had taken a wrong direction. After some time, I saw him mounted on a high rock in the distance, shouting and signaling with all his might till I got up to him. He was very much frightened, as he said that if he had lost me he never could have got on. Though the day was by this time pretty far advanced, we succeeded in making a circuit of the basaltic wall, and struck a deep ravine which in the distance so much resembled the banks of the Columbia, that I at first thought I had missed my way, and had come upon the river.

When we reached the edge, I saw that there was no water at the bottom, and that there could be no doubt of my having at last arrived at the Grand Coulet [Upper Grand Coulee]. With great difficulty we descended the bank, 1000 feet; its width varies from one mile to a mile and a half; and there can be no doubt of its having been previously an arm of the Columbia, which now flows four or five hundred feet below it, leaving the channel of the Coulet dry, and exposing to view the bases of the enormous rocky islands that now stud its bottom, some of them rising to the elevation of the surrounding country.

This wonderful gully is about 150 miles long, and walled-in in many places with an unbroken length twenty miles long of perpendicular basalt 1000 feet high. The bottom of this valley is perfectly level, and covered with luxuriant grass, except where broken by the immense rocks above mentioned; there is not a single tree to be seen throughout its whole extent, and scarcely a bush; neither did we see any insects, reptiles, or animals. Having found a beautiful spring of water gushing from the rocks, we encamped near it. After we had rested ourselves, we commenced an examination of our provisions of dried salmon . . . Much to our regret, we found that it was perfectly alive with maggots, and every mouthful had to be well shaken before eating; so full of life indeed had the fish become, that my man proposed tying them by the tails to prevent their crawling away. Bad as the salmon was, our prospects were made still more gloomy by the fact that there was but a very small supply left, and that we had a long and unknown road to travel before we could hope for any help. A thunderstorm came on during the night, and in the whole course of my life I never heard anything so awfully sublime as the endless reverberations amongst the rocks of this grand and beautiful ravine. There is hardly another spot in the world that could produce so astounding an effect.

August 4th—We followed the course of the [Upper Grand] Coulet, lost in admiration of its beauty and grandeur assuming a new aspect of the increased wildness and magnificence at every turn . . . Our journey now would have been delightful, if we had had anything like good food. We had plenty of grass of the best quality for our horses, delicious springs gushing from the rocks at every mile or two, and camping grounds which almost tempted us to stay at the risk of starvation [on this day or the next, Kane sketched Steamboat Rock].

August 5th—Towards evening we began to see trees, principally pine, in the heights and in the distance [Steamboat Rock/Northrup Canyon vicinity], and I concluded that we were now approaching the Columbia River. I pressed forward and before sundown emerged from the gorge of this stupendous ravine, and saw the mighty river flowing at least 500 feet below us, though the banks rose considerably more than that height above us on each side. This river exceeds in grandeur any other perhaps in the world, not so much from its volume of water, although that is immense, as from the romantic wildness of its stupendous and ever-varying surrounding scenery, now towering into snow-capped mountains thousands of feet high, and now sinking in undulating terraces to the level of its pellucid water.

Two Indians were floating down the river, on a few logs tied together. They were the first we had encountered for many days; and on our hailing them, they landed, and climbed up to us . . . I gave them a little tobacco, and hoped to get some provisions from them, but they said they had none, so we were obliged to make our supper on the salmon as usual. We descended the bank, and camped for the night on the margin of the river.

August 6th—We continued [eastward toward Fort Colvile] along the shore for twelve or fifteen miles, under the rocky banks, which towered over our heads fourteen or fifteen hundred feet. In some places, immense ledges hung over our path, seemingly ready to crush all beneath them . . . At last, with great difficulty, we succeeded in gaining the upper bank, and entered upon a wild and romantic district, studded here and there with small clumps of trees, which gradually increased in thickness . . . we saw a couple of Indians. As soon as we were perceived, they sent a canoe over to us, offering to assist in swimming the horses across, as they assured us that the shortest and best route to Colville was on the other [north] side. We accepted their friendly offer, and camped alongside them on the other side. Both Donny and myself were dreadfully fatigued from the length of our day's travel, the labour we had gone through, and the weakness under which we suffered from the want of sufficient food. These Indians . . . were all kindness, presenting me with plenty of fresh salmon and dried berries . . . one of them proposed to accompany me as a guide to Colville . . .

August 7th—Started very early in the morning with the guide, and made, what is called in those parts, a long day. We were continually ascending and descending [in the mountains north of the Columbia] . . .

August 8th—Started again very early for the purpose of reaching Colville before night. Came to a high hill overlooking the Columbia for many miles of its course, and sat down on its summit to enjoy the magnificent prospect, and give a short rest to the horses . . . We proceeded on until we were within a mile of Kettle Falls, where we swam across in the usual way, holding on by the tails of our horses; and just at dusk we were kindly received by Mr. Lewis [at Fort Colvile].[17]

From his western explorations, Kane produced scores of sketches and paintings, establishing a reputation as one of Canada's great masters.

Lt. Richard Arnold, Pacific Railroad Survey, 1853

In 1846, the year that Kane arrived in the region, Great Britain and the United States finally divided up the Oregon Country by establishing the international boundary at the 49th parallel, where it remains today. For two decades, both Great Britain and the United States had "jointly occupied" the vast "Oregon Country." (Russian and Spanish claims to the region had been eliminated through diplomacy by the mid 1820s.)

The Oregon Country included present-day Washington, Idaho, and Oregon, about half of British Columbia, and parts of western Montana and Wyoming. However, few Americans resided in the region until the 1840s, when large numbers of immigrants began arriving over the Oregon Trail, settling primarily at first in the Willamette Valley and the Puget Sound lowland. In a few years, however, more and more Americans began appearing east of the Cascades. According to the treaty agreement, however, the HBC and British citizens were allowed to continue their activities in the Columbia Basin for a time.

In 1853, another official United States exploring group visited the Grand Coulee as part of an extensive investigation of the entire Northwest region. The origins of this exploration was the result of two interconnected events—(1) in 1853, the U. S. Congress authorized $150,000 for government surveys of five east-west railroad routes across the continent between Mexico and Canada; and, (2) also in that year, Congress formed Washington Territory out of the northern half of Oregon Territory.

Major Isaac I. Stevens, a West Point graduate, was appointed governor of the new territory, superintendent of Indian affairs, and given command of the northern railroad survey. With a budget of $40,000, Stevens received authorization to investigate potential routes between the 46th and 49th parallels from the Mississippi River to Puget Sound (or, essentially what is now the northern tier of states from Minnesota to Washington).

A full complement of soldiers, scientists, artists, cartographers, and aides accompanied Stevens as he proceeded west across the northern Plains and mountains to assume his duties as governor in Olympia. Numerous detachments from Stevens's westward-moving main group, as well as other assigned parties coming east from the Pacific slope (particularly from Ft. Vancouver) and through the Cascades, investigated numerous potential routes for a railroad, while also conducting other scientific and geographic investigations in the Cascades, Columbia Plateau, Bitterroots, northern Rockies, and the western Great Plains.

In the autumn of 1853, Lieutenant Richard Arnold of the Fourth Artillery, U.S. Army, directed one of these detachments to Fort Colvile. Meanwhile, Stevens also arrived in the upper Columbia country after his extensive travels across the northern prairies and through the Rockies and Bitterroots. On October 29, 1853, Stevens ordered Arnold to proceed from Fort Colvile to Fort Walla Walla via the Grand Coulee, which Stevens said it would "be well to examine." The main Stevens party, in the meantime, continued on to the Walla Walla valley via the Palouse River route and down the Columbia to Fort Vancouver.

Arnold meanwhile "obtained the best guide in the country," stating that this man "was born in this country, and has travelled the route for the last fifteen years" (which is another indication of the HBC's frequent use of the Grand Coulee route). On the morning of November 14, Arnold's party left Fort Colvile by following an old Indian trail along the banks of the Columbia, which allowed Arnold to make a rough survey of the river's course.

Several days later, as they approached the Grand Coulee, Arnold noted:

> When within two miles of the mouth of the Grand Coulée, the trail . . . divided. One passed over a rocky bluff about two hundred feet high; the other continued along the river to the mouth of the coulée. To save time and distance, I conducted the train by the former, sending the observers to take particular observations after leaving the river . . . The trail leaves the river . . . and passes nearly south. After an ascent of two hundred and forty-three feet, we arrived upon a level plain which commands a fine view of the coulée . . . its walls were about eight hundred feet high.[18]

In 1950, Theo. H. Scheffer, while working out Arnold's locations, concluded that the lieutenant's viewpoint was "on the plateau, above [the modern town of] Grand Coulee . . . where the party camped on the evening of November 17, 1853; probably at the Delano spring."[19] Upon leaving camp the next morning, the trail down the Upper Grand Coulee led south about six miles to where, according to Arnold, "we came to a fine lake about sixty feet broad, which had no visible outlet." This could have been any one of three or four lakes that had hidden outlets through the basalt in the Northrup Canyon vicinity.

"From this lake the trail had a gradual rise to the south." Here, as Arnold's party passed through the greater part of the Upper Grand Coulee this day, he reported it "was twenty miles in length." Arnold's detachment camped that night at McEntee Springs, present day Coulee City.

(It is interesting to note that George Gibbs, one of Stevens's scientists, learned from an HBC Indian that a buffalo bull had wandered into the Grand Coulee from the western Plains some years before. Gibbs stated: "I was told in 1853, by an old Iroquois hunter, that a lost bull had been killed twenty-five years before in the Grand Coulée; but this was an extraordinary occurrence, perhaps before unknown."[20] Other early writers also mentioned that the Indians occasionally reported finding old bison bones in the region.)

On the next day, the trail continued over a very rocky course for six miles to enter Dry Coulee, which Arnold described as "the second coulée in size." (By this juncture, of course, Arnold's route had diverged eastward away from the entrance of the Lower Grand Coulee, which apparently had no practicable horse trail through its full length. The Lower Grand Coulee's rugged talus slopes and its chain of lakes would have been extremely difficult for the party's saddle and pack horses to scramble around.)

Continuing on, Arnold's pack train reached the main trail to the Walla Walla country: "Traveling through this [Dry Coulee], we again entered the Hudson's Bay trail, near a high rocky mound [Black Butte]."

Forging ahead, Arnold arrived at what appears to be Crab Creek, described as 10 feet wide, about 2 feet deep, and filled with large boulders. After following down it, the party encamped on the west bank, probably not far north or east of where the Moses Lake airport is located today. For the next day, Arnold reported:

> After traveling a few miles, I crossed this stream and passed [east of] a fine lake [Moses Lake], about six miles in length and one in width; it was fringed with alder bushes and filled with wild fowl—ducks, geese, and white swan. Along the eastern bank of this lake I again commanded a view of the range along the western bank of the Columbia as far north as the Pisquouse [Wenatchee] river. This view, taken in connexion with the information I have obtained from my guide, leads me to

believe that the country bounded on the east by my line of march, on the north and west by the Columbia, on the south by a line passing through the mouth of the Pisquouse river and the southern extremity of the second coulée previously spoken of, is filled with coulées running in every direction, and ranging from one to fifteen miles in length. Leaving this lake, I travelled through drifting sand-hills for three or four miles; these sands continued westward as far as the eye could distinguish. I then entered a rocky valley and continued until nightfall, when I found a brook affording sufficient water for the animals and cooking purposes.

From here to Fort Walla Walla, Arnold appears to have continued to remain on the HBC's main trail southward. Leaving Crab Creek and its basalt, rimrock-lined drainage, Arnold skirted the eastern edge of the Saddle Mountains to Eagle Lake, and went on down to the Columbia and the mouth of the Snake. At the end of his exploration, Arnold reached the "fort after dark, on a dark and stormy night" and "took up quarters in the Hudson's Bay buildings," and closed his note taking.

After settling affairs at Fort Walla Walla, Arnold soon set out overland to The Dalles, where he discharged his "guide and packer" and proceeded with the rest of his "party to Fort Vancouver, and thence to Olympia."[21]

Endnotes

1. Anderson's 1867 map, in the holdings of the British Columbia Provincial Archives, Victoria, has been published by the Okanogan County Historical Society (Washington); for a discussion of its significance, see Bruce A. Wilson, "Hudson's Bay Brigade Trail" and "Early Map Shows the Brigade Trail," *Okanogan County Heritage* 4 (September 1966): 3-8. See also, Alexander C. Anderson, *Hand-Book and Map to the Gold Region of Frazer's and Thompson's Rivers, with Table of Distances* (San Francisco, 1858), map.

2. Frederick Merk, ed., *Fur Trade and Empire: George Simpson's Journal . . . 1824-25*, revised ed. (Cambridge, Massachusetts: Harvard University Press, 1968), 132-33.

3. T.C. Elliott, "Journal of John Work, June-October, 1825," *Washington Historical Quarterly* 5 (April 1914): 101-02.

4. *Ibid.*, 101-03.

5. *Ibid.*, 106.

6. F.M. Buckland, "The Hudson's Bay Brigade Trail," *Sixth Report of the Okanagan Historical Society* [British Columbia], 1935, 16.

7. Bruce A. Wilson, "Hudson's Bay Brigade Trail," 5.

8. Alexander Ross, *The Fur Hunters of the Far West* (Norman: University of Oklahoma Press, 1956), 31-32. Ross's two volumes of his reminiscences—*Adventures of the First Settlers on the Oregon or Columbia River*, covering the years 1810-13, and *The Fur Hunters of the Far West* for 1813 to 1825—originally were published in London in 1849 and 1855 respectively. They are essential to an understanding of the early history of the Pacific Northwest in the 1810s and 1820s.

9. David Douglas, *Journal Kept by David Douglas during His Travels in North America, 1823-1827* (London: Royal Horticultural Society, 1914), 161, 208-09.

10. Samuel Parker, *Journal of an Exploring Tour beyond the Rocky Mountains . . . in the Years 1835, '36, and '37* (Ithaca, New York, 1842), 300-04.

11. *Notices and Voyages of the Famed Quebec Mission to the Pacific Northwest* (Portland: Oregon Historical Society, 1956), 34.

12. *Ibid.*, 30-35.

13. O.B. Sperlin, ed., "Document—Our First Horticulturist—The Brackenridge Journal," *Washington Historical Quarterly* 22 (April 1931): 44-46. For written accounts by other members of the Johnson detachment see, Charles Wilkes, *The United States Exploring Expedition*, Vol. 4 (1844), 416-74; and J. Neilson Barry, "Pickering's Journey to Fort Colville in 1841," *Washington Historical Quarterly* 20 (January 1929): 54-63. See also, "Lt. Robert E. Johnson, 1841," *Okanogan County Heritage* 6 (December 1967): 5-12; and Dee Camp, "An Account of a U.S. Exploration of the Okanogan Country," *Okanogan County Heritage* 26 (Winter 1987-88);18-20.

14. Charles Wilkes, *The United States Exploring Expedition*, Vol. 4, 436-37, quoted in Edmond S. Meany, "Grand Coulee in History," *Washington Historical Quarterly* 15 (April 1924): 88-90.

15. Theo. H. Scheffer, "Voyageurs and Explorers in the Grand Coulee: The First Adventurers Striking into the Far West Scouted this Natural Phenomenon and Marveled at Its Grandeur," Spokane *Spokesman-Review*, January 29, 1950. Scheffer was a botanist with the Washington Department of Agriculture and lived in Puyallup, Washington—he was not a local historian or resident of the Grand Coulee area. After retirement, he became interested in the Grand Coulee locality and wrote articles which were published in the magazine section of the *Spokesman-Review*.

16. Nat Washington of Ephrata, Washington, has tentatively identified Paul Kane's route through the rugged terrain east of the Lower Grand Coulee, as well as the three closely grouped features Kane identifies as a "small lake of exquisitely cool fresh water" on a "table land" in a natural "amphitheatre." Washington has located a small terrace, an unnamed lake, and a basaltic cliff corresponding to Kane's description, and likely itinerary, situated just north of Dry Coulee in the SW 1/4, Section 36, T24N, R27E. These features are located 3½ miles south of Sun Lakes State Park. Washington suggests that the beautiful little unnamed lake might justifiably be given a name—i.e., Kane Lake.

17. Paul Kane, *Wanderings of an Artist among the Indians of North America: From Canada to Vancouver's Island and Oregon through the Hudson's Bay Company's Territory and Back Again* (Toronto: Radisson Society of Canada, 1925), 202-14. Much of Paul Kane's art is reproduced in J. Russell Harper, ed., *Paul Kane's Frontier: Including Wanderings of an Artist among the Indians of North America, by Paul Kane* (Austin: University of Texas Press, 1971). For a general discussion of early artists in the Pacific Northwest, including several who visited the Grand Coulee (Paul Kane in 1847, John Mix Stanley in 1853, and Alfred Downing in 1880) see, William H. Goetzmann, *Looking at the Land of Promise: Pioneer Images of the Pacific Northwest* (Pullman: Washington State University Press, 1988).

18. "Report of Lieutenant Richard Arnold, U.S.A., of His Route from the Mouth of Clark's Fork, by Fort Colville, the Grand Coulée, and the Mouth of Snake River, to Wallah-Wallah," *Pacific Railroad Explorations and Surveys, to St. Paul and Puget Sound*, Vol. 1, *House Executive Document* 91, 33d Cong., 2nd Sess., 1855 [791], 284. See also, *Ibid.,* 619-20; Meany, "Grand Coulee in History," 91; and "Lieutenant Arnold's Report," *Pacific Railroad Explorations and Surveys, to St. Paul and Puget Sound*, Vol. 12, *Senate Executive Document* 46, 35th Cong., 2nd Sess., 1859 [992], 137-39.

19. Sheffer, "Voyageurs and Explorers in the Grand Coulee."

20. *Pacific Railroad Explorations and Surveys, to St. Paul and Puget Sound*, Supplement to Volume I, *Senate Executive Document* 46, 35th Cong., 2nd Sess., 1859, 138.

21. "Report of Lieutenant Richard Arnold, U.S.A.," 285-86. For an excellent overview of the Stevens explorations, see Kent D. Richards, *Isaac I. Stevens: Young Man in a Hurry* (Pullman: Washington State University Press, 1993 [originally published 1979]).

PRICE ONE DOLLAR AND FIFTY CENTS

HAND-BOOK

AND

MAP

TO

THE GOLD REGION

OF

Frazer's and Thompson's Rivers,

WITH

TABLE OF DISTANCES.

·By ALEXANDER C. ANDERSON,

Late Chief Trader Hudson Bay Co's Service.

TO WHICH IS APPENDED

CHINOOK JARGON—LANGUAGE USED

Etc., Etc.

PUBLISHED BY J. J. LE COUNT,

SAN FRANCISCO.

Entered according to Act of Congress, in the year 1858, by Alexander C. Anderson, in the Clerk's Office of the District Court of the Northern District of California.

Beginning in 1858, wealth seekers utilized Alexander C. Anderson's guidebook when traveling through the Big Bend country to Canada's gold fields.

VII
Gold Rush Travelers

IN THE 1840S AND into the 1850s, relations between the Plateau people and the Hudson's Bay Company remained good. In fact, a number of Scottish and British gentlemen traders and many French Canadian and eastern Indian employees married into, or otherwise were closely related or allied to, regional tribes. In this period, American missionaries, traders, stockmen, packers, Indian agents, and, eventually, soldiers began making inroads into the region, first in a trickle, but in greater numbers after the mid-century mark. Soon, discharged soldiers from frontier army posts established after 1849, such as The Dalles or Fort Vancouver, likewise joined the ever increasing trickle of men seeking economic opportunity on the Columbia Basin frontier.

The major historical catalyst that changed the Northwest forever was the quest for gold, which was destined to bring about the period of greatest use of trails in the Big Bend and Okanogan areas. Gold fever in the Northwest would draw world-wide interest, bringing a cosmopolitan immigration by land and sea, and from near and far. Before it was over, gold seekers would explore "every nook and cranny of this vast region," triggering the settlement and development of the interior northwest United States and British Columbia, and intensifying tension with Plateau peoples.

In 1853-54, small amounts of gold were found along eastern Oregon's Burnt River, and the Yakima, Pend Oreille, and Coeur d'Alene rivers farther north in Washington Territory, but a significant strike had not yet materialized. There were rumors of gold being present in Canada too. At the time, the U.S. Army's Major Benjamin Alvord reported in a letter to the Portland *Oregonian*, appearing April 16, 1853, that "Not enough [gold] has yet been found to repay the labor of procuring it."[1]

The real start of the gold rush era came with discoveries near Fort Colvile in the spring of 1855 and on the Kootenai River about the same time. The resulting influx of miners would play a significant role in a final showdown that had been developing for some time between the interior tribes and incoming white Americans.

The Cayuse War, 1847-50

In fact, before the miners arrived, limited open warfare already had occurred several years earlier, south of the Snake River and in the Umatilla locality, in a conflict known as the Cayuse War. On November 29, 1847, a portion of the Cayuse tribe had attacked the Waiilatpu Mission near present-day Walla Walla. They killed 14 whites, including the famed missionaries Marcus and Narcissa Whitman, and captured 47 others, mostly children attending the Whitmans' school. Included among the captives were the young half-breed daughters of the well-known Rocky Mountain frontiersmen Jim Bridger and Joe Meek, plus other children, often orphaned and left by passing wagon trains. Eventually, the surviving hostages were ransomed with trade goods by the HBC's Peter Skene Ogden and taken to the lower Columbia.

The reasons for the Cayuse attack were complex. Eastern Indians arriving during the fur trade era had aroused the Cayuse about future American encroachment. The warnings were confirmed when increasing numbers of Americans arrived in the Northwest each year beginning in 1843, passing through Cayuse lands on the Oregon Trail. A measles epidemic spread with the incoming Americans and obviously affected more Indians than whites. Cultural differences were a key factor contributing to the Whitmans' death. A Cayuse medicine man, for instance, could be put to death if his patient died, and Marcus Whitman treated Indians stricken with measles who later did die. In addition, Indians believed that whites, and Whitman in particular, had the power to control or release disease. Finally, the winter of 1846-47 was the harshest the Indians could remember, which the Cayuse viewed as an omen of worse things to come.

After word of the destruction of the Whitman Mission reached Salem, Portland, and other Willamette and lower Columbia settlements, the Oregon provisional government sent a militia force of about 500 men eastward to battle the Cayuse in 1848. (It is noteworthy that, due to the 1846-48 Mexican War, significant numbers of U.S. Army troops did not arrive in the territory until 1849, too late to directly participate in the Cayuse conflict). After several engagements and the occupation of the Walla Walla valley by these territorial troops, the Cayuse withdrew to surrounding areas, beyond the reach of the volunteers. For the next two years, the Cayuse suffered hardship and destitution before the tribe agreed to give up five warriors as the murderers and bring the conflict to a close.[2]

Virtually all of the important military campaigning occurred to the south of the Big Bend, but the tribes north of the Snake, while generally remaining neutral, closely watched events unfold. Interestingly enough, some fighting broke out between the Cayuse and Yakima when the latter tribe refused the Cayuse's insistence that they join in the war against the whites.

The war affected the HBC too, though the Cayuse apparently were hostile only to the Americans, and not the British and French Canadians. The New Caledonia brigades, of course, had been utilizing the Okanogan trail down to Fort Okanogan for the past two decades, from 1826 to 1847. But in 1848, with the outbreak of hostilities in the Walla Walla country, the HBC thought it too hazardous to send a flotilla of York boats down the Columbia. Furthermore, the Oregon Treaty of 1846 had established the international boundary at the 49th parallel, and the HBC decided it was time to move much of its operations north of the line. Consequently, no large New Caledonia cavalcade ever again traveled down the Okanogan valley to join the annual downriver brigade to Fort Vancouver. Afterward, Fort Okanogan decreased in importance, generally falling into disrepair before final abandonment in 1860.

Yakima War, 1855-58

The Cayuse War of the late 1840s was a localized conflict, but the Yakima War, lasting from 1855 to 1858, was a much larger conflagration and involved numerous Plateau groups. Previously, the Yakima, Sinkiuse, Palouse, Spokane, Coeur d'Alene, and other more northerly "horse Indians" mainly had stood to the side, watching developments. Located away from the main immigrant route, these peoples had not been subjected to the same degree of white encroachment that the Cayuse had. But by 1855, all Plateau tribes felt increasingly uneasy about the continuing white advancement.

The causes of the conflict were complex and deep rooted, and emotions had reached the melting point at the time of the Walla Walla Treaty Council in the early summer of 1855. The immediate reason for the eruption of hostilities, however, was a gold strike on the upper Columbia in Washington Territory, which brought several hundred miners through the Columbia gorge and the Cascade passes and on toward Fort Colvile. Consequently, in the summer and early fall of 1855, some miner/Indian clashes occurred and an Indian agent was murdered north of The Dalles in the

Simcoe Mountains. The war now was on, though it would not be until 1858 that some of the most significant events connected to the conflict occurred directly in the Big Bend locality.

In the first major engagement, in October 1855, Yakima and Klickitat warriors defeated Major Granville Haller and his command of 84 regulars in the Simcoe Mountains. Haller was forced to return to The Dalles with significant losses. A follow-up expedition of 334 U.S. troops and militia, led by Major Gabriel J. Rains, fought a skirmish at Union Gap in the Yakima valley, but the action was indecisive. The Indians scattered and the command returned to The Dalles. Meanwhile, militia troops organized by Governor Stevens conducted a campaign in the Walla Walla and the Blue Mountains areas, where heavy fighting occurred in late 1855, and again in 1856. In the spring of 1856, militia columns commanded by Colonel Thomas Cornelius skirmished with Palouse warriors in the southern Big Bend. These volunteer soldiers proceeded to White Bluffs and Priest Rapids, before turning back to the south.[3]

By mid-1856, the trouble in the Yakima country subsided following a bloodless, well-executed demonstration by U.S. troops under Lieutenant Colonel George Wright, and with the establishment of Fort Simcoe, located a few miles north from the site of Haller's defeat. During this period, the U.S. Army felt that it was the military's duty to protect Indians as well as whites, and that advancing white settlement was basically responsible for Indian troubles. Consequently, the U.S. Army closed the interior to American ranchers and settlers until the Yakima and other hostile bands withdrew to the sizeable reservations established in the 1855 Walla Walla Treaty. Somewhat incongruously, miners were allowed to remain in the region. (In 1858, however, other gold seekers would begin arriving in the region in even greater numbers, which would significantly contribute to the mounting crisis in Indian/white relations in that key year.)

Through 1857 and into 1858, the regular army continued to believe that a decisive battle in the interior was unnecessary, despite continuing desultory raiding, and minor harassment and ambuscades. Throughout this period, in fact, most of the Nez Perce and many elements of the other Plateau tribes, even the Yakima, favored peace or were lukewarm about fighting. Prominent among the war leaders, however, were Kamiakin and Qualchan of the Yakimas, who exerted great influence on the elements in other tribes that believed in resorting to arms to drive out the Americans.

By mid 1858, the U.S. Army's peace policy abruptly changed, particularly because of events in the Palouse country. On May 6 of that year,

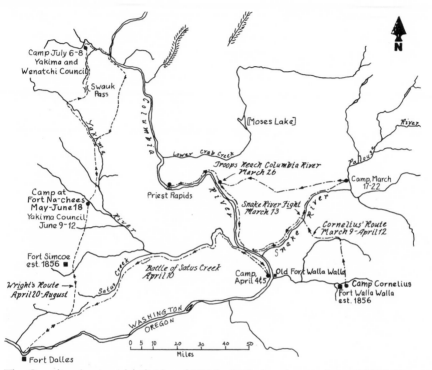

The Cornelius (territorial militia) and Wright (U.S. Army) campaigns of 1856. From Trafzer and Scheuerman, *Renegade Tribe* (1986).

Lieutenant Colonel Edward J. Steptoe and a command of over 150 mounted soldiers, packers, and Nez Perce Indian guides left the U.S. Army's Fort Walla Walla (established in 1856 near present-day Walla Walla) to search for Indian cattle thiefs, to parley with the Spokanes, and to investigate reports of increasing Indian hostility toward American miners around Fort Colvile.

Steptoe's mounted command traveled northward through the heart of the Palouse country. Near modern-day Rosalia, perhaps 600 mounted warriors—Spokanes, Palouses, Coeur d'Alenes, Yakimas, and elements from other tribes—met the troops and warned Steptoe not to continue north. Steptoe obliged, but, regardless, a bloody running fight developed the next day, May 17. After an all-day battle, the command, having suffered considerable losses, was surrounded at nightfall on a hilltop with only three bullets left per man. Under the cover of darkness, the troops quietly abandoned their position to attempt a desperate dash for the Snake River. After a 70-mile flight, alternately riding and dismounting to walk the horses, they reached the Snake a few miles below the mouth of the Clearwater, where friendly Nez Perce canoed the exhausted soldiers across to safety and guarded the tired horses. In a few days, the dispirited command arrived back at Fort Walla Walla.

Three months later, on August 6, 1858, Colonel George Wright with a mixed command of infantry, cavalry, and artillery, and a large pack train left Fort Walla Walla and headed north with revenge in mind. The 700 well-trained regulars, 33 Nez Perce chiefs and scouts wearing army uniforms, and 200 civilian packers guiding a long baggage column, were well equipped with ammunition and supplies. The soldiers carried rifles having a longer range than the Indians' HBC trade guns; in the Steptoe battle, "musketoons" used by a large portion of the troops (dragoons) had proven ineffective because of their short range.

A ferry crossing and a fortified post on the Snake's south bank (named Fort Taylor after an officer who fell in the Steptoe fight) had been established at the Snake/Tucannon confluence for this campaign. During the construction of Fort Taylor, some desultory skirmishing and long range shooting had occurred between the troops and opposing Indian scouts watching from the north shore. Here, Wright's baggage train and command were ferried across, while the mounts swam the river. The long column proceeded northeast toward the Spokane country, through blackened prairie deliberately burned by the Indians to reduce forage for the army's horses and pack animals.

In early September, Wright met and decisively defeated the warring tribes in the battles of Four Lakes and Spokane Plains, and shortly captured 800 or 900 Indian horses. While asking for unconditional surrender, Wright regrettably ordered the slaughter of the horses to prevent them from falling back into their owners' hands. The various tribes gave up, and a small number of the Indians were hanged, including the Yakima warrior Qualchan, long recognized as one of the most intransigent foes of the whites. The soldiers returned to Fort Walla Walla via Fort Taylor, which was abandoned in early October 1858. The post and ferry were turned over to a Palouse chief.

At the same time these events were unfolding, large brigades of miners were proceeding north through the Columbia Basin to newly discovered gold fields on Canada's Fraser River. This movement of miners, along with the Steptoe and Wright campaigns further east, exerted great pressure on the local tribes and made 1858 a crucial year in the interior—as will be described later in this chapter.

It is interesting to note that a surprising number of future Civil War leaders, both for the North and the South, saw duty in Washington Territory in the 1850s. Phil Sheridan distinguished himself as a junior officer in the Yakima campaigns in 1855; in 1853, Lieutenant George B. McClellan explored the eastern Cascades for possible railroad routes; Ulysses S. Grant served at Fort Vancouver in 1852-53; Major Robert Garnett, one of the first Confederate generals to fall in the Civil War, commanded Fort Simcoe; Captain James J. Archer, later a Rebel general captured at Gettysburg, also served at Fort Simcoe; even Governor Stevens, a West Point graduate, became a Union general and fell in an action subsequent to the Second Battle of Bull Run in 1862; and there were numerous others.

Fort Nez Perces (HBC's Fort Walla Walla)

One historical feature that became a casualty of the Yakima War was the old HBC fur trading post at the junction of the Columbia and Walla Walla rivers. Though originally known as Fort Nezperces or Numipu, by the 1850s it had long been identified as Fort Walla Walla. After the Hudson's Bay Company abandoned the post at the outbreak of hostilities in the fall of 1855, Walla Walla warriors pillaged the deserted buildings. They returned a second time in the winter of 1855-56 to set it on fire, though the resulting damage was only partial.

During the U.S. Army's ensuing campaigns in the interior, a portion of the post was rehabilitated to serve as a supply depot (1857-60). Here, river traffic connected with pack animals and wagons using the Overland, or Nez Perce trail, to the U.S. Army's recently established Fort Walla Walla and the fledgling commercial center arising outside of the new fort's gates. (Beginning in 1859, sternwheelers quickly began replacing York boats and sailing barges in hauling cargo and passengers on the river.)

Due to the army's activities and the gold excitement to the north and the east, the mouth of the Walla Walla, now frequently called Wallula, almost overnight became the key hub in the region for stagecoach and wagon freight lines and Columbia and Snake river ferry traffic. The docks, warehouses, and other facilities soon erected at this site would long play a key role in the development of river traffic, and eventually even rail transportation, in the interior Northwest.

Fort Nez Perces, established by the North West Company in 1818, had been reconstructed once or twice and perhaps even moved by 1832. In 1841 it burned down, but the HBC rebuilt it in adobe, copying the construction technique used by the Whitmans at their mission located 23 miles to the east, up the Walla Walla River. Some of the timber used in the rebuilt structure was cut in a sawmill at another American mission established by Henry and Elisa Spalding on Lapwai Creek in what is now Idaho. The Spalding Mission, like the Whitmans', dated from 1836. The lumber was floated down the Clearwater and Snake rivers, and hauled out of the Columbia at the fort site.

After its abandonment and burning by Indians, remains of the adobe stockade and the northeast bastion stood for many years. (The massive Columbia River flood in the spring of 1894, the greatest on record, swept over the site, but did not wipe away all trace of the fort. In the early 1950s, the National Park Service authorized an extensive archaeological salvage of the site prior to the filling of the McNary Dam reservoir. Today, some of the fort's foundation stones and a pair of historical markers are displayed alongside U.S. Route 395, about one mile northeast of the original site, which now is flooded.)

Many significant persons in western history, such as Jedediah Smith, Kit Carson, and John C. Fremont, among others, visited the post between 1818 and the 1850s, but the list is far too long to mention here. Despite the rapid decline of the fur trade in the 1840s, the HBC had continued to man the post for the Indian trade and as a supply point.

Beginning in the mid 1840s, American immigrants traveling on the Oregon Trail often diverted to Fort Walla Walla for provisions or assistance on their long trek to the lower Columbia River country. After 1846, when the region came under the sole control of the United States government, the HBC was allowed by treaty to continue operations here on American soil, which it did until the fort's final abandonment and destruction by Walla Walla tribesmen in 1855-56.

The Fraser River Gold Strike

In the nineteenth century, news traveled fast between the gold fields of the West, and men in the established diggings (initially, the Sierra Nevada of California) were ready to drop their shovels and head for richer (they hoped) strikes elsewhere. These were the circumstances in 1858, when word spread down the Pacific Coast to California about a major gold strike far to the north in the Fraser River country of western Canada. The news grabbed the attention of thousands of men in California mining camps and towns, as well as settlers in the newly established settlements of the Willamette valley and the Puget Sound country.

Various claims have been made as to who initiated the Fraser gold rush. Truth is, the original discoverer probably never will be known. It is plausible, however, that William Peon, a chief of the Fraser River tribe, made the original strike in 1857 on Necoman Creek, which flows into the Thompson River about 10 miles above its mouth. Peon took about $500 in gold dust to the fledgling settlement of French Canadians and Americans in the Colville valley. There, he bought supplies from Francis Wolff and J.T. Demers, who had opened a general store several miles southeast of Ft. Colvile in direct competition with the HBC. (Wolff was a discharged soldier who had packed in merchandise from the little commercial center and boat landing at The Dalles on the lower Columbia). Peon voiced such flattering accounts about the Fraser gold fields that Wolff and others decided to see it for themselves.

Consequently, in the spring of 1857, Wolff and 18 miners whom he later said he outfitted with goods, set out for the Fraser River country, where, as Peon had predicted, they found gold. After selling his goods, and combining the proceeds with the earnings of a business associate, Wolff carried about $5,000 in gold dust to The Dalles by early 1858. It is documented that at least a couple of other miners and a packer with a string of mules likewise traveled to or from the northern mines about this time, via the Big Bend country.[4]

The Fraser River stampede had begun. The word was out; gold fever spread down the Columbia to Portland, Salem, Olympia, and on to Victoria, San Francisco, and the Sierra Nevada mining camps. Soon, a cavalcade of bedazzled gold seekers came traveling overland and by ocean steamer and Columbia River sternwheeler, on foot, horseback, and by wagon, to the interior Pacific Northwest.

For a time, Ft. Colvile as well as 20 or so scattered French Canadian farms, a couple of stores, and two gristmills in the Colville valley supplied much of the provisions to the gold fields to the north. Later, The Dalles became a main supply point, with goods coming by steamboat up from Portland and then overland via the Big Bend trails.

"Trail North—1858"

A recent writer, newspaperman Ted Van Arsdol of Vancouver, Washington, has prepared a remarkable historical account of the Fraser gold rush, titled "Trail North—1858," which was published in the *Okanogan County Heritage* in 1969. (It is noteworthy that the *Okanogan County Heritage*, an invaluable source, contains a wealth of information not only for the gold rush era, but also about many other events and persons in eastern Washington frontier history that generally have been overlooked.)

Relying primarily on rare facts gleaned from early newspapers published in California, Oregon, and Washington Territory, Van Arsdol describes the large numbers of travelers, the Indian-white clashes, and the general excitement in the Columbia Basin during the heyday of the Canada gold rush. In the next few pages, we will take the liberty of drawing heavily on excerpts from Van Arsdol's fine, ground-breaking account, as well as providing additional commentary:

> The Fraser River gold discoveries in Canada stirred the imaginations of many thousands and the events of that year altered the future for a large section of country, as well as providing an exciting chapter in the lives of swarms of adventurers. They relived the days of '49, which were described in one miner's song:
>
> Oh I remember well, the lies they used to tell
> Of gold so bright it hurt the sight
> And made the miners yell.
>
> The Okanogan Country, astride a major inland passageway to the north, came to public prominence for the first time in 1858. For it was here that armed parties of miners were beset by Indians who were determined to keep out the influx of gold-hungry whites . . .
>
> The bulk of the mining parties, coming from the south, had a choice of routes before reaching this area, [either] coming from the Yakima direction or traveling east of the Columbia, up through the Grand Coulee area . . .
>
> Some parties from Puget Sound crossed the Cascades from Seattle and other towns, but they too had to swing north into the Okanogan . . .
>
> Indians still made up the main population east of the Cascades . . . lately they had been relatively quiet. However, before 1858, relatively few white persons had passed through the country—[the] Colville gold rushes of 1854-55 were an exception . . .
>
> Although there had been little intrusion by miners into the Okanogan, the trail north which they were to use had been trod for many years by the fur traders.[5]

It should be pointed out, however, that during the Fraser River gold rush, greater numbers of miners and supplies came by ocean-going steamers to Victoria, British Columbia, and Bellingham Bay on Puget Sound, and proceeded on to the mines via Cascade Range/Fraser River routes. Thus, the Victoria/Fraser routes surpassed the Columbia Basin trails as the main approach to and from the mines. Regardless, the Columbia Basin saw its full share of activity. It should also be noted that in this era there were frequent reports about gold prospects in the eastern Cascades, particularly in the Yakima, Wenatchee, and other drainages to the north.

Alexander Caulfield Anderson's Guide-Book

Alexander Anderson, whom the reader will remember from chapter VI, had retired from Hudson's Bay Company service in 1854, but took up the pen to write about the great Northwest region that he knew so well. Being thoroughly familiar with the Columbia Basin and Okanogan trails (and the Bellingham Bay/Fraser route as well), Anderson took advantage of the gold excitement and wrote a *Hand-Book and Map to the Gold Region of Frazer's and Thompson's Rivers, with Table of Distances*. Printed in San Francisco in 1858, it sold for $1.50 to miners and suppliers headed for the new diggings.

Several other authors eventually published guides to the Canadian mines as well, and these were distributed throughout North America and in Europe. Anderson's *Hand-Book*, though, appears to have been the most useful of the early guides, and certainly was so in regard to routes in eastern Washington.

The mining parties traveling north from The Dalles had a choice of two main routes, and both were used extensively. The first left The Dalles following the road being built by the U.S. Army's Captain Dent over the Simcoe Mountains to Fort Simcoe. This trail then led northeast striking the Columbia at about Priest Rapids. It crossed the Columbia and continued north along the river for 25 miles before turning to the Upper Grand Coulee. The other route used by miners was the familiar fur traders' route leading north from Fort Walla Walla, and also to Grand Coulee.

According to Anderson's *Hand-Book* (with additional commentary from another knowledgeable informer, simply identified in the text as "N.B."):

> Every facility of Steam Navigation exists between Portland and the Dalles. The transit between these two points is performed in part of two days, the intervening night being passed at the Cascades, where

travelers are well accommodated. An attempt is being made to extend steamboat navigation as far as the Priest's Rapids, sixty miles above Walla-Walla, and one hundred and ninety from the Dalles; but the success of this project is thus far undecided [this was accomplished in 1859].

With horses there are two routes to the Priest's Rapids: One crossing the Columbia River at the Dalles, passing over the dividing ridge to the Yackama Valley, and continuing across until the Columbia is again struck at the point in question, where the Columbia is recrossed to its left bank. (N.B.—This trail in crossing the Yackama Valley, joins the trail which parties from Puget's Sound, crossing by the Nachess Pass, would necessarily follow. The necessity of crossing to the left bank at the Priest's Rapids, arises from the impracticable nature of the country on the right side, between that point and Okinagan.)

The other route is by following the left bank of the Columbia from the Dalles to Walla-Walla, crossing the Snake River at its mouth, and thence continuing along the Columbia to the Priest's Rapids. (N.B.—There are several modifications of the latter portion of this route, some of which are shorter; but I instance this for simplicity.)

The first described route is much the shorter, as the Great Bend of the Columbia River is cut off by it. But the double crossing of the Columbia is a serious obstacle; and the Yackama River, when high, is a troublesome impediment.

For this reason, I should prefer the longer route by Walla-Walla; and the more so, as it is passable at all seasons, which the other is not, owing to snow in the mountain.

There is good grass by both routes.

From the Priest's Rapids the Indian trail is followed up some twenty-five miles, when it strikes off the river, and enters the *Grande Couleé*, an extraordinary ravine, the origin of which has been a matter of much speculation . . . The bottom of this ravine is very smooth; and affords excellent traveling; good encampments are found at regular intervals. After following it for about sixty miles, the trail strikes off for the Columbia, at a point a few miles beyond a small lake, called by the *voyageurs*, *Le Lac a l'Eau Bleue*. (N.B.—It is necessary to camp at this lake. There is a small stream twenty-five miles or so before reaching the lake, which is another regular encampment; and again another streamlet about thirty miles short of that last mentioned, where it would likewise be necessary to encamp . . .

Striking off from the point mentioned, in a direction about N.N.W., the trail reaches the Columbia a few miles above Fort Okinagan, which post is called twenty-five miles from the Grand Couleé. Ferrying at the fort (the horses being swum), the trail ascends the Okinagan River, cutting points here and there.[6]

Joel Palmer, an important early entrepreneur and stockman, pioneered the first wagon road north from Priest Rapids in 1858, along the river as described in Anderson's *Hand-Book*. He proceeded on north, however, via Moses Coulee, rather than Grand Coulee. More about Palmer, a well-known figure in Oregon history, will be presented in the next chapter.

Miners' Brigades, 1858

Now to continue with Van Arsdol's account from the *Okanogan County Heritage:*

A full compilation of parties traveling north . . . in 1858, is not possible. Travel started on a small scale, and built up later when miners arrived from Oregon and California and as the arrival of the troop reinforcements in the Pacific Northwest helped abate the Indian problem. David McLoughlin, who headed one of the larger parties, wrote from The Dalles in late June that several small parties had passed through the Indian country without trouble. Ike and L. Moyce were among the earlier travelers, leaving Portland in mid-March and taking mules and provisions via steamboat to The Dalles, where they departed overland. They camped at Walla Walla for five days . . . and required eight days traveling from Walla Walla to the mines. In a letter, they wrote they had found the grass was good and they had no trouble with Indians. "The Indians ferried them across the streams for small presents, handkerchiefs, shirts, etc." At Fraser River they were making $40 to $50 a day mining . . .

Tracing the dramatic trail of the gold hunters in its entirety, by land and sea, in detail, and relating the Fraser River mining activity are beyond the scope of this article. However, a few comments will help set the stage for a detailed discussion of the happenings in the Okanogan area.

One typical comment about the gold "fever" that gripped the [California] populace was printed in a Butte, Calif., paper: "The people can't be kept from Frazer River . . . The stage keeps going away, filled full of impatient fortune seekers" . . . [Another paper of the day reported that] in two days, at least 250 men bound for Fraser passed through Oroville, Calif. on the way north. They were moving along at a "perfect rush, whooping and yelling as they pass along the road" . . .

Many of the California people . . . traveled by Klamath Lake then kept east of the Cascade mountains . . . One well-mounted and armed party of 500 Frenchmen, divided into companies in military style, [moved] north to Fraser on the inland route. These were former California miners, and many had served in the Crimea during the war with Russia.

The Dalles . . . had become a major outfitting center for miners heading on the long journey north . . . on what later was known as the Cariboo Trail. In May it was "all that a frontiersman would desire—a regular 'hurrah camp'" as one observer noted [Charles Frush]. "Pack trains, miners' and quartermaster's wagon trains were preparing to start, some on very long journeys into the heart of a hostile, savage country. All was mirth and merriment, no one appearing to care for or fear the dangers that lay across the trail" . . .

To the end of May an estimated 300 persons had passed through The Dalles en route for the northern mines of Washington Territory and the Fraser River. From 400 to 500 men were fitting out at The Dalles at the time for the trip, and numbers were arriving and leaving almost every day in early July. Nez Perce and Cayuse Indians offered several hundred horses for sale . . . The news of the defeat of [Steptoe's] soldiers from Walla Walla in the Palouse country in May was a shock, but on one boat on which miners were offered a refund and a trip back to Portland, none accepted the offer.

As the miners trekked on into Washington Territory, out of the country served by newspapers, they generally passed into obscurity, as the "news" that was made in the Okanogan vicinity [generally] was [only] by parties which had difficulties with Indians. However, it is easy to visualize long trains of mounted men and pack animals along dusty routes, building up to a peak in the summer . . . about the time or shortly after the troops were defeating the combined tribes in battles to the east of the Okanogan.

The attitude of the Indians of the interior naturally was of prime interest to prospective miners in 1858. These Indians were described by a writer . . . "as athletic, fine-looking men. He also commented: . . . "These Indian tribes are well supplied with horses and livestock— many of them too are well armed—and from the best information we can obtain it is believed that they will make that country their Thermopylae, and resist to the last all nearer approach of the whites."

The attitude of the Indians was learned at first hand by one of the first parties to get into difficulties in the Okanogan. At the mouth of the Yakima River, California and Oregon miners encountered some Indians and questioned them. The gist of the report, as printed by the *Oregon Argus* of Oregon City, Ore., on July 3, 1858, was: "They said that since the fight with Steptoe all the big chiefs had met, had a big talk and concluded that the soldiers and Bostons [Americans] should not pass through their country, but the French and Hudson Bay men could. They said the streams were so high that we would be compelled to go by Priest's Rapids, and there the main body of Indians was collected on both sides of the river, and the balance were watching the Colville Trail, but they would be sure to get us."[7]

Upon hearing this, an Indian guide and some of the Oregon and California miners abandoned the trip, but 23 Californians bravely decided to push on, even though they already had been informed while passing old

Fort Walla Walla that Steptoe had been defeated in the Palouse country. Most of the miners were on foot with packhorses. A French Canadian served as guide, who recommended that they travel west of the Columbia to avoid meeting war-like tribesmen.

However, as they proceeded north toward Fort Okanogan, alarmed Indians followed, harassing them, particularly at stream crossings, and the French Canadian guide was drowned. After passing Fort Okanogan, tension continued to mount. Finally, apparently in the Palmer Lake vicinity in the Okanogan valley, a gun battle erupted when 20 to 50 Indians attempted to grab and run off with several of the miners' rifles. These warriors, joined by the miners' Nez Perce guide, also ran off with most of the miners' horses. One miner was killed and scalped, and another wounded, and the party entrenched. After darkness, they scattered into the mountains, and made their way to the mining settlements after much travail and hunger, though it is possible that several more men were killed.[8]

Around this time period, other hostilities are known to have occurred in the Columbia Basin and adjoining areas. For example, also in the spring, a larger party led by Mortimer Robertson was attacked on the west side of the Columbia below the Wenatchee River and had to turn back. (Later, in August 1858, Robertson again returned north with an even larger brigade.) At Fort Colvile, as word arrived of Robertson's defeat, armed and painted warriors of the upper Columbia area insisted that the miners there abandon the country.

> One source lists the Robertson party losses in the first, abortive trip as two men drowned in the Yakima River, one killed by Indians, one miner dead of exhaustion and several wounded. Of the approximately 77 miners, 20 carried rifles and the others were armed with shotguns and revolvers . . .
>
> Whether this was typical armament for a Fraser-bound party is uncertain. One writer declared that all Americans heading into that region were equipped with the universal revolver, "many of them carrying a brace of such, as well as a bowie knife." They also were carrying "more or less" baggage across their shoulders, according to the writer.
>
> Robertson was in Portland in early July and spoke to a large crowd assembled in front of a hotel there to provide aid for the party, which had lost all of its horses and "chattels" in the fighting. Robertson told "of the dangers to be overcome, and the rich prospects of gold they had found but a short distance above Fort Simcoe." The Portland residents contributed approximately $1,000 for the second trip . . .

The hostile showing of the Indians probably tended to hold up some of the parties in the Dalles area, but most miners were persistent and the main change seems to have been that the travelers formed into larger parties before moving on north.[9]

The most famous party passing north, and gaining notoriety for falling into an ambush in July 1858, was led by David McLoughlin, the son of the former HBC Chief Factor, Dr. John McLoughlin, and his beloved half-breed wife. David McLoughlin, who like his father also had worked for the HBC, was 36 years old in 1858, and had participated in the 1849 California mining excitement. Because of his experience in the region and his natural ability, he was a logical choice to lead a large group of miners assembling at The Dalles. Reportedly, 400 miners already had crossed on the Deschutes ferry, heading for the trails north.

The McLoughlin party was organized into companies, with military-like duties. This was a typical measure for large groups of travelers all across the West, whenever danger was present. They set out on July 5, reaching old Fort Walla Walla, or Wallula, in several days' time. Here, their numbers were augmented by additional miners, including some of the men who had stayed behind when the ill-fated group of 23 miners described above had set out to the north.

On July 13, the McLoughlin party left Fort Walla Walla headed for the Grand Coulee country. To continue in Van Arsdol's words:

Even before the McLoughlin party left Wallula, Indians had succeeded in driving off some of the horses, on July 9.

The strength of the party has been variously listed as 150 to 185, and the number of horses and mules totaled around 400 . . . a contemporary account from the *Oregon Statesman* . . . related that almost all had revolvers, the group had 90 to 100 rifles and 20 to 25 other "heavy arms." The party also was supplied with three months' provisions, mining tools and plenty of ammunition.

Most of this party was from California. Some Oregonians, Frenchmen, half-breeds and "camp followers" also were in the expedition.

After crossing Snake River, the party cut across country and went through Grand Coulee. One day from Fort Okanogan, one member of the party who was lagging behind was killed by the Indians.[10]

The key pioneer chronicler, A.J. Splawn (1845-1917), provides further details about the route of the McLoughlin Party in his reminiscences, *Ka-Mi-Akin: The Last Hero of the Yakimas*, printed in Portland, Oregon, in 1917. (Splawn also provides interesting details about the Indian/miner clashes in the Wenatchee area mentioned above. Beginning in 1861, Splawn spent a lifetime traveling the trails of the Interior Northwest. His book is must reading for anyone interested in Columbia Basin frontier history.)

According to Splawn, the McLoughlin party proceeded north as follows, obviously on the old HBC trail:

> Keeping on the right side of the Columbia, they crossed the Snake river at its mouth and went to the site of the former town of Ringold, then struck northerly to Crab Creek through a coulee by Scooten springs [skirting the eastern end of the Saddle Mountains to Crab Creek]. By way of Crab creek they came to Moses lake, went north to Soap lake and then to what is now known as Dead Man's Spring, just south of Coulee City.

Deadman Spring, located six miles south of Coulee City near Dry Coulee, reportedly is the place where the Californian who lagged behind was murdered. He became a fatality because he was always slow in "getting under way" each morning, as Splawn explains:

> He had been repeatedly told that he was taking too many chances in lagging behind. The warning seemed to have no effect on him, and one morning, when the start was made, he was still lingering, fussing with his pack. He never caught up with the party.
>
> Just what happened to the man . . . I learned from Lo-Kout, who was one of a party of [Yakima and Sinkiuse] Indians lying in wait to steal horses of the expedition. Ow-hi's band of Indians, he said, was camped at We-nat-sha, both Moses and Qual-chan being with the old chief, when a rider brought in word of the McLoughlin party when they were on [lower] Crab Creek. Qual-chan and Lo-Kout with fifty warriors at once set out to intercept them and either give battle or steal the horses. Catching sight of the white men on upper Crab creek, they realized that the force was too large to attack and sent back to camp for re-inforcements, while they hung on the trail of the expedition. The vigilance of this party of experienced men, however, gave the Indians no show. They could have killed the man who lagged behind on two different occasions, but thought it better not to molest him, believing that if it were seen that he could follow behind in safety, the vigilance of the company might be relaxed.
>
> When no re-inforcements arrived, the Indians decided to quit and return to We-nat-sha. Moses and Qual-chan then remembered the man who was always behind. Hiding in the rocks near the white men's camp, they waited until the rest of the party was out of hearing, then crept up and shot the laggard. Both Indians fired, but it was thought that Qual-chan's bullet killed him, and that he was therefore entitled to the scalp, horses and outfit.[11]

Returning to their Wenatchee stronghold, the Yakima war leader Qualchan received word from Yakima chieftain Kamiakin, now in the Palouse country, to bring his men to join in battle against Colonel Wright's forthcoming expedition to the Spokane area.

The Sinkiuse leader Moses, on the other hand, wanted to revenge his brother, Quil-ten-e-nock, who had been killed earlier in the spring in one of the clashes with miners south of the mouth of the Wenatchee River. Moses was convinced that some of these same miners were now in McLoughlin's party. He traveled to Chelan to speak with a cousin, the Chelan chief In-no-mo-se-cha. The Chelan leader "thought favorably of an attack" on the whitemen "when they should reach the Okanogan and immediately set out to stir up the Okanogans to avenge Quil-ten-e-nock, who had been a great favorite" among the tribes. In-no-mo-se-cha was successful in forming a sizeable coalition of Okanogans and Chelans to join the Sinkiuse for an attack, and went to the mouth of the Okanogan River to meet and spy on the white invaders.[12]

Meanwhile, McLoughlin's party had passed through the Grand Coulee and reached the Columbia. At this point, Francis Wolff recorded information that might reveal who the murdered miner was:

> When we were going from the river to the H.B.Co. Fort we noticed an Indian with a horse of our party, dressed in the owners clothes who we suppose had returned to W.W. by the name M. Hillburn who had been killed without our knowledge before we had reached the river. He with others had been warned not to stragle behind but to keep closely up for the Country was not safe . . . [T]his was the first casualty and put us on our guard."[13]

After a long, tense, night-time conference, the chiefs agreed to assist the party in crossing in Indian canoes for payment, but warned that they would attack the whites later. The whites crossed the river in canoes opposite to the old fort, while the livestock swam over. As sometimes occurred in such ventures, a few horses drowned or were swept away. The next day, the miners continued up the Okanogan with an "advanced and rear guard of 25 men each."

Now, to continue Van Arsdol's story:

> One account states that the travelers from the south took over the old buildings at the fort after Indians appeared. However, there was no other unusual action until July 29 after the miners had traveled up the trail to a point near the mouth of Tunk Creek . . . [to] a defile later

known as McLoughlin's Canyon [located on the east side of the Okanogan valley several miles south of present-day Tonasket].

Well-armed and mounted men were in the vanguard and the rear, with the pack train stretched out for over a mile or more on the trail between.

The Indians, numbering around 200, according to information provided by some of the war party to A.J. Splawn in later years, had picked the canyon for an ambush, had felled trees across the trail and piled up stone breastworks on cliffs. At least part of the Indians were armed with Hudson's Bay Co. [trade] guns.

Miners had noticed a great number of footprints near the mouth of the canyon and were wary on that account. An Indian was discovered with a gun pointed at one of the men of the vanguard, and shooting soon was general, with Indians bobbing up from behind rocks. Some of the miners occupied a hill commanding the entrance to the canyon, and others retreated to an open plateau during the fighting. They set up breastworks with their packs, and herded animals inside the area. Indians hovered around until dark and fired many bullets into camp without much damage.

However, the party already had suffered its fatalities . . . contemporary news accounts would indicate . . . three dead and five wounded.[14]

One eyewitness with the McLoughlin party, the same Francis Wolff who had helped start the gold stampede in the first place, recalled part of the action this way:

We entered the mouth with the guard in advance and had proceeded about 100 yards when one of the men noticed some wilted bushes and thinking strange of it went to examine them when the Indians behind it suspecting that we had noticed their ambush fired. Then shots came from the sides and in rear of us, evidently trying to drive us into the Canyon. Men threw themselves from their horses and those not killed or wounded returned the fire.

My horse on which I had my cantenas [small box-like gold/money containers] with $2000 gold dust . . . got away from me and ran up the canyon about 75 yards toward the Indians. I went for him and got him and returned with him to our line.[15]

Now to return to Van Arsdol's telling of this story:

At night, McLoughlin's party saw the Indians in a war dance on a hill not far away and heard their whoops. The Indians also had set fire to trees and grass in the neighborhood. It was an uneasy night for the whites, who did not know how many Indians besieged them.

During the night, some of the miners made a raft or rafts, and the miners later rafted baggage across to the west side of Okanogan

River. Many provisions were soaked and damaged in the crossing. On the day following the fight, the horses were driven downriver and forded to the west side. After the last of the miners, formed into a skirmishing party, had returned from the east bank, the miners traveled about two miles and camped.

The miners remained in this camp about two days, and during the time one group returned to the canyon, and retrieved and buried the three dead miners. They discovered that the Indians had abandoned their positions at the canyon, and were able to examine the stone fortifications which the natives had prepared in the ambuscade. While at the new camp, the miners prepared litters for two of the most badly wounded men.

McLoughlin's party traveled north on the west side of the river for about one day and camped at 3 p.m., made a circle with packs and turned out their animals to graze, when mounted Indians attempted unsuccessfully to stampede the animals.

Shortly after this, a parley was arranged between leaders of the Indian war party and the miners.

One of the chiefs said he favored peace but could not control his braves. He had lost a brother in the fight with Robertson's party, and said the white men came into Indian country without his approval, killed the wild game and fired guns in camp, which was an Indian way of proclaiming war.

A "treaty" supposedly was entered into shortly afterward, with terms permitting the party to pass through, but calling for the miners to provide clothing, tobacco and blankets for the Indians. These supplies were distributed. The chief talking to McLoughlin hedged somewhat by promising that there would be no shooting, but he could not stop bad men from stealing, and he advised the miners to be wary against thefts and stampedes.

That night or the following night is probably the time that . . . [one chronicler] recalled his hair "really stood on end." He had spread out his blankets and was asleep in the camp near [present-day] Oroville, dreaming of home, when "it seemed that the 'Lower Regions' had broken loose."

"We jumped out of our sleep, dazed," he wrote. "It was pitch dark, and the rifles were cracking all around us, the men yelling like mad."

It turned out that a mounted party of Indians had attempted to stampede the animals. They were driven off, but not before getting three to six head. The Indians had fired guns while riding through, and the whites considered this an infraction of the treaty.

The same night Indians succeeded in driving off a band of cattle four miles away. These belonged to or at least were destined for Francis Wolff, who had asked his partner to send cattle to meet the party en route to Fraser River. The cattle and pack train had almost reached Lake Osoyoos, apparently from the Colville Trail, when they were taken.

On a day shortly afterward the miners surprised a small group of Indians on the Similkameen River "jerking" or drying meat from two head of cattle reportedly stolen from Wolff. One . . . escaped, according to one version of the party's adventures, and told the tribesmen that the captives were to be hung. Within a relatively short time, Angus MacDonald, chief trader at Fort Colvile, arrived in the McLoughlin camp. He was en route to Fort Yale or Fort Hope with numerous furs, and he said the Indians had threatened to kill two "Bostons" . . . in his train and cut up all his furs if the prisoners were not freed. McDonald promised to use his influence to secure a safe passage for the whites, if they would turn the Indians loose. The Indians were released, and McDonald remained with the miners until they reached the forks of Fraser and Thompson rivers.

One of the wounded men died on Fraser River, making a total of four fatalities from the skirmish with the Indians.

A complaint heard after the trip was that the French and half-breeds had kept almost entirely out of the fight . . .

Alfred Hodge, one of the travelers, said that 30 days were required for the trip.

Thus concluded the most famous incident on the Okanogan trail in 1858. Other brigades of frontiersmen, of course, continued to head north in this period, and experienced difficulties. For example, in August 1858 the aforementioned Mortimer Robertson, whose brigade had been forcibly turned back in the spring by Indians at the Wenatchee, returned northward again via Fort Simcoe and Lake Chelan. This time, Robertson led an even larger party consisting of 700 mules and horses and 300 well-armed men, including Mexican and French packers.

Played-out horses were left along the rugged route by the long column, and an armed clash with Indians broke out six miles past Lake Chelan, with one straggling miner killed and a dozen horses run off. After the large brigade spied the newly dug graves from the McLoughlin Canyon fight, other clashes occurred with warriors at Okanogan Lake and on the Similkameen, before the miners finally reached the Canadian gold fields.[16]

Combined HBC/Major Owen Brigade, May-June 1858

Three months earlier, just as Steptoe's command met defeat in the Palouse country, a combined HBC and American brigade had set out from The Dalles, headed toward Fort Colvile via the HBC's Big Bend trail. This is an example of a brigade that passed through earlier, and met with better luck, than did the McLoughlin or Robertson parties, albeit they went to Fort

Colville, rather than the Okanogan. Charles W. Frush, an American with this party, has left a fine account of the journey. According to Frush:

> In the month of May, 1858 . . . Among the many parties packing bucking "cayuses" and braying mules that beautiful spring day [at The Dalles] were two that had long, wearisome marches ahead of them. One was the Hudson's Bay "brigade" of seventy-five packs in charge of a Mr. Oglesby, with George Montour, a half-blood, as interpreter, and ten Colville Indians as packers and herders, on its way to the Hudson's Bay Company's Fort Colville on the banks of the mighty Columbia River, near Kettle Falls. The other was a government outfit composed of sixty-five head of animals, about twenty-five with packs and the balance loose, in charge of Major John Owen, of Fort Owen [in Montana's Bitterroot valley, not far from modern-day Missoula], who had been appointed United States Indian agent for the Flathead, Upper and Lower Pend d'Oreille, and Kootenai tribes or bands of Indians, with your humble servant as a kind of brevet Second Lieutenant in command of the mess box . . . In addition there was a colored boy for cook and four Flathead Indian packers. When the words "All Ready" were given we mounted, and for awhile there was some lively bucking and stampeding, but after the first day's drive the ponies were all very docile.
>
> Our trail was what early pioneers knew as the "Buffalo Trail," and was used by the Indians from this side who made yearly trips to the east of the Rocky Mountains. It crosses the Des Chutes River near its confluence with the Columbia, thence over the rolling prairie, crossing John Day River, and on to the banks of the Columbia again, which it traverses to the mouth of the Snake River . . . here the trouble began. There was no drift or timber anywhere in sight to make a raft, and the Indians, what few were left in their camp . . . did not seem disposed at first to ferry us over in their canoes, but after a little . . . talk, they consented and we drove the animals, after unpacking, into the swift waters of the Snake which was about half a mile wide, very rapid and with the spring rise just commencing, but all safely landed on the other side; then with the aid of eight or ten canoes we soon had over all the stores and "riggin" and of course felt much elated over our good luck and sent our old Walla Wallas back with their canoes well pleased . . . [with] the liberal amount of tobacco we gave them for their services.

The next day, the large cavalcade of 140 horses proceeded north from the mouth of the Snake River to the Ringold locality, just below the commencement of the White Bluffs. As Frush relates:

> May 30, 1858. We traveled along the Columbia River, over a sage brush flat, for some twenty miles and camped on its banks near the

White Bluffs. This evening we heard startling news. A Nez Perce Chief, named Jesse, came to our camp, and through George Montour, the Hudson's Bay Company's interpreter, we learned of the great battle Colonel Steptoe had had with the Indians out on the prairie . . . This news gave us the "blues," especially the fact that the soldiers were defeated, Captain Taylor and Lieutenant Gaston killed and also a number of privates. The whole command retreated to Walla Walla leaving the Indians masters of the . . . very country we had to go through.

At this camp I experienced my first game of bluff played with Indians. About dark some seven or eight canoes loaded with Yakima warriors landed near our camp. They were painted and rigged up in first-class war style . . . Our few Indian packers and the interpreter took the situation in and suggested that we [stage a war dance] . . . So we built a large campfire out of sage brush and grease wood, and all of us, the Major included, formed a circle and with one hand holding a raw-hide, with a stick in the other, batted that raw-hide and yelled and danced until we were nearly exhausted. This act, the interpreter said, was intended to show these Yakimas that we were not afraid . . . to my utter surprise when I turned out in the morning . . . They had . . . gone away during the night. I must confess I felt pleased, and so would anyone, from the fact that there is less danger in thumping the raw-hide . . . than trying to dodge their bullets.

The animals were driven into camp and packed and we started, and nothing transpired during the two days following until we reached the Spokane River, near its mouth.

Having proceeded from the Columbia northeast across the Big Bend, via Crab Creek and probably turning east at Black Butte, they fell in with some Spokanes or their allies. The warriors were heartened by the recent Native American victory over soldiers in the Palouse country and by successes against miners in the Wenatchee or Okanogan areas.

On arriving here we learned there had been a fight between a large party of miners, who started from The Dalles for the Frazer River country via the Okanagan canyon [perhaps Robertson first clash at Wenatchee or the Palmer Lake fight; see above], and the Okanagans, their chief, Quilt-ta-mina, being killed.

This was a serious affair to us, and, if it had not been for the influence held by [the Indian packers and] Montour, the half-blood with these people, your writer would not now be penning these lines. We were allowed, however, to move camp unmolested, but a fearful yell of defiance met our ears from forty or fifty painted [warriors] . . . who, I presume, thinking we might not appreciate their clemency, rode along on either side of our party for some distance, and kept up their war-whoop to remind us that we were getting off cheap.

However, upon reaching the expected relative safety of Fort Colvile two days later, the column was surprised to encounter 500 or 600 Indians gathering outside the post to celebrate the victory over Steptoe. Frush, despite being naturally apprehensive under these circumstances, took the time to observe the traditional war-dance of these people:

> We [had] jumped out of the frying-pan into the fire . . . I have seen many an Indian war-dance since . . . [but never] anything that equalled this affair. A great many of them were entirely nude, some painted half red and half black, and some daubed all over with white mud, a kind of pipe clay, and then spotted with red. All were armed with Hudson Bay guns, rifles, or with bows and arrows, and were drumming and singing, with an old [grandmother] . . . in the center of a circle they had formed, who would recite the daring feat some brave had performed and, shaking in the faces of the warriors the swords and pistols and other trophies they had taken from the officers and men killed in the fight, tantalize them by telling them to go and do better.

Some time later, Captain Owen chose a date to leave the post, hopefully undetected. The Americans packed "while the stars" still were shining, and upon leaving the post at daybreak, shortly broke "into a dead run." Alert warriors, however, arose from their camp, took pursuit, and dashed into the train "lassoing seven or eight" horses, then dropped back, letting the column to continue on its way.

After a couple of other incidents with Indians in the next few days, both of a hostile nature as well as decidedly friendly acts, Owens, Frush, and the pack string successfully crossed through the mountains to their destination, the Bitterroot valley.[17]

The Final Act

In the summer of 1858, as miners continued to outfit at The Dalles and leave for the long journey north, U.S. Army reinforcements arrived from other regions of the West to join Colonel George Wright's command at Fort Walla Walla and Major Robert Garnett's force at Fort Simcoe for a showdown with the warring tribesmen.

By mid-summer 1858, Garnett and Wright had orders for a two-pronged attack to the north in an attempt to subdue the hostile elements once and for all. Wright's orders focused on the Palouse/Spokane region, whereas Garnett's directives centered on the area between the Cascades and the Columbia River. General Wright's Spokane campaign, with victories at Four Lakes and Spokane Plains in September 1858, already has been outlined earlier and will not be repeated here.

A few words, however, need to be said about Major Garnett's expedition, which more directly impacted the tribes that had resented and resisted, both overtly and covertly, the passing miners' brigades. On August 7, the day after Wright left Walla Walla, 8 officers and 306 enlisted, 225 pack animals, and 50 herders and packers under the command of Major Garnett left Fort Simcoe. Staying west of the Columbia River, they proceeded north through the Yakima and Wenatchee drainages to Fort Okanogan:

> Some Indians believed to have taken part in attacks on miners were shot on the trip north. By the end of August, Garnett was on the Wenatchee. Of the 25 Indians wanted for attacking miners, the major reported 10 executed, five at large in the Cascade Mountains and the rest . . . "are now opposite Fort O'kanagan, some distance back from the river, and on their way, the Indians say, to either the mountains north of that place in the British possessions, or towards the Blackfoot country."[18]

In this successful campaign, the army too suffered some casualties. Second Lieutenant Jesse K. Allen was killed, perhaps accidently shot by one of his own men, in a predawn attack on an Indian village in the upper Yakima valley. Some days later, Private Liebe of C Company, 9th infantry, was killed while straggling behind the column, 50 miles north of Fort Okanogan.[19] At this cost in Indian and soldiers' lives, the 1855-58 Indian war in central Washington was concluded.[20]

The passage of miners through the Big Bend country during this time, of course, was not just one way. A number of the wealth seekers and merchant packers going north in the spring and summer returned over the same route in the fall to the lower country. A main reason for the return flow of men, according to Joel Palmer, was that "in consequence of the high price of provisions and other necessary supplies, miners generally prefer[red] returning to the lower country to winter." (Significant numbers of excited gold seekers continued passing this way in 1859, and again in 1860. Van Arsdol has documented this flow of men and livestock, but, regrettably, this information has yet to be published.)

Van Arsdol rightfully concludes that the "impact of the mining 'stampede' in bringing about the final defeat" of the warring elements of the interior tribes has not been sufficiently recognized in the standard accounts written about this period of history. However, along with Steptoe's retreat in the Palouse country, the miners and their clashes with warriors clearly were a catalyst for action, leaving "no alternative for the U.S. Army but to complete the conquest" of the Inland Northwest.[21]

Endnotes

1. Leslie M. Scott, "The Pioneer Stimulus of Gold," *Quarterly of the Oregon Historical Society* 27 (September 1917): 147, 151.

2. For a complete historical overview of the Cayuse tribe, see Robert H. Ruby and John A. Brown, *The Cayuse Indians: Imperial Tribesmen of Old Oregon* (Norman: University of Oklahoma Press, 1972).

3. Cornelius's brief Big Bend campaign is described in Clifford E. Trafzer and Richard D. Scheuerman, *Renegade Tribe: The Palouse Indians and the Invasion of the Inland Pacific Northwest* (Pullman: Washington State University Press, 1986), 69-71, 206 map. For a detailed account of U.S. Army operations in the Yakima War, see H. Dean Guie, *Bugles in the Valley: Garnett's Fort Simcoe* (Portland: Oregon Historical Society, revised ed. 1977); see pages 148-86 for the Civil War record of many of the officers. Militia activities in the Yakima War are described in Kent D. Richards, *Isaac I. Stevens: Young Man in a Hurry* (Pullman: Washington State University Press, 1993 [originally published 1979]). See also, B.F. Manring, *Conquest of the Coeur d'Alenes, Spokanes and Palouses* (Fairfield, Washington: Ye Galleon Press, 1975 [originally published 1912]).

4. Portland *Democratic Standard*, July 1, 1858. Also see, "Handwritten Record: Ambush at McLoughlin Canyon and other Adventures of Francis Wolff," *Okanogan County Heritage* 2 (June 1964): 7-12.

5. Ted Van Arsdol, "Trail North—1858," *Okanogan County Heritage* 7 (March 1969): 19-20. Van Arsdol has updated some passages especially for presentation in *Forgotten Trails*.

6. Alexander C. Anderson, *Hand-Book and Map to the Gold Region of Frazer's and Thompson's Rivers, with Table of Distances* (San Francisco, 1858), 11-14.

7. Van Arsdol, "Trail North—1858," 21-24.

8. *Ibid.,* (March 1969): 24-25, and (June 1969): 13-14.

9. *Ibid.,* 14-15.

10. *Ibid.,* 16.

11. A.J. Splawn, *Ka-Mi-Akin: The Last Hero of the Yakimas* (Portland, 1917), 108-09.

12. *Ibid.,* 109.

13. "Handwritten Record: Ambush at McLoughlin Canyon and other Adventures of Francis Wolff," *Okanogan County Heritage* 2 (June 1964): 10

14. Van Arsdol, "Trail North—1858," 16-17.

15. "Handwritten Record . . . Francis Wolff," 10. For an additional firsthand account of the attack (though recorded 43 years later, in 1901), see the reminiscences of Robert Frost, "Fraser River Gold Rush Adventures," *Washington Historical Quarterly* 22 (July 1931): 203-09.

16. Van Arsdol, "Trail North—1858," 17-19, 21-22.

17. Charles W. Frush, "A Trip from the Dalles of the Columbia, Oregon, to Fort Owen, Bitter Root Valley, Montana, in the Spring of 1858," in *Contributions to the Historical Society of Montana*, Vol. 2 (1896 [reprinted by J.S. Canner, Boston, Massachusetts, 1966]), 337-42.

18. Van Arsdol, "Trail North—1858," 20.

19. Guie, *Bugles in the Valley*, 119, 125; and Major R. S. Garnett, "From Fort Simcoe to Fort Okanogan with the 9th Infantry," *Okanogan County Heritage* 12 (Fall 1974): 12. At Fort Okanogan, Garnett was told that 10 miners altogether had been killed at different times along the Okanogan.

20. For an insightful account of Garnett's campaign by a key participant, see Martin F. Schmitt, ed., *General George Crook: His Biography* (Norman: University of Oklahoma Press, 1960), 57-68. In the Wenatchee campaign, Crook distinguished himself as a young subordinate officer in the pursuit of the warriors accused of attacking miners. Afterward, as the column turned back toward Fort Simcoe, Crook was ordered to conduct an exciting and eventful reconnaissance by canoe of the Columbia River down to Priest Rapids. He wrote, "I don't know that ever in my life I enjoyed a trip with such keen zest and pleasure." Crook earned general's stars during the Civil War, and later became an especially noted leader of troops and Indian scouts in the Indian wars of the 1860s-80s.

21. Van Arsdol, "Trail North—1858," 20, 25.

The Hudson's Bay Company's Fort Okanogan in 1853, by John Mix Stanley. The Canadians vacated the post in 1860, at a time when the Big Bend/Okanogan route to Canada was just beginning to be called the "Cariboo trail." *Pacific Railroad Explorations and Surveys, Vol 12*

VIII
Cattle Drives and Sternwheelers

EVEN BEFORE THE END of the Yakima War, stockmen from the lower Columbia River country had started driving cattle into the Columbia Basin. Reportedly, by July 1858, hundreds of cattle were passing through Oregon City or Portland on the way to the new mines in Canada, either via the Puget Sound/Fraser River route, or up the Columbia, either by boat or overland, and then driven northward across the Columbia Basin. These early cattlemen, along with the miners and packers, used the various primary routes through the Big Bend—e.g., Priest Rapids road, HBC Grand Coulee trail, Colville road, etc., and variations thereof.

In the first years of the large cattle drives, 1858 to 1861, the mining camps usually provided a lucrative market for cattle—first in Canada's Fraser and Thompson gold fields, and then the Cariboo mines even farther north. The year 1861 saw a peak of activity on what was coming to be called the Cariboo trail, following the old HBC route north to the Okanogan. (A variation, however, crossed between the lower and upper Grand Coulee at McEntee Springs and extended northwest across the prairie toward the Okanogan, thus bypassing the Upper Grand Coulee altogether.)

After 1861, however, the main thrust of this movement of livestock shifted toward the Snake River country when gold strikes in the Clearwater, Salmon River, Boise, and John Day areas of Idaho and northeast Oregon brought the greatest surge of miners into the Columbia River drainage. Gold strikes in western Montana after 1862 likewise contributed to traffic in this direction. Nevertheless, activity northward on the Big Bend routes remained quite brisk into the mid 1860s.

Pioneer ranchers had long recognized the advantages of raising livestock on the bunchgrass prairies of the interior. By late 1861, there were as many as 10,000 head of cattle grazing in the Umatilla and Walla Walla areas, though the harsh winter of 1861-62 caused severe losses. Stockmen were poised to spread the livestock industry northward throughout the

Yakima valley and the Columbia Basin, turning their herds into the bunch-grass hills alongside Indian-owned herds that already roamed there. Large bands of sheep too would soon follow. In addition, Indian horses, usually called "cayuses," also thrived in the region and were widely herded and sold. Eventually, in many regions of the West, the term "cayuse" came to mean any hardworking range horse of native or common origins.

Along with the swarms of miners, the large cattle drives, and the establishment of military posts and their attached fledgling commercial districts, the coming of steam navigation on the Columbia and Snake rivers was part of the quickening pace of economic development and settlement instigated by the gold rushes. Steamboat routes on the rivers soon proved to be essential links to the region's trail system.

Steamboats on the Rivers

Sternwheelers appeared in the southern Columbia Basin about a decade after commercial navigation originated in the lower Columbia River country. Two impassable natural obstacles initially barred steam navigation into the interior—the massive Cascade Rapids in the Columbia River gorge, and the Dalles and the horseshoe-shaped Celilo Falls just east of the Cascade Range. Up to 1858, Indian canoes, HBC-type York boats, and, most recently, flat-bottomed barges with sails conducted a colorful commerce through these waters, with portages around the falls. But these kinds of craft could not adequately fulfill the supply and transportation needs of the U.S. Army in its campaigns in the interior, nor the succession of quickly developing mining camps in the mountains of Canada and Washington Territory.

Soon, frontier entrepreneurs, particularly the precursors of the famed Oregon Steam Navigation Company from the fledgling commercial center of Portland, Oregon, constructed improved railroad portages around these barriers. They also brought in shipwrights to the "middle river" (i.e., between the Cascades Rapids and The Dalles) and the "upper river" (i.e., above Celilo Falls) to build remarkable, shallow draft steamboats for upriver hauling.

The *Colonel Wright*, the first "upper" river sternwheeler, was completed in 1858, at first primarily to haul freight under government contract to the U.S. Army's main supply point at Wallula. Shortly, this famous sternwheeler explored routes further upstream to Priest Rapids, as well as up the Snake—first to the mouth of the Palouse, and then later to the Clearwater.

According to the classic regional account of navigational development, *Lewis & Dryden's Marine History of the Pacific Northwest* (published in 1895):

> Early in [1859] . . . the *Colonel Wright*, the first steamer on the upper Columbia, commenced to run, opening up to settlement a vast domain that prior to this time was almost as inaccessible as the wilds of Africa. The *Colonel Wright* was launched October 24, 1858, at the mouth of the Des Chutes River, and, like most of the pioneers on the steamboat routes, made a fortune for her owners before others could interfere with the trade . . . The *Colonel Wright* . . . by connecting with the Oregon Steam Navigation steamers on the middle and lower river, landed passengers in Portland thirty hours after leaving Walla Walla, a feat which was considered remarkable at the time . . . The *Colonel Wright* was 110 feet long, 21 foot beam, and 5 feet hold.[1]

The vessel, of course, was named for the now famous Colonel George Wright of the 9th Infantry. It was captained by Len White, a navigator with extensive pioneering experience on Oregon rivers. In the months before the *Colonel Wright's* maiden voyage, White had gone upriver in a bateau to personally investigate the upper river's channels, rapids, and harbors.

The first trip to the mouth of the Walla Walla was financed by the U.S. Army in April 1859, "with a dozen passengers, the owners of the boat and fifty tons of freight to make a trial trip."[2] Captain White masterfully guided the sternwheeler through the upper river's whitewater obstacles, including the Umatilla Rapids, which were the most dangerous along this stretch of the Columbia. The Umatilla Rapids consisted of three separate reefs at half-mile intervals. The trip was a resounding success, and, soon, the steamboat men pushed ahead plans for building additional steamers (especially when gold strikes sparked an increased impetus in developing a lucrative commercial transportation system in the interior).

During the rest of the year, the *Colonel Wright* made hauls between the Deschutes and Wallula, normally three times a week. Also in 1859, with Captain Len White again at the wheel, the *Colonel Wright* pioneered a route up the Columbia to White Bluffs and Priest Rapids; and, during the high spring runoff of 1860, the sternwheeler forged up the swollen Snake to the mouth of the Palouse River. From that point, and from White Bluffs on the mid-Columbia, packers hauled supplies and equipment for the Canadian mines, as well as to the U.S. Army's Fort Colville, established in 1859 near present-day Colville, Washington.

The exploration up to Priest Rapids in 1859, however, disappointingly proved that the rugged reefs and extensive whitewater of this locality were a formidable barrier. In the years to come, few sternwheelers challenged the Columbia at this point, though the rivermen's interest in the northern Columbia remained high. Relatively smooth sailing, however, normally was encountered up to White Bluffs. More will be said shortly about this and other early efforts to improve the transportation link by water to the Cariboo trail.

The details of the *Colonel Wright*'s next major exploratory voyage, this time to the Snake/Clearwater junction, are illustrative of steamboating in this era. In June 1861, with the legendary Captain Len White again in charge, the *Colonel Wright* set out from the mouth of the Deschutes laden with supplies and excited passengers for the newly discovered Clearwater mines. After stopping at bustling Wallula, the boat continued up the Columbia and entered the Snake. Halting by a large log, which had been carried downstream by high water, the crew and some passengers disembarked to cut up the tree for firewood. Discovering a large nest of rattlesnakes under the dead tree, the men jumped lively, making war on the reptiles. A shortage of wood for the steamers' engines was a recurring problem in this treeless region, until contractors, probably including some Indians, began stacking cut wood at strategic points along the rivers.

Proceeding to the Palouse (the *Colonel Wright*'s turn-around point in 1860), the boat's paddle wheel severed the low-lying rope of a recently established ferry. After a two-hour struggle through Palouse Rapids, the sternwheeler reached the Tucannon. Here stood Colonel George Wright's abandoned Fort Taylor, then consisting only of a single cabin, an earth embankment, and a solitary soldier waving his hat as the boat steamed by. Shortly, the *Colonel Wright* encountered mounted Indians, who gamely gauged the boat's speed by galloping alongside on shore. Not desiring to navigate in darkness, Captain White halted for the night in the deep upper canyon of the Snake. Before retiring, the crew and passengers spent the warm evening hours listening to banjo music and singing.

Under way at daylight, the boat approached a newly established ferry at Alpowa Creek by 8 A.M. Gathered there waiting to cross was a large crowd of men and pack animals heading east on the Nez Perce trail to the diggings. Other miners and pack strings, likewise all part of the first great surge toward the Clearwater country, were strung out along the route on both sides of the river. As the sternwheeler approached, men came down to the shoreline cheering, waving hats, and firing guns into the air, while Captain White answered with toots from the steam whistle. The *Colonel*

Wright continued to the forks and up the lower Clearwater, to unload at the head of navigation.

The upriver voyage required 3½ days, but the downstream trip to the mouth of the Deschutes took just 18 hours. As the sternwheeler passed the Palouse, Captain White shouted to the ferryman that he need not replace the cable. On this score White was wrong, because ferry crossings here and elsewhere on the Snake and Columbia were destined to remain for many decades to come. With the advent of steamboats, however, Columbia and Snake ferrymen often would have to mount their cables on high towers on either shore to allow river traffic to pass underneath. During the next several weeks, the *Colonel Wright* made two more highly profitable trips into the lower Clearwater, but, as the water fell during the summer, a new, more practicable, landing had to be established at the Clearwater/Snake junction and, consequently, Lewiston was founded in 1861.

Other steamboats soon appeared on the upper river, plying the waterways to the Palouse, Lewiston, and White Bluffs, some of which were the *Okanogan* in 1861, *Tenino* and *Spray* in 1862, *Nez Perce Chief* and *Kiyus* in 1863, and *Owyhee, Webfoot,* and *Yakima* in 1864, and there were others in later years. In late October 1863, the *Nez Perce Chief* set a record for the richest cargo, carrying out $382,000 in gold dust.

At the trailhead landings, steamers unloaded not only miners, packers, merchants, cattle, horses, mules, wagons, provisions, and mining equipment, but also a liberal sprinkling of gamblers, dance hall girls, and vaudeville-type entertainers. Rubbing shoulders in this cosmopolitan population were Indians, Americans of native born, immigrant, and Black ancestry, adventurers from Canada, Europe, and Mexico, and Chinese from the Orient. In 1861, 10,500 persons came up the Columbia headed for the mines; 24,500 in 1862; 22,000 in 1863; and 36,000 in 1864.[3]

In 1865, the indomitable *Colonel Wright,* with another noted riverman at the wheel, Captain Thomas J. Stump, attempted to navigate through Hells Canyon of the Snake River, but was turned back. The harrowing trip was too much for the veteran explorer of Umatilla Rapids, White Bluffs, and the Clearwater; the *Colonel Wright* returned to Lewiston worn out and soon after was dismantled.[4]

As the gold fever brought thousands of men rushing up the Columbia, new boom towns joined Walla Walla (originally called Steptoeville) as the focal points for transportation and commerce in the interior. These included Umatilla below the Umatilla Rapids, Wallula at old Fort Walla

Walla, and Lewiston at the Snake-Clearwater junction. Depending on the time of year, heavily laden steamboats had to deal with low water, dangerous snags, ice flows, shifting sandbars, or springtime floods; and, at all times, the many rapids were a hazard. Sometimes, during the low water stage late in the year, steamboats could not navigate through the treacherous Umatilla Rapids or other sections of whitewater. Among other places, Ice Harbor about 10 miles up the Snake, and Cold Springs Harbor situated above Umatilla, frequently were used by sternwheelers as havens from threatening ice packs in the winter.

As early as the 1860s, the U.S. Army Corps of Engineers began long-term efforts to reduce navigational hazards on the Columbia and Snake. This entailed mapping channels, rapids, and rocks, dredging channels, blasting out dangerous rocks, and setting ringbolts wherever needed for lining steamboats through the swiftest whitewater. In these decades, dozens of rapids along the Snake-Columbia system were identified with graphic and colorful names (e.g., "Rapids No. 22" or "Perrines Defeat," four miles up the Snake, no doubt was named for some exciting episode perhaps now long lost to history). These improvements were not affected without hazard. At Umatilla Rapids in the 1870s, for instance, a powder barge exploded as men were blasting out rocks.

Joel Palmer's Wagon Road, 1858-60

It was during the 1858 mining excitement that Joel Palmer, a prominent and well-known Oregon pioneer, took a wagon train across the Big Bend country, a feat he was destined to repeat in 1859 and 1860. Palmer's past experiences had made him an ideal person for this endeavor. Having crossed the Great Plains as an immigrant in 1845, he later wrote a popular Oregon Trail guidebook. He also served as a fair-minded and understanding Superintendent of Indian Affairs during the Cayuse War of the late 1840s and again in 1853-56, which, of course, were critical periods in Indian/white relations. Always exhibiting an adventuresome entrepreneurial spirit, he had taken the first wagons from the Willamette valley to California during the California gold rush. As an experienced and capable wagon master and trader, Palmer proclaimed a preference for utilizing oxen as draft animals in rugged, primitive country.

Intrigued by the financial possibilities of supplying goods to the Canadian mines, Palmer spent much of his time from July 1858 until late 1860 en route to and from, and trading in, Canada's Fraser, Thompson, and Similkameen gold fields. Palmer and other packers recognized the fact that the majority of the mining supplies for the camps was being sent via Victoria and Puget Sound, whereas lesser amounts were packed north through the Columbia Basin. It was clear that the distance from Portland through the interior to the mines was shorter than the Puget Sound routes, and transportation costs potentially could be less if a wagon road was pioneered east of the Cascades. Palmer felt he was the man to build the road. Leaning on civic pride and promises of economic prosperity, Palmer actively promoted and raised capital for his venture in Portland.

Accounts differ as to the make-up of the first outfit led by Palmer in 1858, but the most reliable appearing source indicates that "Palmer organized and led a party of over one hundred men, twenty wagons, and seventy-five pack animals."[5] Like other parties traveling to the mines in the last year of the Yakima War, miners and packers apparently joined together and organized under Palmer for mutual protection during the journey. On this 1858 trip (or perhaps it was during the next journey in 1859), Palmer appears to have personally led nine wagons, each with three or four yoke of oxen.

Due to his Cayuse War experience, Palmer certainly must have had a familiarity with the geography of at least the southern part of the Columbia Basin. Also, as was common for travelers in this era, he knew the Indians, mixed bloods, and whites who could provide information about the trails.

Though it is known that Palmer's party proceeded north from the mouth of the Walla Walla, their exact course through the Big Bend in the summer of 1858 is not clear at this time. Reportedly, however, the rugged terrain forced the abandonment of wagons, and a false rumor spread down the Columbia that Palmer's outfit had been massacred by Indians. Palmer, obviously, made careful observations along the way, and the venture to the Canadian mines appears to have proved lucrative in the accumulation of gold dust. Certainly, by the time he returned to the lower Columbia, he was contemplating a more determined effort at road building in the succeeding year of 1859.

Fortunately, the historical sources describing Palmer's 1859 and 1860 trips are fairly precise in regard to the route he followed. The trek he had envisioned was north via Priest Rapids, through Sentinel Gap, along the east bank of the Columbia, into Moses Coulee, down Foster Creek, across the Columbia, and on up the Okanogan valley.

By this time, of course, steamboat transportation above Celilo Falls was a fresh born reality. As previously related, in the spring of 1859 the *Colonel Wright* starting plying the rough waters of the Columbia as far as the mouth of the Walla Walla. As Palmer left The Dalles in 1859, the recently launched *Colonel Wright* was going to play a significant role in his plans. Palmer had contracted with agents of the *Colonel Wright* to haul supplies and equipment upstream, giving Captain Len White the opportunity to further pioneer an upriver route, this time to Priest Rapids.

A.J. Splawn, who knew the Big Bend country as well as anyone ever has, effectively outlined Palmer's 1859 venture as follows:

> General Joel Palmer shipped a cargo of miners' supplies, consisting of provisions, tools, etc., to Priest Rapids . . . on the steamer *Colonel Wright* . . . His ox teams and wagons were driven from The Dalles, Oregon, over the old immigrant road to Walla Walla, over across the Snake river and on up the Columbia by White Bluffs to the foot of Priest Rapids, where the steamer's cargo had been unloaded. Loading the wagons, they struck out up the river. About eight miles above this starting point they encountered the rocky bluff on the east side of the Columbia at Saddle mountain, known by its Indian name as La-cos-tum.
>
> Here they engaged two canoes of about equal size; placing them side by side at a distance corresponding with the width of the wagons, then lashing poles across the ends to keep them steady, they placed them endwise to the shore; then after laying down boards in the bottom of the canoes to prevent the tires from splitting the bottoms, they lifted and rolled the wagons into them, having previously taken the loads out. They had no difficulty in making this portage [avoiding the steep, rocky bank of the Columbia] of about two miles to the mouth of Crab Creek . . . driving their cattle around the narrow Indian trail through the rocks.
>
> Here they yoked up the oxen and hitched them onto the wagons and proceeded on the Indian trail up [the east side] of the river. A few rocky points had to be worked before the wagons could pass, but they kept moving on for about twenty miles where the river cuts into the mountain; here they had to build a grade from the river up to the top of the plain, which took a few days' labor. From here on the country for a short distance presented no obstacles until they reached the vicinity of [present-day Trinidad on the Columbia] . . . where they took an easterly course for a short distance and turned up a ravine, and, finally, over a high ridge, then turned northerly and entered Moses coulee [called "the Little Coulee" by Palmer] . . . following up this coulee north about twenty miles to an alkali lake [today's Jameson Lake vicinity], which is about one mile long. The shore of this lake is generally soft, and . . . some trouble to the wagons; there was a fine spring at the upper or north end of this lake. From this point they abandoned the coulee and traveled in a northwesterly course over a high plateau covered with bunch grass to a spring sixteen miles. From

there their course was the same until they struck Foster creek and down that to the Columbia . . . and followed down about six miles to Fort Okanogan . . . here they crossed the Columbia in canoes as they did at Saddle mountain. They had been following a large Indian trail from the time they had first struck Moses coulee. From here on they virtually followed the Hudson's Bay company's brigade trail up the Okanogan river . . . in 1861, the writer traveled over much of the route taken by Palmer's wagons, and the tracks were yet plain.[6]

It appears that Palmer's trading venture in Canada in 1859 again was a financial success. The Salem *Statesman* later reported he was having a "streak of golden luck."

W.H. Barron, another traveler to the mines, was interviewed by the Portland *Oregonian* in the winter of 1859-60. The resulting account, appearing January 28, 1860, provides another view of activity on the Priest Rapids road in 1859. Newspapermen in this era, of course, retained a great interest in the mines and trails, and frequently published reports about them. Barron had recently returned from Canada to The Dalles.

After talking with him, the writer for the *Oregonian* made the following recommendations to travelers:

> Pack trains may safely leave The Dalles early in March in ordinary seasons. The journey should be made from The Dalles to Quesnel (Canal) in 30 days. Anderson's Hand-book and Map will be found to supply reliable information. Mr Barron recommends that pack-trains should ferry the Columbia at The Dalles, take the road to the Yakima Valley and to Priest Rapids, there to cross to the east bank of the Columbia . . . or to follow up the west bank of the Columbia as the voyageur may prefer.
>   Gen. Palmer—we believe—passed to the east bank of the river at Priest Rapids, when he went to Fort Alexander with his train but we have reason to believe that packers would find it to their advantage to remain on the west bank, and by some little work at one or two points, so improve the trail as to make it a good one.[7]

In the following year (1860), Palmer made another trip north, keeping a diary that has been preserved for posterity (a typewritten copy of the diary now is in the holdings of the Oregon Historical Society).[8] Firsthand travel accounts such as this are rare, of course. As Palmer's diary clearly indicates, moving wagons, livestock, and mule trains upriver from Portland and across the Big Bend country to the Okanogan was no mean feat. It is noteworthy that Palmer, a frontier entrepreneur, was quick to write down personal expenses and fees for accommodations and transportation.

He also frequently mentions a number of other packers and pack strings moving north at this same time.

Here are excerpts from the diary, beginning on April 2, 1860, in Portland:

> [April] 2. Started on *Carry Ladd* for The Dalles at 7 A.M. . . . Reached Dalles in the evening.
>
>   [April] 3. Went to [Deschutes] . . . on steamer [$]3.00. Returned to Dalles . . . on stage 1.50. Meals at [Deschutes] .75. Steamer took part of our goods, balance to be loaded on sail boat.

From April 4-9, while in The Dalles and Deschutes localities, Palmer busily made arrangements and settled accounts with river transportation agents, while his men moved wagons and livestock upriver. Cold, blustery weather hampered their efforts. On April 8, Palmer payed his $6 "tavern bill" in The Dalles, preparatory to proceeding upriver.

> [April] 10. Took stage for [Deschutes]. Fare . . . 3.00. Breakfast .50. At [Deschutes] took steamer [*Colonel Wright*] for Priest Rapids at 10 A.M. Laid up at dark near Willow Creek [approximately halfway between the Deschutes and Umatilla Rapids]. Weather windy and cold.
>
>   [April] 11. Morning pleasant but cold. We reached Wallawalla at 5 P.M. and discharged the freight for this point and loaded up such [on the *Colonel Wright*] as go to Priest Rapids. Packers are campt three miles from this.
>
>   [April] 12. This morning we started up the river [on the *Colonel Wright*], but could only go 6 miles on account of low water [the annual spring run off had yet to commence]. At this distance, that is half way between Wallawalla and mouth of Snake River, is a rapid, which at low water cannot be ascended, too many rocks. We returned and discharged freight and shall pack Alexandrine freight from here . . .
>
>   [April] 13. Packers came in and commenced arranging packs.
>
>   [April] 14. Two trains started, to wit, Mr. Smith and Lafay and Boshnia. Dobson and McKay and Cameron [pack trains] remain until tomorrow.

More details have come to light about two of the pack train leaders— Dobson and McKay—mentioned here and later in Palmer's diary while traveling north to Alexandrine, British Columbia. McKay's outfit consisted of a bell mare and 34 mules, and eventually was sold in British Columbia for $5,150. Dobson's pack string included a bell mare and 32 mules, and likewise later was sold in Canada, for $4,750. The selling of these outfits, obviously, took place after the merchandise carried by the mules was delivered in the mining camps. While traveling through the Big Bend country, the diary, the steamer could not pass over the rapids during the early spring low water.

> [April] 22. This morning train starts and goes up and crosses river above point of rocks [Sentinel Gap] where Mr. Davis has a ferry . . . Here we found Norris with the wagon and 2 mules waiting for a load . . . I swappt Roan for a horse and got badly cheated.
>
> [April] 23. As we need several horses, I purchase another from Mr. Davis and one from an Indian. For the former I gave $50, and for the latter $30. We start and travel about 15 miles. Ballard's cook attempted to build a fire—wind blew . . . [and set fire to] the cargo and burned and destroyed about 5 hundred lbs. flour, 100 beans [and] blankets.
>
> [April] 24. This morning we start the teams a little after 7 A.M. The trail travels to the bluff . . . George, Dwite and myself go on to Willow Springs, taking three pack animals, which we reach late in the day. The wagon remains with Ballard's train.
>
> [April] 25. We start at 8 A.M. and travel to Big Spring in [Moses] Coulee. Here we meet three returning miners. Nothing of importance to communicate. Men are making from 2 to 5 dollars per day; from 40 to 50 at work. The great bulk of miners have gone on to Quesnel River . . .
>
> [April] 26. Today we travel to Cottonwood Grove, where we overtake McKay and Dobson' and LaFay and—oshine and Barron and Dupuy's train. The later have 12 head cattle. My party, according to my directions, had called upon the Indians Mose and the Okanogan chief to obtain the two horses previously left in their country . . .

Cottonwood Grove was located along Foster Creek, where the Moses Coulee and the Grand Coulee trails came together. It was here that Palmer met the pack trains again, after parting from them at Ringold. These packers had taken seven or eight days to make the trip on the old HBC trail via the Grand Coulee area.

> [April] 27. This morning I rode on to [the Columbia River] ferry, which is about 5 miles above the fort [Okanogan], in advance of the train, to make arrangements about ferrying . . .
>
> [April] 28. McKay's and Smith's and LaFay's train start on. This morning Dobson's train remain until Ballard comes up, so as to exchange packs. Windy, but sun shines very warm. The entire party have crossed the river. We overtook Ephraim's road party. Miners are still returning. River is rising slowly.
>
> [April] 29. Not hearing from Ballard's train or the . . . wagon, I crossed the river and went back to Cottonwood Grove, expecting to meet them. Here I met an Indian with a note from Newman, saying that Norris mules were lost and that Norris was back hunting them.

it appears that the Dobson and McKay outfits generally ɪ
together as they moved northward on the old Hudson's Ɓ
trail.

> [April] 15. This morning McKay and Dobson left with theiɪ
> went up the Snake River, where they found the other trains . .
> [Snake] ferry is a poor one. We swam the mules . . .
>
> [April] 16. This morning several of the mules were not fɔ
> until 9 A.M. We then finished crossing [the Snake] and traveled ab
> 10 miles. I walked.
>
> [April] 17. 4 mules of Dobson's train could not be found. All t
> other parties went ahead some 15 miles and campt [in the Ringoɭ
> vicinity]. George and myself had but one horse between us. I rode
> little, but preferred walking, as the horse was poor. At dark Dobson
> came up, but had not found the mules.
>
> [April] 18. Mckay went back with Dobson to hunt for mules.
> His train remains till all can come up. The other three trains go on by
> the Grand Coulee trail. George and myself take one mule, with trunk
> and mess chest and go ahead. We camp about 15 miles below the
> [Priest] rapid.

As indicated above, it was at this camp site in the Ringold vicinity
that three of the pack trains, including Dobson's and McKay's, left Palmer
to proceed via the old, well-used Hudson's Bay trail around the eastern end
of the Saddle Mountains and north to Moses Lake and the Grand Coulee.
Palmer, meanwhile intended to follow the wagon route that he had pioneered toward Moses Coulee, and to rendezvous with wagons coming over
The Dalles/Fort Simcoe trail.

> [April] 19. At 2 P.M. we reach the [Priest] rapids. Teams and Ballard's
> train were campt ten miles on the trail towards Simcoe. We leave mule
> and horse, cross the river and to their camp.
>
> [April] 20. We spend the day packing and arranging loads for
> teams to haul to Wallawalla, for if our other goods cannot come up
> the river by boat for 3 or 4 weeks, we can't wait here. So we send them
> to Wallawalla and abandon going to [Similkameen] with [wagon]
> teams.
>
> [April] 21. Today the teams start for Walla Walla and the [pack]
> train for the rapids . . . We take 4000 lbs. of flour in the care of
> Thompson and Co. . . .

From this account, it is not clear how many wagons Palmer sent back
to Wallula because the *Colonel Wright* could not reach this point with the
merchandise and goods that the wagons were to haul. As related earlier in

Soon after, Ballard's train, and Newman with wagon came up and campt at the Grove. I remained with them . . .

[April] 30. At dark last evening, Norris came up, but didn't find the mules. He tracked them to where he thinks they crossed the Columbia, near the foot of Sand Hill, 10 miles above the point of rocks . . . We went to the ferry and crossed the Columbia. Arranged the packs.

From here Palmer followed north through the Okanogan, trading along the way, and reached "Alexandrine" on May 31, 1860. However, Palmer found fewer miners and an overstocked market. He sold out at a loss, and, after this time, Palmer's entrepreneurial interest shifted south to the Columbia/Snake corridor.

Cattle Drives, 1858-68

In meeting the subsistence requirements of miners in Canada, Palmer and others of his same adventuresome ilk eventually transported thousands of tons of equipment, supplies, and provisions and drove numerous herds of livestock northward. Significant numbers of cattle, horses, and sheep came up the Columbia on sternwheelers, but probably more were driven overland to the mines, following in the tracks of the miners.

As related, the mining excitement started with the 1858 Fraser strike. In the summer of 1860, stunning reports arrived from Canada about an even greater gold strike, this time in the Cariboo Mountains farther north in central British Columbia. More excited prospectors arrived by the boatload at Victoria, and others hurried up from The Dalles, clamoring to get to the mines. As a result, the Cariboo country "came to be greatly prized by stockmen south of the border."[9] To supply the Cariboo camps (and, in 1861, the newly discovered Nez Perce mines as well), hundreds of animals were being moved rapidly up the Columbia by boat and on foot, or through the Cascade passes, in the spring of 1861.

An article appearing in the Portland *Times* in this period explicitly describes this excitement:

> There are now 1500 head of beeves on the road from the Dalles to the northern mines. C.K. Dawson is here with 6000 dollars from the mines, buying cattle and mules for the upper mining country. There are 150 yoke of cattle on the way from this valley bound for the northern mines. Mr. Thomas has 200 head of beeves on the road for these mines; Murphy & Allen have started from the Clikitat valley with 300 head of beeves for the mines; Mr. [K]Nott has 180 head of beeves on the

Yakima, and 300 head in this valley [of western Oregon], destined for the northern mines; John Todd & Grover have 300 head of beeves in Yamhill county, destined for the northern mines; Harry Love is now on the way with 150 head of beeves for the Nez Perce mines.[10]

Drives on the Cariboo trail were constant in 1861. Also in this year, young Jack Splawn first entered the eastern Washington cattle business. He had hired on with pioneer stockman Major John Thorp of the Yakima valley to drive cattle north up the Cariboo trail. In this, and later years, many of the herds were allowed to graze in the bunchgrass hills and plains for a time, before being driven further north or east.

The newspapers of the period frequently reported on this activity. The following entry in November 1861 is typical: "Mr. Knott, an Oregon drover, started from Portland with 1300 head of cattle for the Cariboo mines," with plans to winter them "in the vicinity of Kamloops, and push forward to the diggings early in the spring."[11]

By 1862, it was reported that at least several thousand head were wanted annually in the mines. Stockmen were quick to fulfill this need. One of these men, George Masiker, left The Dalles in April 1862 with a herd of 61 horses for the Fraser River. His intention was to sell them to packers, freighters, miners, and Indians in the north country.

Masiker's diary is of special interest not only because his experiences were typical for the times, but because it also reveals the route he chose to follow, and one which was popular with stockmen and suppliers in this period.[12] Masiker left The Dalles on April 29, crossing to the north side of the Columbia. From there, his retinue continued on north to the Yakima valley, arriving on May 9, where they were ferried across the Yakima River, paying the toll keeper $23. From there, the band traveled to the Columbia River, arriving at the White Bluffs ferry landing on May 14. Here they had to wait a few days while a pack train ahead of them crossed over. Three days later, Masiker's cavalcade finally was taken across for $24.

From White Bluffs, Masiker traveled over to Crab Creek, which he called Crevice Creek, and camped one night. He next encamped at the head of Moses Lake, and then at Cottonwood Springs (present-day Coulee City; at this point, herders could cross the Grand Coulee to the west and continue northwesterly over the high plateau toward the Okanogan). Upon reaching the Columbia River, he sold 3 horses for $50 and crossed on "Dancing Bill's Ferry." The cavalcade then proceeded down the Columbia to the Okanogan River, and followed it northward toward Canada. On May 28, Masiker camped on "half-breeds" creek on the Similkameen

River, having passed through British Columbia customs that day, paying a $60.55 duty.

Masiker remained in Canada selling horses until August, whereupon he made his way to the coast and shipped for Olympia on board the *Northern Light*. He landed in Olympia on August 28, and booked passage on a carriage for Portland. He arrived in Portland on August 30, and was back at The Dalles by September 3. For his trouble of driving 61 horses to the Fraser River country he made $2,638.75—an excellent financial return in 1862 and indicative of the kind of money that could be made on the frontier, at least during "boom times."[13]

J. Orin Oliphant, the noted chronicler of the Pacific Northwest stockmen's frontier, has summarized the traffic over the Cariboo trail, particularly from 1861 until its demise in 1868. Oliphant also reports on the presence of California cattle, and even some livestock from points as far away as Salt Lake City. (Interestingly, during the great California gold rush of the preceding decade, considerable numbers of Oregon livestock had been driven in the other direction, i.e., south to the Golden State.)

Here are excerpts from Oliphant's definitive work, *On the Cattle Ranges of the Oregon Country*, published in 1968:

> To help meet the needs . . . both north and south of the international boundary, cattle drives from California began relatively early . . . The heavy losses of cattle in Oregon and Washington during the winter of 1861-62 no doubt stimulated this movement . . . for in March, 1862, a newspaper in Walla Walla was quoting The Dalles *Mountaineer* as saying that "large trains of mules and droves of cattle are now on the way from California for Salmon River and the Cariboo country". . . . We get a further glimpse of this movement when we read of the arrival in the Walla Walla Valley in July, 1865, of some four hundred head of cattle from California; and a letter written in Wallula in August, 1866, provides an interesting, though narrow, perspective of the driving of cattle from California to the northern mines during the preceding six or seven years. Here we are told that 650 head of cattle belonging to Jerome Harper and J.H. Parsons had recently arrived at Wallula from Marysville, California, and had safely swum the Snake River. This herd was en route to Cariboo. Harper and Parsons were said to be "heavy cattle dealers" who, since 1860, had been driving "from 600 to 1,000 head every year" from California to British Columbia.[14]

There is no question that Northwest livestock, rather than California cattle, remained predominant in the northern mining regions. However, after 1861, with the concurrent gold strikes in the Bitterroots and northern

Rockies, the historical records are not always clear about the division of livestock to each of the mining areas. It must be recognized, however, that the Cariboo country "offered as rewarding a market as any" in the mining regions:

> During the next three years [1862-65], while the Cariboo market was rising to its zenith, great numbers of cattle were moved from western Oregon to the country east of the Cascades. Many of them eventually went to Cariboo, but, because of the vague language used in describing this movement, we cannot tell precisely how many went to any one of the markets then available . . . Occasionally, we learn the precise destination of a given band. We know, for example, that early in May [1862] . . . James Heatherly and A.J. Welch left Lane County "with 800 head of sheep and between three and 400 head of cattle for Cariboo" . . . Whatever may have been the destination of such bands of cattle, a trustworthy newspaper estimated, on October 25, 1862, that 46,000 head of cattle had been taken from western Oregon across the Cascades during the preceding summer . . .
>
> The Cariboo market continued to be an attractive one to American drovers. Some cattle from Oregon went there in 1863, and perhaps even more in 1864 . . . Meanwhile, many persons had gone from the Walla Walla Valley to the Willamette Valley to purchase cattle and horses for the upper country, and early in May, 1864, a Walla Walla newspaper observed that large droves of cattle and sheep were "still crossing the mountains from the Willamette, destined for the various mining regions of the upper country" . . .
>
> One such herd, which came into the Walla Walla Valley in midsummer of 1864, was ready to set out for the Cariboo market in May, 1865. Other herds also left for the Cariboo market in 1865, and in August some drovers, returning to Walla Walla after having driven a band to Thompson River, reported selling their cattle for seventy dollars a head . . .
>
> By this time the Cariboo market was beginning to decline, and by 1868 it had ceased to exist . . . the yield of these mines had declined so much that the white miners were rapidly selling their claims to Chinese.[15]

Canadian customs records show that more than 22,000 head of cattle entered British Columbia over the Cariboo trail during the period 1850-70, with the peak years being 1862-66. These official figures, however, probably do not reflect the actual number of livestock taken across the border. It has been estimated that during the decade of the 1860s these exports of cattle from all parts of the Pacific Northwest may have, in fact, totaled well over 100,000 head.

By the late 1860s, practically all of the Northwest placer mines were in decline, and towns and population stagnated somewhat for the next decade. The open range of the Big Bend country remained occupied by only a light scattering of settlers and ranchers, some of which were virtual cattle barons, owning herds numbering in the thousands. In the 1870s, livestock was driven west through the mountain passes to Seattle, Olympia, and Portland. However, it would not be until the coming of the transcontinental railroads in the early 1880s that economic development and activity (and population) would surge ahead in eastern Washington.

Endnotes

1. E.W. Wright, ed., *Lewis & Dryden's Marine History of the Pacific Northwest* (Lewis & Dryden Printing Co., 1895 [reprinted 1967 by Superior Publishing Company, Seattle]), 80-81. An extensive inquiry of printed sources and archival collections seems to indicate that no photograph or illustration of the *Colonel Wright* is known to exist—Ron Anglin.

2. Lulu Donnell Crandall, "The *Colonel Wright*," *Washington Historical Quarterly* 7 (April 1916): 126-27. For further firsthand details about the *Colonel Wright*, see "The First Steamboat on the Upper Columbia," *Overland Monthly* 7 (1866): 631-35.

3. Bruce Mitchell, *By River, Trail and Rail: A Brief History of the First Century of Transportation in North Central Washington . . . 1811 to 1911* (Wenatchee: Wenatchee *Daily World*, 1968), 8.

4. For complete coverage of upper Columbia and Snake river steamboating in the halcyon days of the nineteenth century, see Randall V. Mills, *Stern-wheelers Up Columbia: A Century of Steamboating in the Oregon Country* (Palo Alto, California: Pacific, 1947), 80-81, 85-86; Fritz Timmen, *Blow for the Landing: A Hundred Years of Steam Navigation on the Waters of the West* (Caldwell, Idaho: Caxton, 1973), 2-14, 17, 20-21, 141-42; Fred W. Wilson and Earle K. Stewart, *Steamboat Days on the Rivers* (Portland: Oregon Historical Society, 1969 [reprinted from the *Oregon Historical Quarterly*, March and June 1933, and March 1950]), 7-10, 59-60, 84-87, 117; and Wright, *Lewis & Dryden's Marine History of the Pacific Northwest*, 75, 80-81, 107, 115-16.

5. Stanley S. Spaid, "The Later Life and Activities of General Joel Palmer," *Oregon Historical Quarterly* 55 (December 1954): 314. Spaid derived this description of Palmer's party by consulting reports in the Salem *Statesman*, July 20 and August 3, 1858; other pertinent information appeared in the *Statesman* on September 7 and October 26, 1858.

6. A.J. Splawn, *Ka-Mi-Akin: The Last Hero of the Yakimas* (Portland, 1917), 381-82. Splawn's description of Joel Palmer's road building efforts via Priest Rapids and Moses Coulee is based on a long descriptive letter written by Palmer and widely distributed for promotional purposes in Oregon following his 1859 expedition. The letter, titled "Dayton, Oregon, Jan. 28, 1860," originally appeared in the Portland *Oregonian*, February 4, 1860, and the Salem *Statesman*, February 14, 1860. In considerable detail, Palmer described the route to Canada and conditions in the mines at that time. Palmer's letter also has been reprinted in "Gold Trains North," *Okanogan County Heritage* 15 (summer 1977): 14-23.

Due to additional details provided by Splawn in *Ka-Mi-Akin*, Splawn's account of Palmer's explorations is reproduced in the main text of *Forgotten Trails*. It must be noted, however, that Splawn mistakes the year that the *Colonel Wright* first hauled merchandise for Palmer in this road building venture. Splawn claims it was 1858, when in fact it should be 1859. This is obvious because the *Colonel Wright* was still under construction at the Deschutes in 1858, and did not venture upriver until 1859.

Following are pertinent passages from Palmer's original letter of January 28, 1860, describing the route developed through the Big Bend by 1859: "In taking the Walla Walla route [from The Dalles] there is a toll bridge over the Des Chutes and sometimes a ferry over John Day River and one at the crossing of the Snake River. In addition to these the travel from a point some 20 miles above the mouth of Snake River leads from a distance of over 30 miles through a succession of heavy sand hills, in a circuitous route with heading ravines and rounding river bluffs, very fatiguing to animals. The rocky point [western end of the Saddle Mountains], some twelve miles above Priest Rapids, is another objection to this route. It is impracticable for wagons for about three quarters of a mile without some considerable labor.

"Last year [in 1859], we conveyed our wagons around this point in canoes. These ravines, sand hills and rocky points presents no serious obstructions to pack trains. From the Point of Rocks the road follows along the river flats, cutting a few bends, for about 20 miles, when it again turns to the north and enters the Little Coulee [Moses Coulee] . . .

"It then follows northerly through the [Moses] Coulee, about 20 miles to Alkali Lake [today's Jameson Lake vicinity], which is one mile long. Along the narrow margin of this lake is a little marshy bottom, very difficult for wagons to pass until late in the season. It may be avoided, however, by ascending the bluff to the right, about one mile before reaching the lake. From this lake the distance to the Columbia River is 23 miles."

7. The Portland *Oregonian* article, appearing January 28, 1860, has been reprinted in "Barron Championed Inland Route North," *Okanogan County Heritage* 15 (summer 1977): 24.

8. Joel Palmer, "Pocket Diary for 1860" (typewritten copy), Oregon Historical Society Library, Portland.

9. J. Orin Oliphant, *On the Cattle Ranges of the Oregon Country* (Seattle: University of Washington Press, 1968), 63.

10. Quoted, *Ibid.* The Portland *Times* article was reprinted in the *British Colonist*, March 2, 1861.

11. Oliphant, *On the Cattle Ranges of the Oregon Country*, 64.

12. George Masiker Diary, 1862, University of Oregon Library, Eugene.

13. *Ibid.*

14. Oliphant, *On the Cattle Ranges of the Oregon Country*, 68. Also see, Dan Drumheller, *"Uncle Dan" Drumheller Tells Thrills of Western Trails in 1854* (Spokane, 1925), *passim.*

15. Oliphant, *On the Cattle Ranges of the Oregon Country*, 64-66.

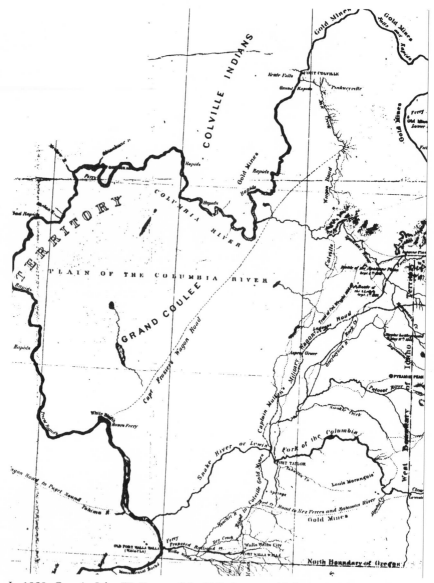

In 1859, Captain John W. Frazer of the U.S. Army established a wagon road between
White Bluffs and newly established Fort Colville. From *Map of Military Road from Fort
Walla Walla on the Columbia to Fort Benton on the Missouri, 1863*

IX
Captain Frazer's Wagon Road

THOUGH INDIAN/WHITE TENSIONS remained high for a time, armed conflict in eastern Washington generally had ceased by the spring of
1859 when a rumor started circulating that Fort Simcoe was to be abandoned, and that troops would be shifted north to establish a new post near
the HBC's Fort Colvile. The truth of the rumor was confirmed in June
1859, when Major Pinkney Lugenbeel and companies A and K, 9th Infantry, started out from Fort Walla Walla, heading up the Colville road via the
Palouse crossing of the Snake. Miner/trader Francis Wolff, veteran of fighting in the Walla Walla valley in 1856 and of the McLoughlin fight in
1858, was one of the civilians with the column.

The general route that they followed north, soon called the "old Walla
Walla-Fort Colville Military road," of course, actually had been long-used
by Indians, and then, later, by traders, miners, and other frontier travelers:

> Cross[ing] . . . the Snake . . . near the mouth of the Palouse . . . The
> road . . . led from the Snake river north along the west side of the
> Palouse [to] . . . . Sheep (or Palouse) Springs . . . in 14 miles. Ten miles
> further on it struck Cow Creek [so named by Angus MacDonald, Chief
> Trader at Fort Colvile, for having killed a cow there to feed the starv-
> ing members of his pack train]. The famous Mullan road [to Mon-
> tana, built by the U.S. Army, 1859-62, and mainly used by packers
> and miners as a pack trail] branched off from the Walla Walla-Colville
> road near the crossing of Cow Creek.
>
> Thence, the Colville road went almost due north to Big Lake
> [Sprague Lake] . . . Three or four miles below the lower end of the lake
> there was a camping place named Lougenbeel [sic] Camp or Lougenbeel
> Springs. Thence, the road was along the east side of the lake past what
> is now Sprague, to Rock Creek and Willow Springs, passing about
> four miles west of Medical Lake, crossed Deep Creek [and continued
> on across the Spokane River to the Colville Valley] . . .
>
> Up to this time there was no white settlement between the Snake
> river and the French half breed settlements near Chewelah and Colville.
> Shortly after the Colville road was established, roadhouses were

established. At the Snake river crossing Hugh McClinchy, the ferryman, had accommodations for a few men. On Cow Creek a short distance from where it joins the Palouse, was a roadhouse established by Henry Wind in 1865 . . .

Another roadhouse at the head of Big [Sprague] Lake was first run by Bill Wilson in 1865 . . . On a little stream called "Fishtrap Creek," running into Big Lake, a man named J.F. Smith settled in a short time . . .

In 1861, Wm. Newman . . . had a roadhouse and station on the Colville Road near Sprague, during the time King Bros. ran the stage and carried the mail to Colville.[1]

In relatively mountainous terrain, at a point about 14 miles southeast of the HBC's Fort Colvile, Captain Pinkney Lugenbeel selected a site next to Mill Creek on which to build the post. The new fort was completed in the autumn of 1859, and, soon, a small, bustling civilian settlement grew up adjacent to it known as Pinkneyville. The army post (located a couple of miles northeast of modern-day Colville) first was called Harney Depot after General William S. Harney, department commander at Fort Vancouver, but the name later was changed to Fort Colville (with the last syllable spelled with a double "l" as compared to the HBC's Fort Colvile which normally was spelled with one "l"). Soon, Francis Wolff became an express rider between the fort and Walla Walla.

Supplying this distant post in the most economical and efficient manner was of considerable concern to the army. Both the old Palouse River route and, shortly, a new road from White Bluffs, developed by the 9th Infantry's Captain John Frazer, were utilized. In the case of either route, the *Colonel Wright*, and later other steamers, were destined to play a key role in hauling equipment, supplies, and men for the army.

This is revealed in a government report dated October 6, 1859, written by Captain George Thomas, a topographical engineer, and sent to J.J. Abert, Chief of the Corp of Topographical Engineers, in Washington, D.C.:

During the past season the steamer *Colonel Wright* had been placed on the Columbia River and has been regularly running between the mouth of the Deschutes and the Walla Walla River, a distance of about 100 miles. Until the middle of July or thereabouts, the *Col. Wright* ran up the Columbia about 12 miles to the Snake River, and thence, during high water, up the Snake River, about 50 miles further, to the Palouse River crossing [furthest upriver point achieved on the Snake until 1861]. Since that time it has been running up the Columbia River to Priest Rapids about 75 miles above [Wallula] . . . that being the highest point to which the river has thus far been navigated by steamboats.

From the Deschutes to Priest Rapids the Columbia is considered navigable, in all its stages, for steamboats, carrying from 50 to 70 tons. Captain W.R. Kirkham, Assistant Quartermaster . . . informs me that in forwarding supplies to Colville during the past season, they were taken by steamboat to the Palouse crossing, on the Snake River, and thence by land 160 miles to Colville, during high water; but since then by steamboat to Priest Rapids, and thence by land to Colville.[2]

Robert Graham, a cabin boy on the *Colonel Wright* at the time, recalled that the sternwheeler normally plied the Columbia between the Deschutes and the Walla Walla, and such points further upriver only as the trade called for. (In the early 1860s following the Idaho and Oregon gold strikes, Boise and John Day freight was usually dropped off at Umatilla; Fort Walla Walla, Lewiston, and Salmon River freight at Wallula; and freight for Colville, the Kootenay and upper Columbia mines, and the Montana trade at White Bluffs.)[3]

It is not known whether or not any white men resided in the White Bluffs area before the summer of 1859, when the U.S. Army and traders like Joel Palmer began utilizing the White Bluffs Landing and Priest Rapids localities as key supply points. Situated at White Bluffs was a principal Wanapam Indian village, named "Teplash" for the bluffs. From White Bluffs, Indian trails spread out in various directions. In 1859, army road finders under Captain Frazer probably utilized part of this Indian trail system, and apparently relied on some Native American guidance, in pioneering the route connecting Fort Colville with White Bluffs.

After the 1859 spring run-off had declined to the point that navigation was impractical on the Snake, the *Colonel Wright*, as related above in Captain Thomas's letter, started landing supplies at White Bluffs instead of at the Palouse. Captain Frazer, meanwhile, developed his road in a northerly direction, passing over the lower, eastern end of the Saddle Mountains, to tie into the old HBC trail just below the present site of O'Sullivan Dam. The new trail eventually diverged northeasterly through the Davenport locality and on to Fort Colville.

Captain Pinkney Lugenbeel had a high regard for the White Bluffs landing and route, as this letter to quartermaster W.R. Kirkham, dated May 25, 1860, makes clear:

Enclosed, I send you a sketch of a good wagon road from Spokane Ferry, to the Columbia River at White Bluffs, a distance of 95 miles. The road is not at all rocky, has an abundance of wood, water and grass and . . . a little cutting of sage brush, is all that is required to make the road very good. The landing on the Columbia River is very good. A wagon train could make the round trip very easily in 11 days. From White Bluffs [through today's Hanford area and on] to the Columbia River opposite the Dalles a good wagon road can be made and I understand that responsible persons can be employed, to deliver freight from the Dalles at White Bluffs, for fifty dollars per ton. By removing your Depot from Snake River [vicinity of the Palouse] to White Bluffs, the dangers of Snake River navigation are avoided and you save the long route between Old Fort Walla Walla and Snake River. Should you determine to adopt this route, Charley, a Son-in-law of [Spokane chief] Big Star, has just been over the road or if you prefer it, I can send Captain Frazer to guide your train from Spokane to White Bluffs.[4]

In another letter, dated June 3, 1860, to department headquarters at Fort Vancouver, Lugenbeel again stressed the advantages of the White Bluffs route: "Should the supplies . . . be carried over this road, they will be received in much better condition and the danger of navigation in Snake River will be avoided."[5]

By the summer of 1860, news about the development of this route had reached the settlements west of the Cascades. On June 22, 1860, the Olympia *Pioneer and Democrat*, enthusiastically reported:

A good road for wagons has been found by Captain Frazer of the Ninth Infantry, from White Bluffs on the Columbia 22 miles below Priest Rapids to the Spokane River, a distance not exceeding 95 miles, making the distance from White Bluffs to Harney Depot [Fort Colville] under 160 miles . . . a saving of land travel will be secured by this discovery of a road to White Bluffs, a point always accessible by steam. White Bluffs will in a short time be an important point as an interport for the upper country.[6]

Civilian interest in the White Bluffs route continued unabated, as is clearly indicated in this December 6, 1860, message by acting governor Henry M. McGill, speaking to the eighth annual session of the legislative assembly in Olympia:

There has been opened during the past summer, a road from Rockland, opposite the Dalles on the Columbia, to Fort Colville, by way of White Bluffs on the Columbia. It crosses the Yakima river at the mouth of the Pisco, and strikes the Columbia about the centre of the [White] Bluffs, eighteen miles below Priest's Rapids.

The great advantages of such a road, in shortening the distance now traveled around the elbow of the Columbia, will be readily seen by a glance at the map.[7]

Captain John W. Frazer

As the army established its supply depot at White Bluffs, the maps and other documents of the time began identifying the White Bluffs route as Captain "Frazer's" wagon road, after the officer who was largely responsible for its development. Unfortunately, relatively little specific information appears to be available at this time in regard to Frazer's activities in the actual laying out and making improvements along this route in 1859 or later. As previously noted, however, Captain Lugenbeel at Fort Colville had recommended Frazer as a guide over this terrain, obviously in recognition of Frazer's knowledge and experience along this route.

A brief biography of Captain John W. Frazer is, perhaps, in order here, not only for his connection to this route, but also because he is an example of the well-educated (for the times) professional soldier that so often served in Washington Territory in this era. Frazer was born in Hardin County, Tennessee, on January 6, 1827, and appointed to the United States Military Academy from Mississippi, entering on July 1, 1845. Graduating July 1, 1849, 34th in his class, he served in various garrisons until promotion to first lieutenant in the 9th Infantry and posted to frontier duty.

He was stationed at Fort Simcoe beginning in 1856, and participated in Garnett's 1858 campaign northward from Fort Simcoe. When Lieutenant Jesse K. Allen was killed in the Yakima valley on August 15, during a surprise pre-dawn attack on an Indian camp, Frazer took personal charge of Allen's body and returned to Fort Simcoe. Fraser was Allen's company commander and a close friend. Fraser remained assigned at Fort Simcoe until the post closed in 1859, and then served at Fort Colville while developing the White Bluffs road.

On March 15, 1861, as the dark clouds of war gathered in the East, he resigned his commission to join the Confederate army. Initially appointed as a lieutenant colonel in the 8th Alabama Infantry, he resigned to serve as colonel of the 28th Infantry, which he led in Kentucky. Appointed Brigadier General on May 19, 1863, and sent to oppose the Federal occupation of east Tennessee, he surrendered along with 2,000 of his men to General Burnside at Knoxville, Tennessee, on September 9, 1863. He remained a prisoner of war until Lee's surrender at Appomattox in April 1865.

Afterwards, Frazer engaged in planting operations in the South for a time, then moved to New York City, where he was in business until his death on March 31, 1906.[8]

Origins of the White Bluffs Ferry

One frontier entrepreneur who had high commercial hopes for White Bluffs was Thomas Howe, a ferryman. Howe must have arrived at White Bluffs by 1860. As became customary in this era, Howe successfully petitioned the territorial legislature to grant him an exclusive right to operate a ferry at White Bluffs. After passage by the legislature, House Bill 33 took effect on January 18, 1861.[9]

It is informative to note a typical ferry rate schedule in this time period, as authorized by the legislature:

```
For each wagon with two animals attached ......................................... $3.00
For pleasure carriage with two horses ................................................  2.00
For man and horse ................................................................................  2.00
For animal packed ................................................................................  1.00
For each head of loose horses or mules ..............................................   .75
For footman ..........................................................................................   .50
For sheep or swine ...............................................................................   .10
```

Cattle, which are fairly good swimmers, normally must have had to swim across, as was customary with the cattle drives on the Cariboo trail. If crossed by ferry, however, cattle perhaps were charged a fee as loose livestock.

Howe remained only a couple of years. By 1863, he was gone, replaced by A.R. Booth. Booth not only ran the ferry, but also operated a trading post and way station. Along with the steamboat men, miners, traders, cattlemen, expressmen, and others utilizing the ferry and the Oregon Steam Navigation Company docks and facilities located here, Booth also developed business connections with the Hudson's Bay Company, which still remained active in the region though it now was solely American territory.

The HBC and the White Bluffs Road

The documentary evidence indicating that long cavalcades of HBC pack animals used the White Bluffs route is clear, for on June 6, 1865, HBC Chief Factor Roderick Finlayson at Victoria, British Columbia, wrote to Angus MacDonald at Fort Colvile stating:

> On receipt of your requisition here we have sent to our agents in San Francisco a list of goods to be shipped via Portland to White Bluffs according to your directions. You will see by referring to the quantity of goods to be transported to Colvile from White Bluffs that it will

amount to about 56 horse loads. You shall be advised through messrs. Richards and McCracken of Portland when the goods will be ready at White Bluffs for transport to Colvile.[10]

Exactly a year later, Finlayson again wrote to MacDonald making arrangements for hauling supplies to posts on the upper Columbia, including Fort Shepherd, a newer HBC post situated on the Columbia River a short distance north of the international boundary. This message also is indicative of the fact that the HBC was making profits as a supplier to miners, as well as trading with Native Americans:

> It is satisfactory to learn that you intend taking your supplies from White Bluffs with our [HBC] horses, thus avoiding the necessity of paying money to others to do so. We hope you have sent the cash and [gold] dust from Fort Shepherd by the party you are sending to White Bluffs, there to be delivered to the agent of the Oregon Steam Navigation Company for delivery to the Bank of British Columbia in Portland.[11]

Again, a year later in May 1867, another chief factor at Victoria sent a letter to A.R. Booth, the ferry operator and merchant at White Bluffs, stating that more HBC supplies and equipment for Fort Colvile and Fort Shepherd were being sent by way of White Bluffs. The correspondence stated that Mr. Hardisty, who was in charge at Fort Shepherd, would send a pack train to White Bluffs for the goods he had ordered.

Christina MacDonald, a daughter of Angus MacDonald who was in charge at Fort Colvile, recalled having once traveled down to the mouth of the Spokane River to meet a brigade coming from White Bluffs. This occurred in the 1860s, and the brigade hauled flour. Interestingly, she noted that the Indian trails were shorter and best for pack train use, even though the U.S. Army had laid out wagon roads in the region by this time.[12]

The Oregon Steam Navigation Company (OSN)

By the summer of 1865, reports of further gold excitement, "centered just beyond the divide of the Rockies in Montana Territory" between Missoula and Helena, began making headlines. "Mines along a six-mile stretch of the Little Blackfoot River paid as high as $200 a day" and "Blackfoot City within a year boasted 21 dry goods and grocery stores, 12 bars and saloons," and all the other attendant features of a booming gold camp.[13]

With people stampeding to the new mining district, lower Columbia River merchants, as was their custom, hurried to send in pack trains to sell provisions and equipment to the miners. Portland entrepreneurs were competing in the lucrative Montana trade with riverboats from St. Louis and wagon trains from Salt Lake City. To indicate how important the upriver commerce had become, the OSN operated 29 passenger steamers, 13 schooners, and 4 barges on the "lower" and "middle" Columbia in 1865, plus a number of additional steamers on the "upper" river.

It soon became evident that the White Bluffs road generally would surpass land-locked Walla Walla (with its attendant lower Snake landings and the Mullan Road) as the best way to get to the Spokane River and on toward the Montana mines. Obviously, this was due to the strategic location of White Bluffs, and because steamboat navigation on the Columbia River to White Bluffs was more reliable than on the Snake River to the Palouse. The shrewd directors of the OSN were poised to use any advantage available in acquiring as much of the Montana trade for as long as possible. They well knew that timeliness was critical in gathering in the wealth of any fast eclipsing gold field. Meanwhile, merchants at The Dalles cooperated with the OSN in making improvements on the White Bluffs wagon road, apparently spending approximately $2,000 on this venture.

Due to the advantages of this route, the OSN located facilities at White Bluffs; by early December 1865, a townsite was surveyed here on the east bank of the Columbia and lots were being offered for sale. The OSN, anxious to further insure its share of the rich Montana trade, organized the Oregon and Montana Transportation Company (OMTC) in the fall of 1866 to work in conjunction with the OSN in offering through steamship and stagecoach service between Portland and western Montana in seven days. With this service, the White Bluffs road earned another name—the "Pend Oreille route."

In the summer of 1865, agents of the OSN had determined that it was feasible to build a steamboat on Lake Pend Oreille in northern Idaho to transport passengers and freight by water over this portion of the route to Montana. It would eliminate a long detour and hard traveling by trail around the west side and upper end of the lake, and could be completed by spring 1866, in time for the next surge of traffic to the mines. The machinery and boilers for this steamboat (and later, two other steamers) would be hauled to Lake Pend Oreille by wagon.

Meanwhile, David Coonc, a freighter with several teams of mules, and his wife, Elizabeth, moved to White Bluffs to haul freight on the White Bluffs road. Mrs. Coonc, in later years, noted upon arriving at White Bluffs: "an attempt was made to start a town there in opposition to Wallula . . . a warehouse and a store were built there" and "there were two white men, bachelors, there, Nevison and Boothe."[14]

Working for the OSN in the summer of 1865, Coonc on at least two occasions hauled "the machinery and materials" for the new Lake Pend Oreille steamer. On the second trip to Cabinet Landing on Lake Pend Oreille, Mrs. Coonc traveled along with her husband on the White Bluffs road,

> riding a mule while my husband managed his ten-mule team with a jerk line. We started in August and it took about three weeks to make the trip, most of the way being over an Indian trail. Our freight was the boiler for a steamboat . . . We returned to White Bluffs and Mr. Coonc sold his mules for ox teams, six yoke.

After wintering at White Bluffs, the Coonc couple left the area—she to Oregon, and David hauled freight to Nevada. (In 1872, however, Mrs. Coonc convinced her husband to return to White Bluffs to pursue the cattle trade: "The cattle were swum over the river and driven to Ringold Bar near White Bluffs. Here we lived three years. There was a large Indian camp up the river near us, but the Indians never molested us. Chinamen were then washing gold in the bars along the Columbia and frequently traded gold to me for flour and bread . . .")[15]

In the winter of 1865-66, the OSN sent carpenters and shipwrights to Lake Pend Oreille to construct the steamer *Mary Moody*. Using lumber whipsawed on the site next to where it was being built, the *Mary Moody*— 108 feet long, with a 20-foot beam, and capable of an 85-ton burden— was launched on April 28, 1866. The first trial run came about two weeks later with Captain Robert Copeley at the wheel.

The *Mary Moody* was the first of three steamers built in this period by the OSN navigate Lake Pend Oreille and the Clark Fork up to the Jocko River in Montana, utilizing a portage system around sections of impassable rapids, much in the same manner as was being done on the Columbia River at the time. The *Mary Moody*'s homeport was Pend Oreille City, which with a population of 25 consisted of a large store comfortably "stocked with Californian and Oregon goods—dry, soft, and liquid," a billiard saloon "of grand dimensions," a modest hotel, and a half dozen private residences, evenly and compactly built of "logs snugly shingled." The store belonged to Z.F. Moody, who was also a principal investor in the little steamboat; it had been named after his daughter. The steamer's route extended from the Pend Oreille City landing up the lake 50 miles to another landing at the foot of the rugged Cabinet Rapids.[16]

According to an outstanding recent study by Bette E. Meyer about the White Bluffs route for the years 1866-70:

> White Bluffs flourished. The powerful backing of the OSN included direct aid and the organization of a portage company for taking freight from White Bluffs to Pend Oreille Lake once the steamer began to run. Operations started with 15 teams of 6 to 8 mules each and increased to approximately 50 teams as the demand rose. Each team carried close to 5,000 pounds.
>
> From White Bluffs it was 15 miles to Crab Creek, which packers followed for 10 miles before proceeding to Black Rock Spring, 25 miles away. This stretch included the longest section without water, 18 miles. Some who claimed to have traveled the route lamented the scarcity of wood and said much of the water in the western portion was alkaline. The water problem was soon rectified, for a well was dug at the halfway point to make the distance to water only nine miles. Rock Creek crossing was 14 miles ahead, Duck Lake another 8, and Buck Creek 2. From there it was 10 miles to Cottonwood Springs (present-day Davenport). The distance from that location to Flag Spring was 15 miles, and 8 miles beyond was Coulee Creek. From that point, the Spokane River and the junction with the Colville Road was but 10 miles farther.[17]

A little past Cottonwood Springs, a fork in the road led to the "LaPray" bridge over the Spokane River and north into the Colville Valley. The other fork led over Deep Creek and Lower Hangman Creek to Spokane Falls, and on to Pend Oreille City.

On February 14, 1866, Jack and Charles Splawn left the Moxee with 160 head of cattle bound for the mines of British Columbia and Montana. Both men were then in their twenties. They drove east across the ridge to the Columbia, striking the river at White Bluffs, and swam the cattle and horses to the other shore. Jack Splawn later claimed that the only occupied thing there at the time was A.R. Booth's house. When Splawn reached White Bluffs on his return trip a few months later, however, he was "surprised to find many new houses, a store, blacksmith shop, and one of those indispensable adjuncts of the border land, a saloon . . . Now it was a busy burg."

Travelers to and from Colville and other points north, of course, also continued to pass this way during these years. In fact, in 1865, the OSN built the steamer *Forty-Nine* to tap into the Kootenay mining trade on the upper Columbia above Kettle Falls and the HBC's Fort Colvile. Named for the international boundary, which, of course, follows the forty-ninth parallel of latitude, the steamboat continued operations into the 1870s, connecting with wagon trains of six-mule teams.

One of the travelers heading for Colville in this period was G. Merrill, who arrived at The Dalles about April 1, 1866, intending to go north for trading, mining, or some other purpose which is not clear at this time. Looking around The Dalles, he saw notices posted up in public places stating that the nearest and best route to Colville was by way of White Bluffs road. It was his understanding that a good wagon road extended the 100 miles from The Dalles to White Bluffs, and the next 170 miles from there to Colville.

Merrill and some companions decided to take the route, but "to our greatest surprise we found it was a humbug as there was no wagon road at all." Various maps published between 1859 and 1865 clearly delineated the route from The Dalles to White Bluffs and on to Colville. To anyone looking at the maps, the route appeared to be a good wagon road, though it also is possible that Merrill and his companions were something of greenhorns and unaccustomed to traveling on rugged wilderness roads. As we will see, they became lost for a time before reaching White Bluffs. At any rate, Merrill has left to posterity a valuable diary, though he wrote entries in it only for the mid part of the journey. Despite being brief, it is a rare and interesting firsthand account of travel on this route in this era. It almost certainly appears that the men were leading pack animals, and not driving wagons.

The diary begins at their fourth camp on the trail, after having left The Dalles and crossed the Simcoe Mountains:

> April 7, 1866. I found myself very lame; my hip was very painful all night. Our course is north running across the valley past the government farm [formerly Fort Simcoe]. Steered for the gap [Union Gap south of present-day Yakima] in the dividing range of mountains that separated the Simcoe and Yakima Valley[s]. Found an Indian who ferried us over the Yakima River. Passed through the gap and around where Thorp lives. Camped near his house.
>
> Left camp 5 early, it being a very pleasant morning. Our course is due east up a portion of the Yakima Valley 15 miles to a spring; crossed Natchez Mountains, found it very warm work getting over them. On descending, found quite a creek which we followed up to the head, crossed over and camped.
>
> Left camp 6. Followed on down the creek for 15 miles. Concluded we were wrong and took off up the mountain due north thinking to strike the trail that some other men had taken who were ahead

of us. After traveling some 4 hours, took off down the mountain in a canyon which we found to be very difficult to descend, but as were suffering for water we had to go down. After a very rough time of it we succeeded in reaching the river and to our surprise found a herd of ponies and a camp of the Natchez Indians from whom we learned that we were off our route. On getting directions we took off down the river; after traveling an hour, saw some Indians coming up the river in a canoe. Ascertained that the ferry boat and trading Fort was below; as we had eaten the last of our grub in the morning, it stood us in hand to get to a trading post. So we pursued our journey down along the river. Soon we saw two Indians coming on horseback hooting and yelling; up they came and dismounted, shook hands and asked for some tobacco. After that they told us we were near a Boston man's store and that we would get there the next day in the forenoon. We hurried on feeling quite hungry. Finally night came and we camped on the bank of the river for the night.

Left camp 7 at sunrise. After going about two miles stopped and made some coffee which seemed to allay our hunger. After 15 miles more we reached White Bluffs where two Indians ferried us across in a canoe. There were 5 in the canoe. The river was very rough, so much that the canoe shipped water often. The Indians seemed to look at it as play. When on land the old Indian got his 50 cents. Each then smiled and said all right. For my part I had no desire to cross any more rivers in such frail looking crafts. White Bluffs is at the head of navigation until up at Colville. There is a boat from Portland to Cascades then a six mile portage, then 50 miles to The Dalles, then a portage of 13 miles, then to White Bluffs, a distance of 200 miles. Then the river is not navigable between the Bluffs and Colville, a distance of 300 miles. White Bluffs is only a trading post, 3 small buildings. We camped at the Fort making camp 8. Very windy all afternoon and cold. Sold Jim's coat for $1. Hustons sold a soldiers overcoat for $2 in trade; pair buckskin gloves 75 cents for new ones. Left White Bluffs April 11.

April 11. For 7 miles very sandy; crossed the [Saddle] mountain. Nothing but a sandy plain called Antoine Plains. Sagebrush 7 miles more; came to water, great deal of alkali, followed for several miles, it was sandy at the bluffs. We gave away pair of blankets, 1 pr. pants, 1 pr. gloves and other articles as we were taking 50 lbs. of flour, bacon and other necessary things. We went to Rock Creek [this probably was Spring Creek which is now submerged by the Potholes reservoir], camped after going 20 miles, found it a very hard days jaunt. No timber, plenty of sagebrush, a few willows along the creek.

April 12. Left camp, walked 28 miles with no water. A level sandy plain, though not very loose so as to make it bad walking. It being cool windy day it was greatly in our favor. As we left the creek, found a finger board, the first one on the route. On it was "Antoine Plante and Contena" with an index hand [Plante's ferry over the Spokane River was located several days' travel away near modern-day Spokane]. This place is the dreariest looking place so far on the road; very seldom seeing even a bird. We have had no timber since crossing the Yakima River and along it there was only a little belt of soft wood. Made Black Rock Springs; found 4 men camping, bound for the same place. They seemed in good spirits.

Left camp 10, clear morning. Last night was very cold. The country is very rough and rocky, very hard walking. The country is destitute of timber. A good deal of alkali. We were bothered a long time about the route; for several hours we were hunting over the hills and not until four o'clock did we succeed in finding the road. Went on to Rock Creek, camped. After a general camp entertainment we all retired for the night feeling gay and happy and determined to let the wide world wag as it would; we would be gay and happy still.

Camp 11 . . . 15 miles.[18]

Unfortunately, as descriptive and revealing as these short passages are, this is all that Merrill wrote in his diary.

Commercial Competition and the White Bluffs Road

In a relatively unsuccessful effort to quell use of the White Bluffs route, and to encourage travelers instead to take the Mullan road, the Walla Walla *Statesman* ran caustic editorials attempting to discredit any route to the mining districts except those passing through Walla Walla's business district. For instance, on May 25, 1866, the readers of the *Statesman* read a testimonial of an unidentified Colville expressman who seems to have run into Merrill's party in April, because he stated:

I met a pack train and several miners who had come by the White Bluff (that is to be) road. They reported it a perfect humbug . . . In fact, it is the opinion of most persons with whom I have conversed, that the whole affair is a deliberate plan concocted for the purpose of swindling all they can this season, knowing it be their last opportunity.[19]

Northern California commercial interests, on the other hand, expressed considerable positive interest in the White Bluffs road. As an example, a San Francisco newspaper, the *Alta California*, pointed out the obvious on February 5, 1866, saying that much of Montana's new found wealth was moving eastward to the Mississippi, instead of westward to California. The editor urged California merchants "to go to the expense to open an all-year road to the Montana mines for the benefit of the local merchants."[20] Along with Portland interests, men from San Francisco invested $11,000 in improvements on the Pend Oreille route in 1866.

In the same issue of the *Alta California* cited above, the San Francisco chamber of commerce published the following information, giving interesting comparisons of freight rates and hauling distances. The White Bluffs rates were lowest, despite the fact that this was the longer route. White Bluff's advantage was due to the fact that steamboat hauling rates were lower than for wagon teams or pack trains, and sternwheelers going this way proceeded farthest upriver:

From S.F. by way of Owyhee & Snake River to Helena, 1,190 miles cost/ton $345

From S.F. by way of Portland & Snake River to Lewiston then by land to Helena, 1,338 miles cost/ton $320

From S.F. by way of Portland to Wallula, thence by land to Helena, 1,283 miles cost/ton $275

From S.F. by way of Portland to White Bluffs thence by land to Helena, 1,370 miles cost/ton $270

The Mullan Road, of course, still saw much use, but the main focus for many commercial interests and travelers in the mid 1860s definitely shifted to the White Bluffs route. Strategically placed Portland, of course, looked to continue to benefit from the gold strikes. Remarkably, only seven or eight days were required to make the trip from Portland to Montana via White Bluffs, or so claimed the advertisements of the times. Considering the great distance covered—the Columbia River, with its many obstacles between Portland and White Bluffs, then the broad, semi-arid plains and rocky coulees of eastern Washington, followed by the precipitous, wooded peaks and mountain torrents of Idaho and Montana—it is no wonder that the Portland *Oregonian* wrote with pride, "Too much cannot be said in praise of the gentlemen who have thus far pushed this gigantic enterprise to a successful end."[21]

Portland businessmen and the OSN actively lobbied legislators for assistance in making improvements in the route. Consequently, Senator James Nesmith of Oregon introduced a bill in the U.S. Congress, asking for $100,000 "to survey, locate, and construct a wagon road from White Bluffs . . . via Pend Oreille Lake, to Helena, Montana Territory." To the displeasure of the road's supporters, the bill was killed.[22]

Washtucna Road, Founded 1867

By the late 1860s, as a nationwide business downturn set in and with the gold excitement faltering, the quantity of provisions, supplies, and travelers coming up the Columbia began a decline. Furthermore, newly arrived settlers in Montana began fulfilling that territory's agricultural needs, and Oregon foodstuffs no longer were marketable there. But more detrimental to the future prospects of the town of White Bluffs was the development in 1867 of a newer and better route to the mines, called the Washtucna road.

> The Washtucna Road . . . soon replaced White Bluffs as the jumping-off place in eastern Washington Territory. Travelers still utilized OSN steamers but now disembarked at Wallula and followed a new route overland, one that stretched across the prairie from Wallula at a 30-degree angle for Fish Hook Bend on the Snake River, about 15 miles away. After four miles of sand, the road was level and paralleled a well-used Indian trail. At Jim Ford's Island, about halfway between the Palouse ferry and the mouth of the Snake, was the ferry crossing. Although travelers used the road without cost, they paid a toll for the ferry . . . Washtucna Lake was the next landmark en route, located some 15 miles north. Two miles long and spring-fed, it was a refreshing stop after the ascent from the river and the overland trek. The road continued around the lake and onward, well posted, ascending to Cow Creek and then dropping to the forks of the Colville and Mullan roads.
> Although the Washtucna route saved only 40 miles in distance, it meant three fewer days of travel for wagons and one day less for pack trains. It had the advantage of sufficient grass and shorter distances between water than other routes. Thus, the journey was not so arduous for men and animals.[23]

By the spring of 1868, the OSN began phasing out its activities at White Bluffs in favor of this new route. The fledgling settlement at White Bluffs, and its hopes, faded. But the boom period for the OSN in Montana was just about over too. High profits continued for a time, but, by 1870, Missouri riverboat traffic became more efficient, resulting in lower hauling rates and prices for St. Louis goods than what Northwest merchants could provide. The competitiveness of suppliers and teamsters out of Salt Lake City likewise stiffened with the completion of the Union Pacific transcontinental railroad in 1869. Rail connections to the East and California proved a boon to Utah mercantilists and outfitters in the Montana trade. Portland's lucrative advantages had slipped away.

These events brought to a close the greatest use of the White Bluffs landing and route. The road fell into disrepair after this period, and Booth was gone by 1870, though other ferrymen continued to operate here.[24] The Hudson's Bay Company too terminated its operations in the region, abandoning Fort Colvile in 1871 and Fort Shepherd in the 1870s (Fort Okanogan had been abandoned in 1860).

In the spring of 1870, word was sent to the OMTC agent at Pend Oreille City to bring the company's two upriver steamers, the *Cabinet* and *Missoula*, down the Clark Fork to Lake Pend Oreille to join the *Mary Moody*. The perilous run, through the Clark Fork's dangerous Cabinet Canyon, was accomplished by Captain Sebastian Miller. The three boats—the *Mary Moody*, *Cabinet*, and *Missoula*—were beached at the lake and in 1876 stripped of machinery.

Endnotes

1. William S. Lewis, *The Story of Early Days in the Big Bend Country* (Spokane: W.D. Allen, 1926), 6-8. In the early decades of the twentieth century, William S. Lewis (1876-1941), of the Eastern Washington State Historical Society, carefully researched historical documents and interviewed aging pioneers. Consequently, he became one of the Inland Northwest's experts on frontier times in the Columbia Basin. Among his other regional works, Lewis also published an interesting account about former U.S. government camels that were used as pack animals, albeit in small numbers, on Pacific Northwest trails in the 1860s; see William S. Lewis, "The Camel Pack Trains in the Mining Camps of the West," *Washington Historical Quarterly* 19 (October 1928): 271-84.

2. Captain George Thomas, Topographical Engineers, to J.J. Abert, Chief, Corp of Topographical Engineers, Washington, D.C., October 6, 1859, U.S. Congress, *House Executive Documents*, 1859-60.

3. Robert Graham papers, Box 2, File 30, Eastern Washington State Historical Society Library, Spokane.

4. National Archives, Washington, D.C. Assorted U.S. Army records, including War Department, Letters Received; Records of U.S. Army Commands, Department of Pacific.

5. *Ibid.*

6. Olympia *Pioneer and Democrat*, June 22, 1860.

7. Acting Governor Henry M. McGill, Message to the Eighth Annual Session of the Legislative Assembly, December 6, 1860, Olympia, Washington Territory.

8. H. Dean Guie, *Bugles in the Valley: Garnett's Fort Simcoe* (Portland: Oregon Historical Society, revised ed. 1977), 184-85; and A.J. Splawn, *Ka-Mi-Akin: The Last Hero of the Yakimas* (Portland, 1917), 101. See also, Francis B. Heitman, *Historical Register and Dictionary of the United States Army*, Vol. 1 (1903). An exhaustive search failed to turn up a diary or any written account by Fraser describing his involvement with the establishment of the wagon road—Ron Anglin.

9. House Bill 33, "An act to authorize Thomas Howe to establish and keep a ferry across the Columbia River at White Bluffs," Laws, Eighth Session of the Territorial Legislature, Olympia, Washington Territory.

10. Chief Factor Roderick Finlayson to Angus MacDonald at Fort Colvile, dated Victoria, June 6, 1865, HBC B.226/b/26.

11. Chief Factor Roderick Finlayson to Angus MacDonald at Fort Colvile, dated Victoria, June 6, 1866, HBC B.226.

12. Chief Factor W.F. Tolmie to A.R. Booth, White Bluffs, Columbia River, dated Victoria, May 10, 1867, HBC B.226/b/35, fo.317; and Christina MacDonald McKenzie Williams to William S. Lewis, May 28, 1921, Eastern Washington State Historical Society Library, Spokane.

13. Bette E. Meyer, "The Pend Oreille Routes to Montana, 1866-1870," *Pacific Northwest Quarterly* 72 (April 1981): 76-77. This is an excellent recent study outlining the Oregon Steam Navigation Company's role in developing the White Bluffs road to tap into the lucrative Montana mining trade in the late 1860s. Meyer's article will be frequently cited here.

14. Elizabeth Ann Coonc, "Reminiscences of a Pioneer Woman," *Washington Historical Quarterly* 8 (January 1917): 17.

15. *Ibid.*, 18-19.

16. Thomas Francis Meagher, "Rides Through Montana," *Harper's New Monthly Magazine* 35 (1867): 570-72; and E.W. Wright, ed., *Lewis & Dryden's Marine History of the Pacific Northwest* (1895 [reprinted 1967 by Superior Publishing Company, Seattle]), 145, 183, 240. Wright, on page 145, claims that the *Mary Moody* "was provided with the old engines from the *Express*."

It often has been assumed by many that the engines of the *Colonel Wright*, which was dismantled August 1865, were later installed in the *Mary Moody*. This is not true. The engines and boiler that Coonc hauled to Lake Pend Oreille came from another OSN boat, the *Express*, and not the *Colonel Wright*. OMTC records for 1866 indicate that the *Colonel Wright*'s engines went into the steamer *Missoula*, which joined the *Mary Moody* on the Clark Fork not long after the *Mary Moody* herself had entered service. Note the following mention of *"Col. Wright* machinery" in the building of the *Missoula* on the Clark Fork in "Record Book of the Oregon Montana Transportation Company, 1866," (Oregon Historical Society Library, Portland):

Steamer *Missoula* Construction

Sept. 8	freight pilot wheel	31.88
Oct. 31	164 lbs. strandirons	49.20
Nov. 8	passage 7 carpenters down	226.00
12	freight 4 bars iron	2.75
30	freight 7 chests tools	32.50
	passage Sullivan	18.00
	210 lbs. iron	16.80
Dec. 20	ps. G.W. Keln on ft	123.35
	of Adams and Co. freight	500.00
	Kermanson & Co. freight	423.87
	Col. Wright machinery	10,000.00
	[Total]	11,424.35

17. Meyer, "The Pend Oreille Routes to Montana, 1866-1870," 79. Otis W. Freeman, in "Early Wagon Roads in the Inland Empire," *Pacific Northwest Quarterly* 45 (October 1954): 130, described the OSN's White Bluffs Road as follows, from west to east: "The road climbed over the eastern ends of the Saddle Mountains and Frenchman Hills and then northward to the Crab Creek bottoms, keeping to the east of Moses Lake. After following the creek to a site near the present town of Odessa, the route continued northeast to Cottonwood Springs, a camping spot now the site of Davenport . . . The road then went from Davenport on north of Reardan, east over Deep Creek and lower Hangman Creek to Spokane Falls, and on to Lake Pend Oreille."
18. G. Merrill Diary, 1866. Property of Vera Holm, Iowa. Copy in author's collection.
19. Walla Walla *Statesman*, May 25, 1866.
20. *Alta California* (San Francisco), February 5, 1866.
21. Portland *Oregonian*, June 2, 1866.
22. Meyer, "The Pend Oreille Routes to Montana, 1866-1870," 81 (fn. 25).
23. *Ibid.*, 81-82.
24. For a good account about ferry operators, Indians, ranchers, settlers, rivermen, and other occupants of this area in the decades of the late nineteenth and early twentieth centuries, see Mary Powell Harris, *Goodbye, White Bluffs* (Yakima: Franklin Press, 1972). Also see, Robert H. Ruby and John A. Brown, *Ferryboats on the Columbia River: Including the Bridges and Dams* (Seattle: Superior, 1974).

A glimpse of the Grande Coulé
Great Plain of Columbia River
Washington Territory

Sketch by Alfred Downing titled "A Glimpse of the Grande Coulé." As a topographical assistant, Downing accompanied Lt. Thomas Symons in exploring and surveying the Big Bend country in the early 1880s, in a period when the U.S. Army was abandoning short-lived Camp Chelan and establishing Fort Spokane. *Washington State Historical Society*

X
A Boat for Camp Chelan

FOLLOWING THE 1877 Nez Perce and 1878 Bannack wars in Idaho, Oregon, Montana, and Wyoming, the white occupants of the Yakima and Kittitas valleys felt apprehensive about the free-roaming Sinkiuse, Chelan, and other Indians loosely allied under Chief Moses, who yet occupied traditional village sites along the oasis-like watercourses and in the wild coulees of the Big Bend. Being well-armed, mounted Indians, they potentially could muster a formidable force of warriors for striking along the trails, or retreating into the Big Bend's hidden recesses to defend their lands.

Both sides, however, were maintaining what would best be described as a "truce-like" peace. On their part, the Indians, as is perfectly understandable, retained a deep, heart-felt attachment to this ancient homeland of their ancestors; and they, of course, felt as equally apprehensive about the situation as did the whites. Occasionally, stock were run off, or an unoccupied cabin was ransacked or a corral burned (particularly in 1877). Though tensions sometimes reached high levels in the late 1870s and early 1880s, time would prove that cool heads prevailed on both sides. In this period, Chief Moses proved to be an especially astute and capable leader. Eventually, to avoid serious incidents or even armed conflict, Moses and his people moved to the Colville Reservation, north of the Columbia.[1]

This eventual peaceful resolution, however, was not at all apparent in 1879. Spokesmen for Yakima and Kittitas settlers and ranchers pleaded with the army to locate a fort along the Yakima River or in the Priest Rapids locality, but their wishes went unheeded. Instead, the army, in a move that disappointed many civilians, decided to establish a new post on the northern edge of the Big Bend. This action, however, was destined to revive excitement at White Bluffs landing for awhile, which for nearly a decade had fallen on quieter times after the OSN had largely pulled out.

Camp Chelan, 1879-80

The troops designated to establish the new post came from Fort Colville, and the route they took basically was the one followed many years before by the fur companies, between Fort Okanogan and Fort Colvile. After crossing the Grand Coulee, they came down Foster Creek to the Columbia by way of the road built by Joel Palmer, two decades before.

Wenatchee area historian Bruce Mitchell, in an excellent secondary account titled *By River, Trail and Rail*, has summarized the establishment of the original "Camp Chelan," which was destined to be only a temporary post until a more advantageous location could be determined:

> On August 12, 1879, Companies E and I of the Second Infantry began the 212-mile march from Fort Colville to the mouth of Foster Creek, bringing their wagons across the extreme north end of Grand Coulee, and making the 1,500-foot descent from the Big Bend plateau to the Columbia River by a tortuous road down Foster Creek. Arriving on August 28 at the site presently occupied by the town of Bridgeport, and having found "good grazing for the animals, and good ground for camping purposes," they established a camp "to await further orders."
>
> Apparently Lieutenant Colonel Merriam arrived a few days later, for on September 2 he issued Camp Chelan Post Order No. 1 stating that, "Military post (is) hereby established, temporarily in the angle formed by the confluence of Foster Creek and the Columbia River."
>
> [The] . . . contention [by civilians] that a post could be maintained much more economically in the Kittitas Valley than on the Columbia River or Lake Chelan was quickly substantiated. Flour, vegetables, meat, lumber, hay and grain, abundant in the Kittitas Valley, had to be freighted from great distances to the temporary army camp . . . By winter the camp was being sustained in part by pack trains from Ellensburg, at a transportation charge of 8½ cents per pound. James Monoghan of Fort Colville was furnishing hay at $50 per ton and fire wood at $25 per cord, while in Ellensburg the best timothy could be had for $7 to $10 per ton, wood for $5 or $6 per cord, and oats at 1½ to 2 cents per pound.[2]

Since the distance from the new post to Fort Walla Walla was excessively long (i.e., 213 miles via the Palouse ferry), Lieutenant Thomas Symons of the Corps of Engineers received orders to search for a shorter, more practicable route. Furthermore, once he reached Camp Chelan, he had instructions to look for a better location for the post. Symons, a well-educated West Point officer and a capable surveyor, set about preparing for the exploration from Wallula northward.

It was evident to him that the remoteness of the Big Bend's interior generally had deterred settlers from going there; thus the country was, in his words, "very little known." Before setting out, Symons could obtain "little information in regard to it." He believed that the only white "inhabitants were three or four cattle-raisers living along Crab Creek—'Portugee Joe,' living on Kenewaw Run, and 'Wild Goose Bill,' on the headwaters of Wilson Creek."[3]

It seems surprising that Symons could not find sufficient informants, either Indians or white frontiersmen, to guide or tell him about the country. However, there were factors that had contributed to a significant decrease in the area's activity and white population, transient as it was, by this date. The peak of the mining excitement, with its hordes of gold seekers, had passed. Likewise, the teamsters, herders, packers, and OSN men who knew so much about this region had left as well, or were focusing their attention elsewhere. And, of course, the HBC traders and the first soldiers that originally occupied the Indian-war era posts two decades earlier now were gone too.

Symons, leading a detachment of engineers and soldiers, set out from Fort Walla Walla in August 1879, proceeding to Wallula and thence up the Columbia in search of "a practicable route for a wagon-road to the military camp." Upon reaching White Bluffs (see appendix 2), Symons, as planned, led his party east up the bluffs, away from the river. Climbing to the top of the "540 feet high" bluff, he reported:

> From the summit the country spreads out, gently rolling, as far as the eye could reach, to the northeast and east. To the north and northwest a small mountain chain, devoid of timber, stretched itself from east to west across our way. It is called the Saddle Mountain. The country was covered with a luxuriant growth of bunch-grass, with here and there a tract of sage-brush. The soil is of firm and excellent quality. Quite a large number of cattle were seen, all of which had to descend to the river for water.[4]

Proceeding on, Symons and his escort elected to try a short cut "somewhat to the northeast" over the eastern end of the Saddle Mountains, but eventually found themselves "getting into a country more sandy and more rolling," and the "mules and horses had greater difficulty in getting along." They soon were lost, with both men and animals "intensively" thirsting from the late summer heat in the vicinity of where Warden stands today. Finding no trace of water, they desperately turned westward in mid-afternoon of the second day in the quest for water, but, some six miles southwest of Black Rock Springs, picked up the OSN's old White Bluffs road. It "gave indications of having at one time having been well traveled," so they "turned and followed it to the northward, trusting that it would take" them to water.

Two hours later, at 5 P.M., the desperate straits of the animals became unbearable; the men surrendered their saddles and stacked their baggage, leaving it, and proceeded along on foot. On the point of collapse, "about nine o'clock that night" they "came to a small alkali pond, which, vile as it was, seemed like nectar to" the men and their "poor horses and mules." The next morning, they found the "fine" Black Rock Spring, which fed "the alkali pond above mentioned." Actually, this spring with its cold, price-less water, had been used 20 years before by the men of the U.S. Army stationed at Fort Colville.

To continue in Symon's words:

From Black Rock Spring we kept to the north, and in about nine miles came to Crab Creek, which is here quite a stream, flowing through a rich bottom half a mile wide. Up the stream the bottom narrows and becomes a chasm, formed by the perpendicular and overhanging walls of basaltic rock. Lower down the bottom became a marsh, entirely filling the space between the basaltic walls, in which the creek sinks to collect again further below. Where we crossed it the bottom was good, and the descent and ascent from the great table land were compara-tively easy. A goodly number of fine fat cattle inhabited this valley and the adjoining high grounds . . .

Leaving Crab Creek we went nearly northward, taking as a guide the Pilot Rock, a mass of rock about thirty feet high, but which, on account of the general flatness of the country, can be seen for a great distance in every direction. Soon we crossed Kenewaw Run [Canniwai Creek], the dry bed of a winter stream, now containing a scanty sup-ply of water in lakes and springs. Leaving this we crossed shortly after-wards Wilson Creek, a fine little stream flowing through a rich bottom . . . Keeping on over the part of the Great Plain lying between Wilson Creek and the Grand Coulée, a rich rolling country covered with a luxuriant growth of bunch-grass, we descended by mistake into Cold Springs Coulée, down which runs the great trail of the Indians from the Spokane country to the Wenatchee and Moses Lake countries. We climbed out of this coulée, and, passing over the broken and rocky summit between the two coulées, we descended by a long gradual slope of about three miles into the Grand Coulée. The Pilot Rock was right above us, on the western bank, to the north. Here in this vicinity [called the "Middle Pass" by Symons; present-day Coulee City vicin-ity] is the best place to cross the coulée for a road going east and west.

The bottom of the coulée is uneven and more than a thousand feet above the present level of the [Columbia] river. The sides show no water-marks. We went north through the coulée, its perpendicular walls forming a vista like some grand old ruined, roofless hall, down which we traveled hour after hour. The walls are about 300 to 400 feet high. At about seven miles from the [Columbia] river a trail crosses the coulée, and we turned here and went to the west until we struck Foster Creek, down which we kept, following the wagon-road made by the troops which preceded us, to the winter camp [Camp Chelan], and which crosses the coulée at its junction with the Columbia River.[5]

Symon's "Middle Pass," now the site where Coulee City stands, was after the early 1880s known as McEntee's crossing of the Grand Coulee. Here, for an extended period, lived Philip McEntee. McEntee was born in Ireland in 1830, drifted West in the 1860s, and mined for a while at Bear Gulch, Montana. In 1877, he made his way to Washington, and participated in the surveying of the region. With his earnings, he bought cattle and located at the springs, where Coulee City stands today. A log cabin he erected in 1881 stood on what is now the outskirts of town.

In a later report, Symons made additional insightful observations about the Big Bend country after he had conducted further explorations. Here are some excerpts:

This section has never seemed to enter into the minds of people except as a broken and almost desert land, but I speak from knowledge acquired by traveling over nearly the whole of it, and I shall not hesitate to characterize it as a very fine agricultural and grazing section. The country between Crab Creek and the Columbia [to the north] is well watered . . . these streams flow with more or less water, according to the season of the year, through valleys of varying width, in a southwesterly direction, to Crab Creek. The land . . . is of the finest quality, growing the most luxuriant bunch-grass and giving every evidence of being a magnificent grain country . . .

The Grand Coulée is the most singular, prominent, and noted feature of this portion of the country . . . Except at one point it is a deep chasm, with vertical, impassable walls, averaging about 350 feet in height. About midway [today's Coulee City locality] between its extremities these walls are broken down, entirely so on the east, and so much so on the west that a wagon has no difficulty in ascending . . . To the north of this middle pass the bottom is quite level; it has some springs and small ponds, and can be traveled without difficulty. It is in some places four miles wide. The southern portion is very narrow, and the bottom is filled with a succession of lakes, the northern ones being of clear, white, sweet water filled with fish; toward the south the lakes become more and more strongly impregnated with alkali, until the one at the end of the coulée [Soap Lake] is of the most detestable unpalatable nature . . .

I first called attention to . . . Middle Pass in 1879, and located a wagon-road across it in 1880 . . . The southern portion of the coulée from this point cannot be crossed or traversed owing to the lakes and steep walls.

To the west of the Grand Coulée there is another running nearly parallel with it, known as Moses or Little Coulée. This has a number of springs and much good land in it. The land between the two coulées is mostly rich and covered with bunch grass. This Moses Coulée comes to an abrupt end, inclosing a little lake . . .

The Moses Lake or Desert Section . . . is a desert, pure and simple . . . This section is much lower than the remainder of the Great Plain . . .

A large portion is covered with bowlders embedded in a loose, light, ashy soil: other portions are covered with drifting sands . . .

Crab Creek sinks soon after receiving the waters of Wilson Creek, and rises just above Moses Lake . . . at this point the water is passably good to drink. Moses Lake is stagnant, alkaline, and unfit for any use. At its lower end are great sand dunes and sandy wastes.

The water seeps through this sand and rises again a few miles to the south and flows southwesterly to Saddle Mountain, where it is turned to the west, sinking and rising several times. I do not think that it now ever reaches the Columbia. Below Moses Lake the creek water is alkaline, filled with organic matter, and unpalatable.[6]

Now to return to Symons's exploration in 1879. After reaching Foster Creek, Symons along with post commander Lieutenant Colonel Merriam began searching, "pursuant to instructions," for a more suitable location for a camp than the temporary depot the troops then were occupying on Foster Creek. According to Symons:

We examined both sides of the [Columbia] river from the mouth of the Okinakane to Lake Chelan, and decided that the most advantageous sight [*sic*], taking everything into consideration, was at the outlet of Lake Chelan, the plateau on the north side of the lake and river . . .

In a dug-out canoe paddled by old In-na-ma-setch-a, the chief of the Chelans [and apparently one of the Indian leaders in the McLoughlin fight, 21 years earlier], and his two sons, Colonel Merriam and I went up the lake about twenty-four miles, and found it to increase in rugged grandeur and beauty at every paddle-stroke . . . the most grandly beautiful body of water that I have ever seen."[7]

Thus, at the lower end of the lake, the soldiers in 1880 began the difficult and laborious task of building what they expected to be a permanent fort. Merriam in a dispatch from Camp Chelan, dated September 10, 1879, outlined his plans for the new site, and also requested a steamboat for use on the Columbia:

> The site chosen for the camp is about one mile from the Columbia River, and is elevated above it about three hundred and fifty feet, the surface of the lake being about twenty feet lower. A comfortable grade for a wagon road is entirely practicable at a little expense, and one that can be made by the troops in a single day. This opens communications with the Columbia River which should be made the highway for supplies and operations in both directions without delay both for economy and for the efficiency of the garrison, wherever it may be stationed. Unless private enterprise meets this demand promptly, the Quartermasters Department should provide a small steamer with a large proportionate power for navigating the Columbia from Priest Rapids to the post and as far above as might be necessary, thus transporting supplies and troops where necessary; and at the same time the steamer could perform all needful service as a ferryboat opposite the post. The price of such a steamer would soon be spent in the high rates which must be paid for wagon transportation over a region so difficult as this.[8]

The new wagon route that the command developed from White Bluffs, in much of the same area investigated by the Symons party, turned out to be more than 100 miles shorter than the Palouse ferry road—i.e., 103 miles from White Bluffs, as compared to 243 miles from Fort Walla Walla via the Palouse. According to historian Bruce Mitchell:

> After leaving White Bluffs it followed the old White Bluffs-Colville road to a point below Moses Lake where this road divided; then up the east side of Moses Lake, across Crab Creek, past the present town of Ephrata, north between Moses Coulee and Grand Coulee to a crossing of Moses Coulee at McCarteney Springs (a few miles south of the point at which U.S. Highway 2 now crosses the coulee), and from there in a direct line to the hills opposite the mouth of the Chelan River, where it descended to the Columbia River, crossed on a ferry, and ascended the opposite bank to the lake.

On January 1, 1880, Lieutenant Colonel Merriam described his expectations in regard to this new route from White Bluffs to Lake Chelan:

> In announcing my selection of the site for Camp Chelan, I stated that I was then preparing to proceed with a detachment, supplied with tools to open and work a wagon road from Lake Chelan to Priest Rapids or White Bluffs.

Encouraged by information I gathered from some of Moses's Indians, I undertook to find another pass further south and was successful. The pass found is an excellent one and happens to be in the direct line towards the eastern side of Moses Lake; where the road must pass on account of an extensive hill of drifting sand, which blocks the other side and which in fact has made the lake itself by filling up the valley through which Crab Creek flows, back a distance of twelve miles. This detour in our road to the eastward renders White Bluffs more accessible as a landing for supplies than Priest Rapids which is thirty miles higher up the river. Another fortunate circumstance considered with my pass through the Grand Coulee is that it contains a fine spring and abundance of wood. The first wood and water was found after leaving the Columbia, a distance of twenty-seven miles. This itself is indeed a long drive for loaded teams but the road will be excellent, laying all the way over a high smooth grass plateau. In locating this road as shown by the map enclosed, I have traveled three times over the entire route with troops and wagons doing a great deal of handwork cutting grades, removing obstructions, etc. The road is now fairly passable for loaded teams a little way from White Bluffs to within four miles of the crossing of the Columbia River opposite Lake Chelan. It is already a better road than that over which our supplies have passed this season [Palouse route], besides being about one hundred miles shorter. From that point however, a great deal of heavy grading must be done. In those four miles the road must descend a little more than two thousand feet to the ferry, and then ascend again over three hundred feet in the mile and a half between the ferry and the fort. It is extremely desirable in the interest of economy as well as convenience to have this road made practicable all the way to the post at the earliest possible day. It is only by that means that we can escape the ruinous rate paid for freight over the other route. I have already taken steps under instruction from the department headquarters to put a wire ferry in operation for crossing the river and the entire command will be absorbed in the labor of constructing the ferry. I earnestly recommend that an effort be made to procure a small appropriation especially for this military road. Ten thousand dollars justly expended upon it would, I think, construct the grades at the crossing of the Columbia and improve the other parts by removing boulders and making easier grades. Even though this sum may seem considerable, the records of the Quartermaster Department will show how soon that sum would be absorbed by the excessive rates unavoidably paid for freight over the other route [Palouse ferry], to say nothing of the great disadvantages of so long and so difficult a line of communication in the other respects. I have made no allusion to that part of the road between White Bluffs and Ainsworth [a Northern Pacific railroad construction town at the mouth of the Snake, founded 1879], because I suppose it will not be much used by loaded teams. Its principal difficulties are due to the prevalence of sand, the necessary dependence on the Columbia for water, and the scarcity of grass for animals. These difficulties cannot be overcome.[9]

Merriam further outlined the army's White Bluffs route as follows, proceeding south from Camp Chelan to the mouth of the Snake:

From Chelan Lk. to:	Miles	Total Miles	Remarks
Columbia River Ferry	1.5		
Pass of . . . [Moses] Coulee	27.0	28.5	wood/water/grass
Whitman Spr., Badger Mtn.	9.2	37.7	"
Egbert Spr., Badger Mtn.	7.5	45.2	"
Upper Ford of Crab Creek	11.5	56.7	water/grass/sagebr
Moses Lake 1st camp on bluff	6.8	63.5	"
Moses lake 2nd camp on bluff	6.0	69.5	water/grass
Middle Ford of Crab Creek	10.8	80.3	wood plenty
Lower Ford of Crab Creek	10.0	90.3	"
White Bluffs Landing	13.4	103.7	no grass
Head of Long Island, bluff camp	9.4	113.1	water/driftwood
Kuntz corral on Columbia	7.5	120.6	grass on bluff
Splawn corral on Columbia	6.5	127.1	"
Mouth of Yakima on Columbia	6.5	133.6	water/driftwood
Ainsworth	9.7	143.3	no grass

By way of comparison, Lieutenant Symons, who surveyed the Palouse ferry wagon road, came up with measurements via that route from Fort Walla Walla to Camp Chelan. Here are excerpts from his calculations:

From Ft. Walla Walla to:	Miles
Sheep Spring	22.2
Palouse ferry (Snake River)	38.7
Washtucna Spring	52.8
Crab Creek	91.6
Cold Spring	109.5
Mosquito Spring	117.6
Orchard Springs	149.7
Pass of Grand Coulee Springs	167.0
Cow Springs	174.9
Head of Foster Creek	193.2
Mouth of Foster Creek	211.1
Lake Chelan (Site of Post)	236.6

Lieutenant Symons in a letter to department headquarters provides insight into another road planned by the army, which he surveyed from Camp Chelan to Ritzville. He also expresses his views, perhaps a little testily, regarding Merriam's road from White Bluffs to Camp Chelan:

Sir: I have the honor to make the Following report as chief engineer officer of the Department of the Columbia . . .

The first duty assigned me during the fiscal year just passed was to . . . survey, and mark a wagon-road from Camp Chelan, to the nearest most convenient point on the Northern Pacific Railroad, then in course of construction. A study of the map and my knowledge of the country gained during the previous year convinced me that the best point to strike the railroad would be at Ritzville, or somewhere in that vicinity, and that a good and nearly straight wagon route would be found connecting the two points.

On the 12th day of July [1880] I left Vancouver [Barracks] and proceeded with my party to White Bluffs, on the Columbia River, by the special steamer conveying stores to this point for wagon shipment to Chelan. At this point was a temporary depot and camp, under charge of Lieut. C[harles]. H. Bonestee, Twenty-first Infantry. A more dismal place it would be hard to imagine; sand and sage brush near at hand, and beyond only the white cliffs and the brown bare hills to be seen.

I left White Bluffs on July 16, with an outfit, consisting of Alfred Downing, topographical assistant, a four mule team, with Joe Brant as teamster, Corporal Hathern and Privates James Kane and John Reynolds, of the Twenty-first Infantry, and the necessary saddle horses. We went first to Camp Chelan by the road laid out by Lieutenant-Colonel Henry Clay Merriam the preceding fall. A careful survey of this road was made, and we found it to combine in itself about all the bad qualities which a road can possess to be, as represented by teamsters, an abominable road, and well nigh impassable for heavy wagons. Upon it there is very little feed, very little water, and that bad, and a road-bed consisting in some places of sand, but generally of light ashy soil in which large bowlders were very thickly imbedded. The horses' hoofs and wheels would sink freely into the light soil, slipping and stumbling among the bowlders in an exceedingly aggravating and tiresome way.

From White Bluffs to the north our road crossed Saddle Mountain [about 3 miles southeast of present-day Corfu], and took us to where Crab Creek rises after its underground passage from Moses Lake. Beyond this about 4 miles we left the old White Bluffs road and skirted along to the east of Moses Lake. This is a long, narrow body of alkaline water, unfit for any human or animal use, and lying in the midst of as utter and horrible a desert as exists on the globe. It is fed by the waters of Crab Creek after they have made their underground passage near the southern extremity of the Grand Coulee. The creek rises at about a mile above the lake and is crossed at what is known as the Rocky Ford of Crab Creek. From this point the road is very rocky and bad until Tapeta Creek [Topeta Creek] is reached, where it crosses Badger Mountain, and we are once more in the bunch-grass lands.

The next place of importance on the road is Moses Coulee, which is crossed at the fine springs [McCarteney Springs] . . . well up in it at about 25 miles from its junction with the Columbia. While encamped at the Rocky Ford of Crab Creek, and Moses Coulee, examinations were made covering as large a portion of the country as possible, which materially aided in the unraveling of the coulee system of this section. From Moses Coulee to the Columbia we first climbed the high hill to reach the high lands [southeast of Farmer], and then over this beautifully covered bunch-grass plain [for some 30 miles farther] to the summit, overlooking the river. The descent of 2,500 feet to the river [via McNeil Canyon] was terrible, as nothing had been done on the road to improve it.[10]

The documentation of travel and activity on Merriam's road is fairly good. In particular, the diary of John Corless, who was a head teamster at Camp Chelan from May 27 to October 8, 1880, presents an interesting picture of the scene.[11] Apparently it was not until June 28, 1880, that Corless set out on this route for the first time. Note that Corless was leaving Camp Chelan heading south on the new road to White Bluffs:

June 28, 1880, Monday. Quartermaster's packtrain consisting of seventy-eight pack and saddle mules left for White Bluffs this morning at six o'clock a.m. I struck my tent and broke camp sending my wall tent, cook tent and everything pertaining to my camp up to the post [Camp Chelan], going up myself and got everything in readiness as regards mules, harness and rations, to organizing a small wagon train of five wagons. Got all to the river by 3:30 p.m. I then swam twelve mules and crossed the harness, rations, etc. by five. I received my instructions in writing. I signed for some Ordinance Stores and crossed the river myself. Mr. Freidlander received some of his goods today and has opened his store [Freidlander had brought a pack train in from White Bluffs on June 23, making the round trip in 13 days].

June 29th, Tuesday. Men were up this morning at 3 o'clock and got everything in shape as regards wagons, double trees, fifth chains, spreaders, etc., and were on the road by 7 o'clock a.m., taking sixteen sacks of oat feed, two sacks of barley, making in all eighteen sacks of grain for which I gave a receipt to Mr. Freidlander. We drove over to Moses Coulee a distance of thirty miles getting into camp at 8 o'clock; making in all thirteen hours on the road, four of which were spent making the grade up from the Columbia River hill, a distance of five miles. I left one teamster with a light wagon to wait the coming of Dr. Merriam who overtook us just before I got into the coulee [Dr. Merriam was an assistant surgeon, assigned to Colonel Merriam's command]. The road to the camp was a good one. There is water and wood but grass is rather scarce. Weather is quite cloudy and raining in the distance, road quite dusty.

June 30th, Wednesday. I was on the road this morning at 5 o'clock, driving over to Whitman Springs where the teams watered. At 9 o'clock proceeded to Egbert Springs where I made camp at 12:30. Distance from last camp 17 miles; passable good road, good water and grass this camp. This camp is the first mail station out from Lake Chelan. Left one of the team mules [injured] at Whitman Springs.

July 1st, Thursday. Out of camp and on the road at 5:30 this morning and drove over to Rocky Ford, 11 miles. After watering the team, we continued on to the arm of Moses lake, distance 12 1/2 miles, where I made camp at 3:30. Dr. Merriman shot a duck with a rifle at quite a distance. The water at this camp is very poor on account of its warmth and the alkali in it. Distance in all today 21 miles. Road very rocky.

July 2nd, Friday. Started this morning from the arm of Moses Lake at 5:30. Traveled over a very good road to Crab Creek crossing, 11 miles from our last camp. This is one of the mail stations to Lake Chelan. After watering the team mules at this place, we drove 10 miles farther and made camp on another crossing of Crab Creek at 2:15; whole distance 21 miles. The road I pronounce good, the water at this camp is very much impregnated with alkali. One of the teamsters named Hitch left his feed box in camp this morning and another named John Eddings lost an extra fifth chain. I sent a man back after these things, who got into camp just as the teams did.

July 3rd, Saturday. This morning we left our camp on Crab Creek at 5:35 and traveled over to White Bluffs on the Columbia River; arriving at that place at 11:30 a.m. A packtrain in charge of Jack Wilson is laying here putting up cargo. The river is so high that it has formed an island of the place where the storehouse and camp are situated. Consequently, we have to haul the freight in a cart and ferry it across a slough to where the trains are camped. The road today is very sandy and hard rolling. Distance between the two camps is about 13 miles.

The Yakima *Republic*, on July 24, 1880, presents a good view of activities at the White Bluffs landing at about the time that Corless was there:

At White Bluffs—From Mr. Duncan who arrived in town from White Bluffs on Saturday evening we learn that part of our county is looking up since the establishment of the transportation depot by the government. When he left there were some eighty tons of freight in the warehouse waiting transportation to Chelan and other northern points. Six government teams were expected daily, and they were to take away a portion of this freight. He also stated that one of the Small brothers of Walla-walla had obtained the contract for transportation to the post at Chelan and will soon put a number of teams on the road. A force of twenty soldiers and three officers are stationed at the Bluffs for the purpose of protecting government property.[12]

Now, to continue with John Corless's diary:

July 4th, Sunday. Although it is the national day of Independence and Sunday at that, still we are at work loading up the wagon train. Wilson's pack train left this morning on return trip to Lake Chelan with a full cargo of mail and flour. Loaded all the wagons and hauled all but two of them up the big hill. One of the team mules got loose from the wagon.

July 5th, Monday. I left White Bluffs this morning at 6 o'clock on return to Lake Chelan, making the first crossing of Crab Creek by 2:15 p.m., after being delayed on the road for two hours by the upsetting of teamster Clark's wagon on a sliding hill. Turned the team mules into an enclosure for the night. The wind commenced blowing very strongly about sundown and continued nearly all night.

July 6th, Tuesday. On the road at 5:30 a.m. and drove over to the Crab Creek mail station, arriving in camp at 10:30 a.m. I met McGloohlin Packer and Antwain Peoria who were looking for a pack mule which had got away from the main train with a load on. Found the mule about noon. I put her load into a wagon and turned the mule over to teamster Clark to work. Wind blew nearly all day; very pleasant camp.

July 7th, Wednesday. I left Crab Creek mail station this morning at 5:45 a.m. and stopped at the arm of Moses Lake and watered the team at 9:40. Met Tom, the Government mail carrier from Lake Chelan at this place. Continued on the road and made camp at Rocky Ford by 3:15 p.m. This part of the road is very rocky. Wind blowing very high this afternoon.

July 8th, Thursday. On the road again at 5:10 a.m. driving over to Egbert Spring mail station, arriving at the last named place at 10:30 a.m. This piece of the road is very rough and rocky; it is the worst part of the road on the route. I learned from the mail carrier, Miller, that the mule struck with a piece of iron picket pin has died at the next spring above this camp called Whitman Springs.

July 9th, Friday. This morning I left Egbert Creek Station at 5:20 a.m., meeting young Mr. Rogers in a buckboard on his way to Walla Walla. I also met Sergeant Beck with a detachment of men belonging to the 2nd Infantry on their way to Vancouver to shoot in the Creemore Matches. Watered teams at Whitman Springs and came on to Moses Coulee, arriving in camp at 12:15. I saw the mule which I left at Whitman Springs; he was dead.

July 10th, Saturday. I was on the road today at 5:10 a.m. It commenced to rain just as I left camp and rained all day with a cold wind blowing. I did not arrive at Freidlanders until 7:20 p.m. The teams were from 3:15 p.m. to 7:20 p.m. getting down the big hill to the Columbia River. The teamsters as well as myself were wet through when we got into camp.[13]

It had taken Corless nearly two weeks to make the round trip between Camp Chelan and White Bluffs.

The Steamer *Chelan*

As related earlier, Lieutenant Colonel Merriam in his dispatch of September 10, 1879, had asked that department headquarters undertake the effort to provide Camp Chelan with a small steamer. On November 28, 1879, the army fulfilled this request, purchasing a steam launch at Portland for $3,510 and renaming it the *Chelan*.

The *Chelan* was a little less than 60 feet in length, with a 10-foot beam, a 4½ foot hold, and screw-powered. The *Chelan* started upriver from the lower Columbia on December 1, 1879. Steaming to the Cascades and then The Dalles, the smallish boat was transported by the portage railways at both locations, and reached Wallula, December 16. Finding it impracticable to go further at this time of year due to wintertime conditions, the *Chelan* was hauled out of the river to wait out the icy season.

The *Chelan* remained at Wallula until relaunched in the spring, and on May 8, 1880, proceeded toward Priest Rapids, arriving May 10. Here, serious difficulties were encountered. A couple of weeks later, the Walla Walla *Union* reported that the little propeller steamer had to lie at the foot of Priest Rapids after several unsuccessful attempts to pass over the white water, even though the river was then in the most favorable stage for the ascent. A later report added that the boat did pass "Priest Rapids, but Rock Island was too much for her, and after weeks of expensive work, she was dropped back to White Bluffs."[14] In this attempt, the *Chelan* had capsized and was swamped in the river. Undaunted, the army now planned to transport the steamboat by wagon teams, overland to Camp Chelan.

Meanwhile, Colonel Merriam had been away from Camp Chelan all winter on official business, returning only in late May 1880 to the new lakeside post. Merriam's disappointment in some of the ineffective work that had occurred during his absence is evident in his report of June 5, 1880:

> The troops have made a passable track for wagons from the bluff south of the Columbia without attempting to make a uniform grade of course. Loaded wagons are passed down without great difficulty now. But at

some points the descent is so great that a six mule team can scarcely return with an empty wagon . . .

A grade much steeper than I had contemplated has been constructed up the bluff north of the Columbia by Capt. James Miller . . . This grade was so steep that teams were able to haul but half the ordinary load, or about 1500 lbs. for a six mule team. I found it advisable to abandon Capt. Miller's grade and make a new one . . .

No forage is on hand or obtainable in the vicinity, hence our animals depend solely on grazing which reduces their capacity at least one half . . .

There is no public means of conveyance to and from this post. Our mail is brought from Walla Walla by military carriers, via Palouse Ferry and Crab Creek but the route will be changed immediately to the new road via White Bluffs from Ainsworth (Pasco) which will be our nearest Post Office.[15]

By mid July, the *Chelan* was back at White Bluffs being taken apart and readied for transporting overland to Camp Chelan. On the beach at White Bluffs, the boiler and machinery were extracted and the boat cut into two sections for hauling with several wagons by teamsters and soldiers. Lieutenant H.B. Larson and his company of men were in charge of moving the boat. Merriam, meanwhile, prophetically reported on August 9, the *Chelan* "is now supposed to be en route overland . . . The difficulties of this method will . . . prove to be great, and in my opinion, little or no service can be expected of the boat this season."

Relatively few facts have come to light about the start of this remarkable feat—the actual transporting of a steamboat overland. Some information about the crossing of the Saddle Mountains, however, was recorded by local historian Cull White. In the early 1940s, White interviewed a man by the name of Cash McLeod, who was a nephew of longtime Crab Creek stockmen, Sam and Ben Hutchinson. The Hutchinsons had worked for the army at the time the boat and machinery were hauled north. Many times, they told McLeod about letting sections of the boat, lashed to the trucks of heavy wagons, down the steep sides of the mountain by block and tackle, anchored to driftwood deadmen sunk in the slopes.[16]

Some excellent firsthand information exists, however, for the later part of the trip. Again, we turn to Corless, freighting at Camp Chelan:

> August 1, 1880. Received instruction to send one six-mule team and wagon to Egbert Springs to meet Lieutenant Larson who is coming up with the steamboat *Chelan*.
>
> August 18, Wednesday. I crossed the river this morning and started out ten pack mules with twenty sacks of grain to meet Lieutenant

Larson in charge of John Walsot, accompanied by Antwain Peoria. Returned to this side and forwarded some freight to the post for Mr. Rogers. Mr. Grey was sent down from the post to put the ferryboat in good repairs, bringing in three men down with him . . .

August 19, Thursday. Crossed the river with Lieutenant Kinsey and met Mr. Robert, the Engineer of the steam Launch *Chelan*. I brought him over and sent him up to the post to report to Major Forsyth. Three of Small and Putman's teams arriving this afternoon with the machinery of the launch *Chelan*. I crossed the river again to receive their freight which checked on Bill of Lading all right. Quartermaster Sergeant Nolen had the misfortune to miss his footing in getting into the boat and fell into the Columbia but was soon pulled into the boat by Lieutenant Larson and myself, without anything serious happening outside of a wet skin. Lieutenant Larson recrossed the river and returned to his camp at the three mile spring. Mr. Grey and men still at work on the ferry and other boats.

August 20, Friday. Major Forsyth came down from the post this morning and I went over the river with him. We met Lieutenant Larson who had gotten in with some teams. Found blacksmith Nickels at the landing drinking and somewhat drunk. Sent him to camp with his tools and returned to my camp. The first wagon with a section of the launch *Chelan* arrived at the landing at noon and the other section and boiler arrived later. I took Mr. Grey over the river with me to locate a place to unload the *Chelan*. Met Mr. Weeks who is in charge of her; he says that he would put her in the proper position, so we returned to my camp . . .

August 21, Saturday. Mr. Weeks with his men put the bow section of the *Chelan* in position today. I was over the river several times with Lieutenant Larson and Quartermaster Sergeant, trying to get his things together so that he could turn over his Public Property to us, but it was a failure.

August 23, Monday. Mr. Weeks put the stern section of the *Chelan* in position this afternoon.

August 24, Tuesday. Mr. Grey and several mechanics crossed the river from the post today for the purpose of putting the steamer *Chelan* on the stocks and putting her in running order.

August 25, Wednesday. Went over the river this morning and then brought everything over to camp but what was necessary to leave with the steamer, turning over to Mr. Grey anything he needed to carry on the work on the steamer.

August 27, Friday. Mr. Grey and men have the launch in position.

September 1, Wednesday. Sending material over to complete the launch.

September 8, Wednesday. Several of the mechanics who have been working on the launch *Chelan* have been laid off, until the order comes regarding the new post at Spokane [Camp Chelan would be abandoned, to be replaced by Fort Spokane].

September 11, Saturday. Robert, the engineer of the launch *Chelan* met with an accident this afternoon by being caught under the steam boiler and bruising his hip joint considerably.

October 3, Sunday. The steam launch *Chelan* was launched yesterday before noon and it was a success. Today they got up steam and went up the river on a trial trip. Colonel Merriam accompanied her.

October 4, Monday. We are crossing supplies and getting a great deal of stores over the river. The launch *Chelan* commenced towing the ferry over today.[17]

Ironically, all this effort proved for naught, because Camp Chelan was closing down. Here, Bruce Mitchell concludes the story of the *Chelan* and the post it was to serve:

By this time it was becoming apparent to the department commander at Vancouver that the Lake Chelan site possessed numerous geographic and strategic disadvantages. He therefore ordered Merriam and Lieutenant Symons to go in search of a new location, which they found on the south side of the Spokane River, about one mile above its mouth. This site had wood, water, and grazing land nearby, and was close to the developing agricultural area of eastern Washington from which food for the troops and forage for the animals could be delivered to the post at a nominal cost. They therefore recommended the establishment of an eight company post—six of infantry and two of cavalry—to replace the posts at Chelan and Colville.[18]

There is no word about what became of the *Chelan* in the winter of 1880-81, after the soldiers left. During the following summer, however, the Walla Walla *Union*, on July 23, 1881, reported: "Mr. Myers of Fort Spokane" had contracted to sail the craft downriver for $800.

Other information about the *Chelan* comes from Lieutenant Symons. Symons, who in September and October 1881 led topographical engineer Alfred Downing and a small group of Indian boatmen on a grand survey of the entire course of the Columbia River from the Canadian border to the mouth of the Snake River (see appendix 2), wrote that the steamer "was brought down during high water." But, when passing "through the east channel" of the extremely treacherous Rock Island Rapids, "she struck two or three times on account of breaking her rudder, but managed to escape."[19] The fate of the *Chelan* is unknown at this time; an exhaustive search of currently accessible records has failed to locate any information concerning her later days.

The structures at Camp Chelan, too, quickly passed from the scene:

The skeleton of the saw-mill was still visible in July 1886, when a pleasure party from Spokane visited the remains of that short-lived post, and at which time the area had a white population of three permanent settlers: I.A. Navarre, his wife and child. Within a few years, however, the former camp became a part of the town of Chelan which by 1891, had become an important outfitting point for prospectors and trappers, and in later years became the gateway to the spectacular recreational, agricultural, lumbering and mining areas in the drainage basin of the 55-mile lake.[20]

Likewise, with the closing of Camp Chelan, the military had little reason in later years to use the White Bluffs depot or its roads. White Bluffs again largely fell silent.

Endnotes

1. For a full telling of the story of Moses and the Sinkiuse in this period see, Robert H. Ruby and John A. Brown, *Half-Sun on the Columbia: A Biography of Chief Moses* (Norman: University of Oklahoma Press, 1965). At the Wenatchee River in the spring of 1879, territorial governor Elisha Ferry and six companies of troops under General O.O. Howard counciled with Moses and the Sinkiuse, Methow, Chelan, Wenatchee, and other tribal groups. C.E.S. Wood, who was with the command, observed and recorded one of the best descriptions of an old-time Indian horse race ever put down on paper; see, C.E.S. Wood, "An Indian Horse Race," *Okanogan County Heritage* 2 (December 1963): 3-7 [originally published in *Century Magazine*, January 1887].

2. Bruce Mitchell, *By River, Trail and Rail: A Brief History of the First Century of Transportation in North Central Washington . . . 1811 to 1911* (Wenatchee: Wenatchee *Daily World*, 1968), 17.

3. "The Upper Columbia River and the Great Plain of the Columbia," *Senate Executive Document* 186, 47th Cong., 1st Sess., 1882. Publisher Glen Adams of the Ye Galleon Press, in Fairfield, Washington, has reprinted this valuable account; see, Thomas William Symons, *The Symons Report on the Upper Columbia River and the Great Plain of the Columbia* (Fairfield, Washington: Ye Galleon Press, 1967). "The Symons Report" is a key source for Big Bend and Columbia River history and geography.

4. *Ibid.*, 122.

5. *Ibid.*, 122-23.

6. *Ibid.*, 119-21.

7. *Ibid.*, 123.

8. Record Group 98, Records of the United States Army Commands (Army Posts), Post Returns Camp Chelan, Washington Territory, August 1879-September 1880.

9. *Ibid.*

10. *Ibid.* Also see, Alfred Downing, "A Brief Narrative of a Misadventure on the Columbia River [Washington Territory, 1880]," *Northwest Discovery* 4 (June 1983).

11. John Corless Diary, May 27-October 8, 1880, Oregon Historical Society Library, Portland. Corless's account has been edited for presentation in *Forgotten Trails*.

12. Yakima *Republic*, July 24, 1880.

13. John Corless Diary.

14. Walla Walla *Union*, June 18, 1880.

15. "Merriam to Asst. Adj. Gen., June 5, 1880," from Record Group 98; quoted in Mitchell, *By River, Trail and Rail*, 18.

16. Cull White, "The Steamer Chelan," in author's collection.

17. John Corless Diary.

18. Mitchell, *By River, Trail and Rail*, 18.

19. Symons, *The Symons Report*, 44.

20. Mitchell, *By River, Trail and Rail*, 18.

"Old Ben" Hutchinson (1854-1925) at Corfu, Washington, about 1912. Born in old Oregon, Ben along with his brother Sam Hutchinson were among the best known horsemen on the Crab Creek range at the turn of the century. *Lloyd F. Nelson*

XI
Range Riders and Railroaders

RANCHING INCREASED along the routes of the Cariboo and White Bluffs trails after Chief Moses and the Sinkiuse relinquished control of the Big Bend country by 1884. Of course, ever since the fur trade days, decades earlier, many white travelers had passed through the Columbia Basin. Stockmen, packers, and freighters, however, generally had wintered in the "lower country," mainly in Lewiston, The Dalles, Walla Walla, and Portland. Few had stayed permanently, as Lieutenant Symons clearly pointed out in his 1879 survey report.

The first, few, widely scattered settlers along these routes were ranchers and herders—often former gold miners, packers, cattle drivers, or government freighters who had come to know the country during their travels over the dusty trails. By the 1870s, the main focus for Pacific Northwest cattle raising clearly was shifting east of the Cascades, as open range ranching expanded north from the Walla Walla valley and east from the Yakima valley into the Big Bend. Ranchers, however, had fallen on leaner times, since the numerous mountain mining camps had declined and lost most of their population. Instead, stockmen turned to supplying the population centers of Washington and Oregon's coastal regions, and drove their cattle and horses westward through the Cascades passes. This proved to be a lesser market than the mining boom, however.

But then, in the late 1870s, the interior Northwest cattle industry again revived—this time due to events in a different quarter. Following the termination of the Sioux Indian wars and the demise of the buffalo on the northern Great Plains, large numbers of Texas and "Oregon" cattle were sought for stocking purposes in Montana, Wyoming, and Dakota territories, where vast rangelands had opened up.

Large roundups soon became common in eastern Washington, and herds in the southern Big Bend usually crossed at fords on the lower Snake or at its mouth. In 1879 alone, about 72,000 eastern Washington cattle were driven eastward over the Oregon Trail to Wyoming, to be sold to ranchers building up new herds in Montana and adjacent territories or to buyers from Omaha or Chicago. During this period, the isolation of the Northwest cattle ranges was broken and all of the stock raising areas in the West were united.

Interestingly enough, although incoming Texas livestock was most numerous on the northern Plains, ranchers preferred Northwest animals—both cattle and horses—because they were bigger and healthier. Given the boom and bust nature of the frontier economy, this colorful and exciting era of large drives east to the Great Plains was destined to last only about a half decade, generally ending about 1882.

Regrettably, it is beyond the scope of *Forgotten Trails* to fully describe all of the roaming frontier stockmen and half-wild ranchers that came into the Big Bend—at first in a trickle in the 1860s and 1870s, and later in more significant numbers, especially after 1884. It will have to suffice to mention only a few of them. Furthermore, many a pioneer rancher seldom remained long in any one spot, other than perhaps to construct a small log cabin for the winter or to erect a rough-hewn corral to hold half-wild stock. The Big Bend's open range livestock business was as typical as any in the West at the time.

Among the largest and best known outfits, E.D. Phelps and W.I. Wadleigh of the Yakima valley (and later the Okanogan as well) reportedly started pasturing and buying cattle in the Crab Creek country as early as 1869 or 1870. These two "heavy" stock owners and the many men they hired, both whites and Indians, were typical frontier cattlemen of the open range era.[1] A few similar outfits and some other stockmen, including A.J. Splawn, also came in by the 1860s or early 1870s, turning their Durham cattle loose on the open range. White-faced Herefords did not appear until some years later.

Edward O'Roarke, 1880

An unfortunate incident in 1880, which resulted in the death of one of Phelps and Wadleigh's young herders, became a part of Crab Creek range lore, and the origin for the name of two prominent natural features, Deadman Lake and Deadman's Bluff. During April 1880, a 15-year-old lad named Edward O'Roarke was working in a cattle roundup in the channeled scablands south of where O'Sullivan Dam now stands. On this day, the cattle were driven up a narrow defile to the top of a small mesa (now Deadman's Bluff). Once on top, there was no way for the cattle to escape, except down the way they had come up. This being the case, one or two men usually sufficed to guard the route and keep the cattle on top during the night.

On this fateful night, the last watch was given to O'Roarke, who went on duty riding a mule. At sunrise, however, when O'Roarke's relief came to assist him, the young man was not there. Shortly, the men discovered mule tracks leading to the brink of the mesa, and there, below, they saw the lad and his mule sprawled out at the base of the cliff. Sometime during O'Roarke's night shift, the mule and rider stepped off the edge, or were inadvertently pushed over by cattle, and fell some hundred feet to their deaths.

The men's first job was to wash and clean O'Roarke's body before sending him home to Walla Walla. The nearest lake, at that time, was too alkaline, and the cowboys were reluctant to use it. Instead, they carried O'Roarke a short distance south to a lake known for its sweet, clean water. Here they washed and cleaned O'Roarke's body, before wrapping him in sacking material for carrying to White Bluffs. Since this time, the small body of water has been known as Deadman Lake. From White Bluffs, Indians canoed O'Roarke's body down the Columbia to Wallula, as word was sent to his parents at Walla Walla.[2]

Mrs. Laura Tice Lage, author of *Sagebrush Homesteads*, recalled that when she first came to the Othello area with her family in 1906 there was a five-foot-pillar of rocks marking the site where O'Roarke met his death. The skull of the mule also could be seen at the base of the monument. "Two smaller piles of rocks stood on top of the cliff directly above" the fateful site. The rock monument was "a cowboy's tribute and memorial to a lad's courage."[3]

The steep-cliffed, basaltic butte is situated six miles northwest of Othello in Section 7, T16N, R29E, of the CNWR Marsh Unit 1 locality. It is located virtually alongside the old HBC/Cariboo trail. A historical marker and the piled-rock memorial can easily be seen just east of paved Morgan Lake road and a short distance south of the refuge subheadquarters.

Waterhole Homestead Claims

Incoming stockmen, meanwhile, started claiming the best waterholes along the old routes for their base of operations. In the early 1880s, for instance, George Bowker staked a claim at Black Rock Springs. Typically, he made no "improvements" on his homestead; his obvious purpose for filing a claim was simply to control the waterhole for the livestock business.

At about the same time, stockmen selected Black Rock Coulee and Black Rock Springs as the site for one of their regional corrals. The first roundup of livestock was driven here and held between two fences stretching from bluff to bluff, below "Long" lake. Later, a pole corral was constructed opposite to the aspen grove. From the 1880s and on into the first few years of the twentieth century, Black Rock Springs remained the main corralling ground northeast of Moses Lake.

Also in the mid 1880s, horse-ranchers Henry and Milt Gable started wintering at Skooteney springs (Eagle Lakes), the old camp site on the HBC/Cariboo trail. By the late 1890s, Henry Gable had become a large operator, and in addition to herding horses in the southern Big Bend, he also ran them west of White Bluffs and the Columbia River (Gable Mountain on the Hanford Site is named for him.) Twice a year, Henry Gable's outfit rounded up large numbers of horses at the shack and corrals at Skooteney. He remained here until at least 1908.

The McManamon brothers first came to the lower Crab Creek valley in the mid 1880s. Tom McManamon located his ranch just below the site of today's O'Sullivan Dam, and his brother, James, located his ranch where the Columbia National Wildlife Refuge subheadquarters is located, a short distance north of Deadman's Bluff (Tom purchased his place from a H.K. Newland; James acquired his spread a few years later). In 1885, James joined a group of cowboys on a roundup from Whitman County, and rode the range as far up as Wahluke Slope on the Columbia.

In 1886, James and Tom undertook a trip to the Okanogan country, returning over the old Cariboo trail. They crossed the Columbia River at Bridgeport and followed the route south to Ephrata, then known as Indian Graves. From there, they traveled to Moses Lake and into the lower Crab Creek valley. It is noteworthy that both of these ranches were located right along the old HBC/Cariboo trail.[4] As the years went by, horse raising came to make up a large part of the livestock operations, in addition to cattle and sheep raising, in the Big Bend.[5]

Ainsworth and the Northern Pacific Railroad

The completion of the laying of transcontinental railroad tracks to eastern Washington—the Northern Pacific (1883), Union Pacific (1884), Great Northern (1893), and Milwaukee (1909)—did more to bring the Big Bend's frontier era to an end than any other single factor. In the 1880s and 1890s, other "branch" railroad lines likewise spread across eastern Washington.

Railroads brought great numbers of settlers, spurred spectacular community and town growth, and quickened the widespread development of wheat production, especially in the northern Big Bend and the Palouse. For a time, the heart of the range riders' Big Bend country largely escaped these effects, but, by the 1890s, it became clear that major change was sweeping over the region.

A key event in the coming of the railroads was the establishment, in 1879, of the construction town of Ainsworth at the mouth of the Snake River.[6] Founded by the Northern Pacific (NP) to serve white and Chinese construction crews, Ainsworth instantly earned a reputation as one of the Northwest's most notorious frontier towns. In this era, construction workers (often unmarried men) had a reputation for being hard-working and hard-living types, much like those other icons of the frontier—the cowboy, miner, and logger.

Ainsworth, on the Snake's north shore, grew quickly with the establishment of offices, construction yards, and other railroad facilities. However, along with its numerous boarding houses, saloons, dance halls, gambling dens, and other vice-serving establishments, Ainsworth was noted for a high rate of brawling, homicides, and criminal activity. Here, a murdered man could be quietly dropped into the dark waters of the Snake River at night. In its six-year heyday, the town consisted of approximately 100 or more structures. The population averaged 400 men (divided between whites and Chinese), and 100 women and children.[7]

Ironically, the place was named for the upstanding John C. Ainsworth of Oregon Steam Navigation Company fame, who now was a principal director in its successor, the Oregon Railway and Navigation Company (OWRN). The OWRN'S tracks extended from Portland up the south bank of the Columbia to Wallula, where it was planned to meet with the newly built Northern Pacific, completing the transcontinental connection to the Pacific Coast at Portland. (At this same time, of course, vast NP crews also were laying tracks in the Spokane area, in the northern Bitterroots and Rockies, and across Minnesota, North Dakota, and Montana.)

Construction crews from Ainsworth laid tracks south to Wallula and northeast from the mouth of the Snake River up Esquatzel Coulee and on toward Spokane. As the rails were laid down, men on the upper Yakima River to the west and the Clearwater River to the east cut timber in the forests, and sent the logs floating downstream to two sawmills at Ainsworth. Lumber was needed for railway ties and other railroad facilities, and, beginning in 1882, for erecting a railroad bridge across the mouth of the

Snake. Meanwhile, the steamer *Spokane* hauled materials to construction sites or maneuvered rafts of logs and lumber to and from the sawmills; and, soon, the specially built, large sternwheeler *Frederick K. Billings* (launched by the NP at Celilo in 1880) ferried trains across the Snake. The *Frederick K. Billings* was named for the president of the Northern Pacific at the time. For a short period, the railroad terminal on the Snake's south shore opposite Ainsworth was called "Hades," but company officials soon censured the name, substituting "South Ainsworth."

From St. Paul, Minnesota, the Northern Pacific sent out stone-masons to build the Snake River bridge's foundation piers. The rock was quarried many miles up the Snake at "Granite Point" and shipped by steamboat downriver to the construction site. Meanwhile, much of the iron superstructure, prepared in the East, was shipped by sea around South America and hauled up the Columbia. Vast amounts of other construction materials likewise came up the Columbia from Portland. After pushing construction forward at a quick pace, the bridge opened to rail traffic on April 20, 1884. Reportedly, the log girders in the seven span bridge were broad-axed by hand to a fine smoothness. (The bridge remains standing today, though major modifications have been made, particularly in the superstructure.)

Actually, two separate railroads—the NP from St. Paul, and the OWRN from Portland—met at Wallula to establish the first northern transcontinental connection. However, no sooner was the line completed, but the corporate and financial structure that held this arrangement together suddenly collapsed. The Northern Pacific was left with a line terminating in the sand dunes at the mouth of the Walla Walla. To add insult to injury, the NP's great rival, the Union Pacific, gained control of the OWRN and was pushing up from Utah, soon to be a bitter opponent of the NP for Pacific Northwest commerce.

The NP now had little choice but to begin building its expensive "Cascade Division" up the Yakima Valley and over the Cascade Range to Tacoma. Ainsworth, for the most part, had to be abandoned in 1884, and Pasco and Kennewick were established to continue the laying of tracks westward. Most of the machine shops, offices, storage yards, and other railroad facilities were moved to newly founded Pasco, as was the sternwheeler *Frederick K. Billings*, which during the mid 1880s ferried as many as 200 or more railroad cars daily across the Columbia. (A new railroad bridge also was constructed at Pasco in 1887-88; it too experienced extensive modifications over the years).[8]

Saloon owners and other Ainsworth businessmen likewise removed to Pasco, and in some instances entire buildings were hauled by rail or floated on barges to the new town site. For a while, Pasco took on some of the same wild and undisciplined characteristics that Ainsworth had displayed, but the rougher elements soon were drawn westward to the boisterous new camps up the Yakima valley. In 1885, the Ainsworth railroad station closed, and the town was not listed in the 1890 U.S. census. Ainsworth met its unlamented end on October 3, 1898, when Franklin County, on petition from the NP, formally "vacated, set aside and" annulled most of the town plat.

The town stood mostly in what is now Sacajawea State Park on the north bank of the Snake at its confluence with the Columbia.[9] None of its structures remain today, and the town site is partially submerged under Lake Wallula or is covered with trees, brush, or the lawns and facilities of the state park. A state highway marker commemorating the town stands at the north end of the modern Snake River highway bridge about one mile upstream from the site.

An important immediate effect that railroad building had on the Big Bend was the establishment of Connell as a key shipping point for livestock on the Northern Pacific Railroad. In the following decade, Ephrata too became a shipping center for cattle and horses, when, in 1893, the Great Northern completed its line through the heart of the Big Bend to Wenatchee and across the Cascades. The Great Northern was the second of the northern transcontinental railroads to cross the Big Bend (the third would be the Milwaukee, in 1909).

Endnotes

1. Ted Van Arsdol, "Pioneer Cattle Outfit: Phelps & Wadleigh," *Okanogan County Heritage* 4 (June 1966): 15-30. See also, A.J. Splawn, *Ka-Mi-Akin: The Last Hero of the Yakimas* (Portland, 1917), *passim.*

2. Gladys Para, personal communication, 1985. Para is local historian of the Othello area. She is a key source for a wealth of information about the original homestead claimants in the Big Bend country.

3. Laura Tice Lage, *Sagebrush Homesteads* (Yakima: Franklin Press, 1967), 49. This book, by a member of an early Othello-area homestead family (1906), contains much information and lore about the Big Bend area, including photographs and a chart of livestock brands used by herders and horsemen. Another early homesteader's story is Marjorie Faulkner Bonn's, *Hogback* (New York: Vantage Press, 1954); this account focuses on the Connell area in northern Franklin County from 1907.

4. Gladys Para, personal communication, 1985. See also, George F. Beck, compiler, "Black Rock Pioneer Edition," Ritzville *Journal-Times*, 1949.

5. For further colorful information about Big Bend ranchers from the 1880s to the early decades of the twentieth century, see Mary Powell Harris, *Goodbye, White Bluffs* (Yakima: Franklin Press, 1972); E.H. Neal, "Blythe: He Built Manor House in the Desert," *Okanogan County Heritage* 15 (Spring 1977); and Robert H. Ruby, "Blythe: Gentleman Cowboy," *Okanogan County Heritage* 15 (Spring 1977).

6. Marjorie Hales, "The History of Pasco, Washington, to 1915," 21-35; MA thesis, Washington State University, Pullman, 1964. Hale's excellent study also has been serialized by the Franklin County Historical Society (Pasco) in its historical journal, the *Franklin Flyer*.

7. See also, George B. Abdill, *This Was Railroading* (Seattle: Superior, 1958), 46-48; Click Relander, *Drummers and Dreamers* (Caldwell, Idaho: Caxton, 1956): 292-96; and Ted Van Arsdol, "End of Track Town," *Frontier Times* (Spring 1961), 28-29, 63.

8. Marjorie Hales, "The History of Pasco, Washington, to 1915," 21-41; and D.W. Meinig, *The Great Columbia Plain: A Historical Geography, 1805-1910* (Seattle: University of Washington Press, 1968), 257-70.

9. Thomas William Symons, *The Symons Report on the Upper Columbia River and the Great Plain of the Columbia* (Fairfield, Washington: Ye Galleon Press, 1967), 50-51, map 25.

Roping colts near the Saddle Mountains during the great 1906 roundup. *Grant County Historical Society*

XII
The Last Grand Roundup

EVEN AFTER THE arrival of homesteaders in the early twentieth century, much of the Big Bend country remained a vast sea of bunchgrass. Many alert, quick-moving bands of wild horses and free-running, ranch animals yet roamed across the Crab Creek rangeland. It was truly a "horse heaven" for these thousands of horses in the sagebrush and sand country, but their time was running out.

The year 1906 is noteworthy for two key events: the beginning of construction of the Milwaukee railroad bridge over the Columbia River at Beverly, just north of Sentinel Gap; and "The Last Grand Roundup" of range horses. There would be other roundups—one in 1914, and another in 1916 for artillery horses for the French and British during the First World War, and again in 1928, 1932, 1936, and on up to the early 1950s for "canner horses," but none ever compared to the 1906 drive. After four decades of the open range livestock business, the "Old West" was giving way to the new, and the cowboys and wild horses of eastern Washington were on the way out.

During the first years of the twentieth century, land was rapidly being taken up by settlers coming in by railroad. As barbed wire and fence lines spread across the country, closing up much of the range, it became obvious that a tough winter could wipe out thousands of horses. But, due to low market prices and high railroad rates, it did not pay for ranchers and cowboys to catch wild horses and ship them east. A couple of decades earlier, horses and cattle from "Oregon"—meaning both Washington and Oregon at the time—had commonly been driven east to help stock the northern Great Plains after the close of the Sioux and Cheyenne wars.

By 1906, the days of sending Northwest herds eastward were long gone, or so it seemed. But suddenly, that spring, came the startling news that Washington horses were wanted to stock rangeland in North Dakota. Profits would go to the men delivering the first and the best bands of horses to buyers from the Plains! Consequently, ranchers and cowboys in eastern Washington set about organizing a "Last Grand Roundup" of wild horses—an event which would be publicized with much fanfare by newspaper writers across the region and from as far away as Boston.

Thus, in the spring of 1906 a vast cavalcade of wranglers set out to gather up wild horses on the expansive rangeland of the Crab Creek drainage, the Frenchman Hills, and the Saddle Mountains. Traveling along with them to record the event was a cadre of reporters, jovially calling themselves "war correspondents." One of them was Albert Abel McIntyre, owner of the *Big Bend Chief*, a weekly newspaper published in Wilson Creek, Washington. In addition to writing newspaper reports about events in camp and on the trail, McIntyre also gathered information for a book which was published just a few months after the horses were driven in from the range. Titled the *Last Grand Roundup*, the slim volume was printed by McIntyre's own Chief Publishing Company.

McIntyre's volume is one of the best accounts ever written about the Big Bend country for any time period. In its descriptive 88 pages of text, which include illustrations and cowboy poetry as well, are the wranglers, Indian horsemen, ranch owners, early townspeople, and other colorful characters that typified the Big Bend country in a period that was drawing to a close.

Since its publication many decades ago, copies of the original 1906 edition have become scarce. In 1988, this had become apparent to Stuart McIntyre, a grandson of the book's original author. A resident of California, Stuart was researching family history in Washington State when the idea came to him to reprint the *Last Grand Roundup* in commemoration of Washington's statehood centennial. Consequently, in 1989, in a handsome bound volume, McIntyre's original account once again became readily available to readers. (For information write: Stuart McIntyre, The Chief Research Co., 3848 Cresta Way, Sacramento, CA 95864.)

With permission from Stuart McIntyre, following here are selections from *The Last Grand Roundup*. This is by no means a complete rendition of the pioneer newspaperman's story. Readers are encouraged to see the original source for many additional descriptions and stories about the interesting persons, events, and places that characterized the Big Bend country at the close of the frontier era. By 1906, of course, railroad building had expanded feverishly across the region, and, shortly, automobiles and highways would become common, ushering in the modern age. Change was coming fast.

Here, then, is A.A. McIntyre's superb telling of the great, old-time horse drive—an event, that, quite appropriately, can be said to conclude the "Forgotten Trails" era in Big Bend history.[1]

A.A. McIntyre's Narrative

In December [1905] . . . Al Soper, one of the heaviest horse owners at that time, conceived the plan of organizing a big roundup party and instead of spending weeks riding the Moses Lake Desert range, as has been often done, to place enough men in line to drive all the horses before them. His idea was to line the riders out from Ephrata west and drive south to Crab Creek, then to swing round and corral the horses at the mouth of Crab Creek. The plan was discussed by the horse men for some weeks and finally the result of the talk among them was a call for a convention of principal owners at Ephrata . . . At this meeting, which was held early in March, Thomas Burgen was elected foreman of the roundup and given entire charge of all arrangements of the big ride.

About this time Wm. McCarty of Dickinson, N.D., had heard of the curtailment of the range in eastern Washington and came west to buy horses for his range in the Bad Lands of Dakota. He purchased many from Soper & Hull and some from other parties till he had contracted for nearly 2000 head . . .

The date set for the beginning of the ride was April 23, 1906. It was planned to rendezvous at Ephrata and start the long drive from there. In order to get the boys in good spirits the horse men decided to have a few days recreation before beginning the real work. Accordingly the first event was a "buckayro ball" given in the opera house at Wilson Creek on Friday evening, April 20. This party was attended by riders from all parts of the state. It was a motley gathering. Gentlemen in full dress suits danced alongside buckayros clad in the uniform of the range . . . Instead of the drunken revel many had expected from the buckayros, this dance was marked by perfect decorum and the exhibition of hearty good fellowship among all. The supper was a unique affair, served on tin plates, with coffee in tin cups and cream from the tin can, just as the range rider is used to when on the drive . . .

Saturday [April 21] following the party at Wilson Creek was consumed in getting the outfits started toward Ephrata and in talking over the old times by those assembled. Long before night the hotels were filled to their utmost capacity and a hundred or more slept upon the ground in the outskirts of the town. Among the stories told one could gather much interesting history. Ten years ago there were many herds of horses roaming over the south half of the Big Bend country, and along down the Columbia to the Snake river and on up that stream . . . Horses were a drug in the market, and while they [were] inexpensive to raise they were of practically no value to the owners. Many of the horsemen turned their attention more especially to cattle then. About [1900] . . . sheep became the ruling investment, and now many of the old cattle and horesmen have large flocks of sheep which they graze on the mountains in the summer and return here to feed during the winter on alfalfa which grows abundantly. But there are still some good sized bands of horses to be found in the south country, and many smaller ones.

Four or five years ago [circa 1901] C. Lewis, then a large horse raiser, conceived the plan of locating at Moses Lake where he could raise horses, unmolested by civilization and the constant encroachment of ranchers, and grow rich on the increased value of them, owing to the number required to till the soil [in the grain-growing country] to the north of the Great Northern railway. His dream of getting away from civilization was not realized, however, and today can be seen from his ranch dozens of homes of the tillers of the soil he tried to get away from. The supposedly desert land surrounding his ranch is rapidly being fenced and developed into productive wheat fields and orchards. He now owns but few horses. True, he has an excellent herd of cattle, but is making preparations to diminish rather than to increase it.

In fact he has taken up farming and has no less than 2000 fruit trees planted besides his alfalfa fields and other crops.

One peculiarity of western life was particularly noticed while at Ephrata—idea of value of money. A buckayro walks up to the bar, names his drink and invites everyone within the room to join him, and invariably throws his money on the bar before he orders. An eastern man will walk into a saloon, look around, run his hand down into his pocket two or three times, perhaps invite a special friend to drink, or maybe take his stimulant alone, and then ask the barkeep for his bill. This difference follows the two men all through their life. The buckayro wants to enjoy himself and have other folks partake of his pleasure and never figures on the cost. When he has money he pays his bill. When he is broke he hikes to the hills and recuperates his wasted fortunes. The other—well, he counts the cost and remembers there may be a "rainy day."

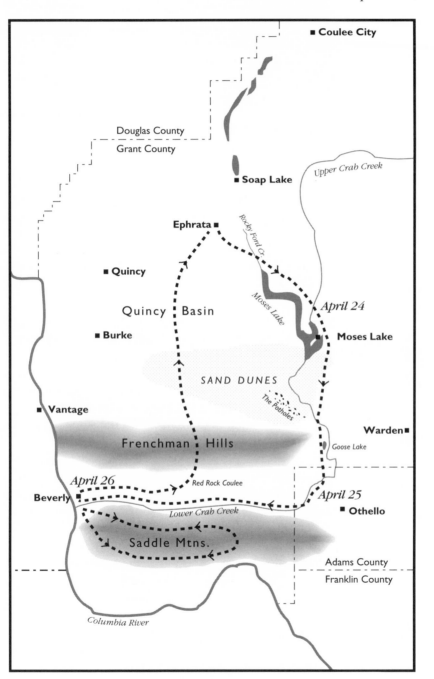

Route of the 1906 Big Bend country roundup.

Sunday [April 22, 1906] was a lively day at Ephrata, over 300 buckayros and sightseers having arrived in the town [running events and a rodeo of sorts were held that afternoon, and alcoholic beverages consumed] . . .

[However] The festivities of Sunday had been so much enjoyed that on Monday [April 23] it was found to be a difficult task to get the boys to begin the ride . . . a conference resulted in a change in the plan of riding and the start was delayed until Tuesday morning. Instead of forming in a long line across the country to drive south it was decided to proceed at once to Crab Creek or Saddle Mountain and there begin the drive. Accordingly Monday was spent in much the same manner as was Sunday. Generally speaking, the buckayro likes liquor when he can get it, and one peculiarity of this gathering at Ephrata was the quantity of beer and liquor consumed and the absence of quarrels among the motley crowd. Several newspaper correspondents had joined the party and were ready to drive for a week or more among the hills and learn something of this last big roundup of horses in the state.

At 6 o'clock in the evening word was passed from the foreman to be ready to move at sunrise next morning . . . Two large cook wagons, drawn by four horses each, bed wagons and a number of hacks with smaller outfits made up the camp.

By daylight [April 24] the big camp was astir. Breakfast, consisting of coffee, baking powder biscuits, potatoes, bacon, butter and eggs, was served by each man taking a tin plate, cup, knife, fork and spoon, and helping himself from the capacious camp kettles filled with the smoking viands. The "night wranglers" had brought in the saddle horses and a sufficient number were lassoed to equip the party for the day, and then began the march. The saddle horses were divided into four bands of about seventy-five each and started off to the south, in charge of several riders to each bunch. Then came the camp outfits and lastly the riders who were not on duty for the day. [The route traveled was the old White Bluffs road that Lieutenant Colonel Merriam had laid out in 1879.]

The first addition to the cavalcade was made at the north end of Moses Lake where old "Tomanowish" and his camp contributed several riders. These Indians are from the Nespelim country . . . and many of them speak fairly good English, while all the buckayros can converse with them in Chinook [jargon].

The first camp was made at the Parker horn of Moses Lake, about twenty-five miles from the starting point. For supper there were biscuits, potatoes, ham, canned fruit and tea or coffee. No tents were used and each man spread his blankets on the ground and slept under the open sky.

The next day's march was still to the south, and after an hour's ride the sand hills at the foot of Moses Lake came into view. These huge, crescent shaped mounds are formed of drifting sand and are continually changing their location as the direction of the wind changes. Among them can once in a while be found bunches of withering grass and stunted sage brush, but for the most part there can be seen nothing but the ever shifting sand piled two hundred or three hundred feet high in places with ravines between, and an occasional sand lizzard or horned toad. The sand flies, however, are numerous and bite savagely. This country is about four miles wide and some six to eight miles long.

Leaving the sand hills, a few miles of sage brush prairie brought the long line of riders down into the canyon of lower Crab Creek [now Marsh Unit 1 of the U.S. Fish and Wildlife refuge], which here is a narrow flat valley occupied by alfalfa ranches alternating with stretches of willows and salt grass pastures. On across the stream and upward over the eastern spur of Frenchman Hill the cavalcade proceeded until four o'clock in the afternoon, when a halt was made in Crab Creek canyon at the foot of a beautiful mesa rising straight up some fifty feet out of the center of the level valley. A smart shower of rain before sundown gave an inviting appearance to the country and the scent of the buckwood and sage mingled in a pleasant perfume. This spot is known locally as the "Bird Ranch" [the lower crossing of Crab Creek] and is about thirty-five miles from the junction of Crab Creek and the Columbia.

Here the party was joined by more newspaper correspondents and increased their number to eight. All the reporters rode horses and by this time were beginning to feel the effects of two days in the saddle. Many were the jests of the boys at their expense, but they were all good natured, jolly fellows and entered into the fun with as much interest as the buckayros, which fact certainly aided them. No kindness which could be shown them was omitted and whenever a rider could do a favor for one of the "war correspondents," as the newspaper men were called, he was sure to do it.

Many of the terms used among the buckayros were the same as Greek or Sanscrit to some of the newspaper correspondents [including Herbert Heywood, sent out by the *Boston Herald*; also present were editor G.T. Rice of the *Ephrata Record*, two reporters from the Spokane *Spokesman-Review*, photographer F.E. Snedecor of Wilson Creek, and others] . . .

On Thursday morning the first riding for horses began. Towering up to the south rose Saddle Mountains, or better known among the horsemen as Crab Creek Mountain. This range rises from 600 to 1500 feet above the level of the canyon, is precipitous on the north side and gently sloping on the south toward the Columbia, with many a deep coulee bounded with precipitous basaltic walls cutting the surface at intervals.

The main body of the outfit, augmented here by the addition of several white men and Indians and Ben Hutchinson's big camp outfit drawn by six horses, pushed leisurely on down the canyon toward the Columbia. At noon a halt was made for lunch and to let the work horses rest. For the most part the trail was a good one, but several times the cook wagons were stalled when crossing the streams and saddle horses were brought into play to help haul the heavy loads out of the mire. Lariats were tied to the wheels, a couple of twists taken about the horns of the saddles, and the way the horses squirmed and struggled showed that they had had practice in the work and enjoyed it much more than their riders. The last five miles of this day's march was through washed sand along the creek, interspersed occasionally with stretches of crumbling basaltic rock, and it was not until nearly sundown that the Columbia was reached. A dozen or fifteen men on fresh horses were sent into the mountains to assist the riders, and about eight o'clock the roar of hoofs and the neighing of the mares and colts heralded the appearance of the wild band. Sweeping down the mountain through a narrow ravine, out of the clouds it seemed in the dim light, came the struggling, plunging mass, followed and herded by the riders, down to the water. The horses were all thirsty and tired and after a drink it was a short task to drive them into the corrals. Many of the riders' horses had given out with the hard work. Some finished the drive on foot, while Owen Minton and John Brookhouse stopped at the "Figure 2" ranch for the night. A large number of [horses] . . . had been started, but in the afternoon when the riders and horses were tired it was difficult to hold them and impossible to overtake them once they got under way in their efforts to escape, and only about three hundred horses were brought into camp. This promiscuous gathering resulted in leaving many orphan colts with the band and fully fifty were shot during the afternoon. While this practice may seem cruel, it is certainly more merciful than to leave the little fellows to slowly die of starvation on the hills while their mothers are miles away in their acustomed haunts searching for them. Several orphans were brought into camp and nearby settlers came and took them to feed on cow's milk until they were able to forage for themselves . . .

The partial failure of the ride on Crab Creek Mountain necessitated a conference of the horse men, and it was finally decided to rest the horses and try again. Accordingly the next day's work was taken up on the south side of the Frenchman Hills, lying to the north of Crab Creek, and gently rolling country. The drive extended only about fifteen miles from camp and at 4 o'clock about four hundred horses were turned into the corrals. The fact that sheep had recently been through the country near the corrals now necessitated the driving of the saddle horses and the wild band some eight miles from camp to feed and required more "wranglers" for the day time and for the saddle herds at night.

Saturday, April 28, was an easy day and foreman Burgen laid the plan for riding Saddle Mountain again. This time about twenty-five riders moved up the canyon some twenty miles from camp, carrying provisions on pack horses, and spent the night there. In the morning, bright and early, they were on the mountain and the first bunch of horses sighted were rounded up and held and succeeding bunches run into them during the day.

At the camp all were about early in the morning and by sunrise a number of riders started out around the end of the mountain with a herd of extra saddle horses to meet their comrades who had gone up the canyon the day before and give them all a fresh mount about noon. This plan met with better success than the first ride, although quite a number of horses still eluded the wily vanqueros.

One bunch, numbering from seventy-five to one hundred head, it is said, and all of them white to gray, or spotted black and white, and bred from Arabian stallions, could not be captured. It is known locally as the "wild goose band," from the gray color and the straight away runs they make. When their leaders decided to pull out, riders had to get out of the way or be run down, and no horses under saddles were able to keep pace with them. It is said that fully half of them have never been branded or felt the swish of a rope about them. It is a beautiful sight to see the long line of gray swiftly rounding a sightly butte, or taking a slide down passes that seem bound to hurl them into the depths below, but they are sure footed and hold to their paths like goats. No effort was made to get them this year, but next season, and with the further encroachment of the farmers on the range, they will doubtless be ridden down with relays of men and horses until they are tired and willing to be corralled from sheer exhaustion . . .

The camp at the mouth of Crab Creek was a delightful one. The Columbia furnished an abundance of fine, cool drinking water, and for grandeur—well, one could travel many a day to find a spot more impressive.

To the west of the camp, over a rise of ground, lies the "Oregon," [Columbia River] here wending its mighty way along the foot of a precipitous cliff on the west, an eastern spur of the Ellensburg Mountains . . . On the east and south of Crab Creek abruptly rises the Saddle Mountain, and to the north of Crab Creek and east of the Columbia lie the gently rolling Frenchman Hills, while the Crab Creek valley stretches away to the east, now a desert stretch of sand and rocks and greasewood, but soon to be turned into beautiful and valuable fruit and garden patches.

Engineers of the Chicago, Milwaukee and St. Paul Railway Company were busy here taking soundings and surveying the approaches and for the contours of a bridge across the Columbia. This is to be the main line of the Milwaukee transcontinental system . . .

Around the camp fire one could hear many an interesting story of the range . . . Herbert Heywood, the representative of the Boston Herald, was one of the party of "war correspondents" and came direct from Boston to see and learn something of the buckayros. The life was new and wild to him. His interest in the country and the customs never fagged and each moment brought new things for him to examine and question about . . .

By the third day, at the mouth of Crab Creek, pocket flasks had been pretty well emptied and many were the wishes expressed for an "eye opener" in the morning. Ben Hutchinson could occasionally "dig a little deeper" in his cache and rake up a few drops of Melwood Rye if he thought one really needed it . . .

Owing to the lack of grass around the camp it soon became necessary to move the big herd to other pastures. Before this was done the horses belonging to Sam Gabriel and Ben Rosencranz had to be cut out of the band and branded, as most of their holdings were to be left upon the range another year. This occupied a couple of days, and Owen Minton, who is deputy tax collector, improved his opportunity to seize a few head of horses and cattle belonging to Gabriel, Rosencranz, the "Figure 2" ranch and others to satisfy the claims of the county . . .

The first move was to Red Rock Coulee, lying some eighteen or twenty miles to the northeast and forming a natural corral. The sides are precipitous and a few men could hold a large band of horses by stationing themselves at the mouth and source of the canyon. Springs furnish an abundance of water and the bottom of the coulee is covered with luxuriant bunch grass. A few days rest for the herd there and the driving in of horses from the adjacent hills by the buckayros and then the big outfit pulled out for the West Lake Corrals, a few miles west of the south end of Moses Lake.

PHOTOGRAPHS
OF THE
LAST GRAND ROUNDUP
IN EASTERN WASHINGTON

While riding with the roundup the editor of The Big Bend Chief secured twenty-seven excellent snap shots of incidents of the ride, including:

1. The Lineup at Ephrata
2. On the March
3. A Halt in the Hills
4. Crossing Rocky Ford
5. Camp of Tomanowish.
6. Soper's Outfit at Dinner
7. Burgeu's Chuck Wagon
8. Chuck Wagons on the Trail
9. Chuck Wagons in the Mire
10. Chas. Howard Gets Busy
11. Heywood Taking Notes
12. Heywood and His Horse
13. Packing Away Orphans
14. Group of Principal Horse Owners

15. The Race at Ephrata
16. Roping Colts
17. Driving in Strays
18. A Bucking Bout
19. A Shot at the Big Herd
20. Ben Hutchinson and His Mount
21. Four Snake River Horse Men
22. Wm. McCarty
23. Bunch of 1000 Horses
24. Watering Chuck Teams
25. Off to the Hills
26 A Last Nip
27. "Asleep in Peace"

Twenty-four of these beautiful and interesting 4x5 Photographs, mounted in an Elegant Imitation Seal Grain Flexible Leather Album, will be sent postpaid to any address in the United States or Canada for $5.00, cash with order.

Any less number than twenty-four supplied, mounted on excellent gray mats for 35c each or three for $1.00, postpaid.

IT IS THE LAST OPPORTUNITY
Which will ever occur to get actual photographs of the wild, exciting life of Washington horse men at work. Send your order now. Address **THE CHIEF PUBLISHING CO.,**
Wilson Creek, Wash.

A.A. McIntyre, editor of Wilson Creek's weekly newspaper, the *Big Bend Chief,* offered for sale 27 "excellent snap shots of incidents of the ride." From McIntyre, *Last Grand Roundup* (1906).

When the outfit reached West Lake news came of the summoning of several of the prominent riders to Waterville to serve as jurors or witnesses on the famous Strodmier case. Strodmier was convicted of stealing cattle and is now serving a term in the penitentiary . . .

As soon as the heaviest work was finished at West Lake the Badger Mountain delegation hurriedly pulled out for their home range . . . After the horses had been rounded in from the Moses Lake Desert range and the principal work of branding done, all the outfits were moved on into Ephrata and on account of lack of [railroad] cars for transportation the wild band had to be held there for some days. Hutchinson, Soper and Burgen brought their outfits with the herd and the town was again a lively, bustling buckayro village.

McCarty had considerable difficulty and spent a good deal of time in order to get a routing for his horses from Ephrata to Spokane over the Great Northern and then transfer to the Northern Pacific, in order to reach Dickinson [North Dakota], his nearest station for unloading. Early in March he had begun negotiations, and frequent trips of the traveling agent of the Great Northern railway, F.W. Graham, were made to Wilson Creek for conferences . . .

At another time McCarty was the guest of several officials of the Great Northern in their special train, where he was offered the hospitality of the road in wines, cigars and other social attributes. When the time came for him to leave he thanked the gentlemen for their genial hospitality and hoped that they would call at his ranch some day where he would do his best to return the courtesy. That was all the impression, in a business way, the display had made on the buckayro, and in the end he won his point and loaded his horses at Ephrata and routed them over the Northern Pacific from Spokane, just as he had started out to do.

The loading of a thousand head of wild cayuses is an interesting sight. Bred and foaled upon the hills, coming in contact with man only to be caught with the lariat, hurled to the ground and burned with the branding iron, these horses look upon him as their worst enemy, and they are as frightened at a hand stroke as the cut of a whip. Crushing up the gang plank between two rows of laughing, yelling, cursing men and boys, the frightened animals will cringe and plunge as though they expected to be tortured. In they go, however, some twenty-eight to a car, the door is shoved to place, the train pulled up a car length and the operation is repeated until the big corral is empty. Wm. McCarty, B.S. Townsend and N.D. Nichols owned the entire trainload of some 800 head. The horsemen of Washington were pocketing the proceeds of years of work and waiting. The trainload left Ephrata on Monday, May 14, and on the Sunday following landed at Dickinson, where they were turned upon the range, some seventy miles away in the Bad Lands . . .

The trip east with the horses was marked with heavy loss. In shipping horses that distance, some twelve hundred miles, shippers always figure from 1 to 3 per cent of loss. On this occasion it reached fully 18 per cent. The railway yards at Missoula, where they expected to feed and water, were filled with cattle on arrival there and the railway company ordered them on to Helena. Here every precaution was taken in feeding and watering but before Billings was reached over one hundred horses were dead. The water supplied them at Helena was from the [mining areas of the] mountains, and is said to contain quantities of gypsum and arsenic, which it is reported, accounted for the large loss. The humane society took the matter up with the railway company, but it was then too late to save the stricken horses. From Billings on to Dickinson there was little loss, although the greater part of the horses were weak and depleted from the "gyp" water and the long confinement and knocking about in the cars.

[Back in Washington,] as soon as the horses had been loaded the big outfit was broken up and each owner took charge of his own camp. They immediately began to ride other parts of the range individually, and for the next two months it was easy to run on to a roundup outfit anywhere on the range, gathering, branding and selecting for the shipments. The next big shipment occured June 15 when McCarty, Townsend and N.D. Nichols of Dickinson took out another train load of nine hundred head. One buyer from Billings shipped twelve carloads, W.H. Thompson found a few carloads of heavy horses for which he paid good prices, Spokane and Seattle received several small lots, while a large number were sold to ranchers and broken for use in the harvest. [In all, about 5,000 horses were rounded up and shipped out of Ephrata in the spring of 1906.]

The ride was not entirely finished until the middle of July when McCarty made his last shipment east . . .

It is a picturesque sight to see a large band of wild horses with the colts coming down to water or grazing on the prairie. And, when one stops to think that this is practically the last of them in Washington, that they are doomed to give way to the tiller of the soil and that their haunts will be turned into wheat fields and fruit ranches, for the moment wishes it were not so.

The old horse men feel the change, too, and while waiting at Ephrata, could be heard speculating as to what they will do now that their wild, free and happy life as horse raisers is at an end. Many of them have ranches and will fence and improve them and continue to raise better horses, although in a smaller way. Others will leave the country and cast their lot with new people and new surroundings. Still others will change their life completely and enter new branches of industry in their endeavor to keep pace with the progress of the world.

Endnote

1. A.A. McIntyre, *Last Grand Roundup* (Wilson Creek, Washington: Chief Publishing Company, 1906); reprinted by Stuart McIntyre as *The Last Grand Roundup* (3848 Cresta Way, Sacramento, California, 95864: The Chief Research Co., 1989). The reprint edition contains the original 88 pages of text with new added sections, including a dedication, preface, epilogue, and index. Selections reprinted in *Forgotten Trails* are from pages 1-2, 5-6, 10, 13-14, 18, 21-22, 25-26, 29, 46, 51-52, 55-56, 59-60, 67.

Photograph taken in the fall of 1956 at Ephrata, Washington. From left to right: Billy Curlew, Harry Nanamkin, and Cleveland Kamiakin, the last surviving son of Chief Kamiakin of the Yakima. *Nat Washington*

XIII
Remembering the Past

FIRSTHAND ACCOUNTS BY Indians describing the routes and sites they used in the Big Bend country are rare. One valuable record that history has left to us in this regard is in the form of a tour that Billy Curlew, a Sinkiuse (or Columbia), made in 1946 with Harold Weaver, forest supervisor for the Colville Indian Reservation.

As already related in chapter III, Billy, whose Indian name was Kul-Kuloo, was born at the big tsuka-lo-tsa root digging camp at Ephrata, perhaps as early as the 1860s, but probably in the 1870s. The Columbia River (Umpa-quotwa) was the wintering place of the Sinkiuse; one large winter village was located below the mouth of Moses Coulee, and another stood just a few miles south of Vantage. In Billy's time, the Vantage camp was the largest and it occupied both sides of the river.

Late in the summer of 1946, Billy visited Harold Weaver at Weaver's office in Nespelem, Washington. At the time, Billy was the chief of the Moses band of the Confederated Tribe of Colville Indians. (The Colville Reservation is located in north-central Washington, stretching across southeast Okanogan County and the south half of Ferry County; its boundaries are the Okanogan River on the west and the Columbia River to the south and east. The reservation was created by an executive order signed by President U.S. Grant on April 19, 1872. The original bands living on the reservation at its inception included the Methow, Okanogan, San Poil, Lake, Colville, Kalispel or Pend d'Oreille, Spokane, and Coeur d'Alene.

(Another Indian reserve—the Columbia Reservation—also was created by presidential directives, on April 19, 1878, and March 6, 1880. It was established west of the Okanogan River for the Sinkiuse and other Salishan Indians of the Big Bend area. However, neither Chief Moses nor any of the Columbias ever moved to the Columbia Reservation. They continued to roam the Big Bend until late 1884, when they finally settled on the Colville Reservation. The Columbia Reservation never functioned as an Indian reserve and was abolished in 1884.)

At the meeting in the forest supervisor's office, Weaver learned about Billy's early years through Billy's interpreter, Harry Nanamkin. When Billy was a young man, his band was under the leadership of Chief Moses.

"Great changes are coming," Billy said, referring to the development of the Bureau of Reclamation's Columbia Basin Project. Before it was too late for him to do so, he wanted to go over the lands that he had grown up in, pointing out what he could remember so that the names of the places would not be lost.

Weaver learned through subsequent conversations that Billy had made annual pilgrimages on horseback to the scenes of his early life in the Big Bend country. Advanced age, however, had prevented such excursions for the last seven or eight years.

In Billy's own words, he "knew and respected every foot of the country." Weaver's work prevented him from touring with Billy until mid October 1946, and then for only two days. During the short time allocated for the tour it was possible for them to visit only a portion of the places that Billy wanted to show Weaver. (Because of this, Weaver considered it urgent that another tour of at least three or four days be organized in the spring of 1947.)[1]

Here is Weaver's account of his first tour through the Big Bend country with Billy on October 15 and 16, 1946.[2]

Billy Curlew's Tour, 1946

October 15, 1946, 8:30 A.M. we left from Billy's house south of the Little Nespelem Creek, about three hundred yards west of the highway to Grand Coulee Dam. In addition to Billy and myself the expedition was comprised of Harry Nanamkin, our interpreter, and Jake Weipa, a friend of Billy's.

The first stop was made at Steamboat Rock in the Grand Coulee. One of the original Indian trails between Chelan, Wenatchee, and Moses Coulee to the west, and San Poil and Kettle Falls to the east, crossed the Grand Coulee immediately south of the rock. The Indian name of the rock is Cha-ka-wa, meaning "something set down in the open." Six to eight miles south of Cha-ka-wa or Steamboat Rock, a stop was made to observe the west wall of the coulee. A spring issuing from the rocks at the base of the cliff and talus slope is named Squo-koht. The Indians camped there to gather service berries and to obtain paint (Tool-man) from the rock cliff above. Apparently the paint consists of some exudation from a rock strata next to an intermittent waterfall below the upper rimrock. Billy

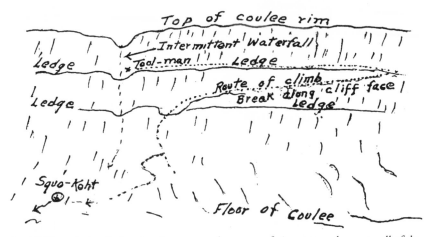

Harold Weaver's sketch showing the route to the source of pigment on the west wall of the Upper Grand Coulee.

informed us that this was the only source of suitable paint in central Washington and pointed out the route by which the coulee was climbed to obtain it. The climb and return trip, he indicated, required approximately one half day for an active man. It should prove an interesting climb for experienced alpinists.

The third stop was made at the south end of the Grand Coulee, approximately 4 miles north of Coulee City. The series of ridges and draws immediately east of the coulee entrance are named Hup-lo-sana. On inquiring concerning the meaning of the name the writer was informed, after considerable discussion between Billy and Harry, that it applied to the corrugation of the inside of a deer or sheep intestine.

The next stop was made at the big spring immediately east of Coulee City. The Indian name is Has-tat-wa-kin. This used to be a big campground on the main trail between Wenatchee, Chelan, and the Moses Coulee to the west, and Spokane and Kettle Falls to the east and northeast. On the prairie, adjacent to the spring, horse races were held. A fine grove of cottonwoods once surrounded the spring, but now scarcely a shrub remains. The source of the spring has been roofed over by a special building and a strong flow of water still issues, to meander across the salt grass flat. On returning to the car from the Has-tat-wa-kin spring, we were greeted by a white citizen from Coulee City by the name of McCann. He told us that his father was one of the original settlers at Coulee City and in the ensuing conversation, he and Billy discovered several mutual acquaintances.

After stopping in Coulee City for a few minutes while Billy visited with an old white friend, the party proceeded to Dry Falls State Park. There, near the present vista house, was an old Indian camp of minor importance. Water was obtained from the spring immediately to the south, the source of the present water supply for the state park buildings.

The next stop was made by the lake on the floor of the coulee at the foot of the highway grade south of Dry Falls. The Indian name of this lake is Squa-quint. The white people call it Park Lake. In early days the Indians, desiring to avail themselves of a boat suitable for the hunting of geese, constructed a dugout canoe at the mouth of the San Poil River. From there it was floated down the Columbia to the present site of Grand Coulee Dam and carried approximately 30 miles overland, through the Grand Coulee, by 16 men. During the night following the launching of the canoe in Squa-quint Lake, however, according to the story a violent storm caused the dugout canoe to be torn from its moorings and destroyed.

One of the earliest white settlers planted an apple orchard immediately north and east of the lake and the present highway. Many of the trees still remain near the old ranch house and dance hall. There, according to Billy, a bear cub was once apprehended while in the act of harvesting apples up in a tree, when barking dogs disclosed his presence.

According to Billy, deer used to be plentiful in the Grand Coulee and in the coulee below Dry Falls and are still present in limited numbers. His brother, when a young man, once shot a deer from a ledge on the coulee wall near Dry Falls. The deer fell a considerable distance to the talus slope below the cliff.

After leaving Squa-quint Lake, the car was parked along the gravel road leading to the east and the party proceeded on foot to Squa-quint Falls in the stream entering the head of the lake from the east. Here, in the spring, the Indians used to catch by hand the native trout ascending the stream to spawn. Approximately 100 to 150 feet below the falls on the south side of the stream is a low basalt cliff with a recess, several feet above the water, containing a natural basin, or water worn pothole. The Indians use to fill the basin with water from the stream, then heated it by rolling in hot rocks. In this hot water they cooked their fish.

From Squa-quint Falls, the party proceeded several miles east along a gravel road to the lower end of a long narrow lake [Deep Lake], lying beneath the precipitous coulee walls, apparently the principal source of Squa-quint Creek. This lake is only a short distance south of Coulee City. The Indian name of this lake is Chul-a-na-nuk. According to Billy it use to be noted for its numerous loons (Ees-wal). At this place the party stopped for a lunch of army K rations.

From Chul-a-na-nuk Lake the route was retraced to Squa-quint Lake and the party proceeded south on the highway towards Soap Lake. To the right of the highway, immediately south of Squa-quint Lake and north of Mu-quis-pum Lake [Blue Lake], Billy showed us an old campground known as Mas-ki-yad. Here, he said, one can hear the water running underground from a large hidden spring. Here, also, he told an old legend concerning a herd of cattle that used to disappear each night under the surface of the north end of Na-quis-pum Lake, then emerge daily to graze on the surrounding hills.

By the highway along the west shore of Na-quis-pum Lake Billy called our attention to the stream cascading from the cliffs above. A sign warned us that the water is impure. Billy said that he used to drink of it frequently when a young man. Perhaps it wasn't polluted then.

South of Na-quis-pum Lake we drove east of the highway a short distance to the shore of a dry lake that Billy called Na-tso-kite. Around this shallow lake, geese, ducks, and mud hens used to nest and the Indians came from Moses Coulee, Wenatchee, Chelan, and San Poil to "gather eggs." Billy said that he believed that the lake was drained after the whites dug another channel for the outlet to Na-quis-pum Lake.

This used to be the site of a large camp. The old trail to Moses Coulee ascended the rim to the west. Along this trail, in the early days, an Indian camped at Na-tsu-kite ambushed another Indian from Moses Coulee. The victim had been visiting at San Poil early in the spring. There he had found a salmon run, much earlier than usual, and after catching all that he could dry and pack on his back had started to return on foot to Moses Coulee. At Na-tsu-kite, he found the camp of an Indian family in rather dire straits for food after the hard winter. It was customary, in those days, for the Indians to share food, especially with anybody who was hungry. The Moses Coulee Indian, however, was a selfish individual who was loath to part with any of his salmon after packing it all the way from the San Poil. Therefore, he merely told the family of the excellent salmon run at San Poil and proceeded up the trail toward Moses Coulee. The head of the family then ran up among the rocks along a short cut and was waiting in convenient ambush when the victim, bent forward under his heavy burden, came climbing up the trail.

After several weeks the Moses Coulee Indians suspected that something had happened to the absentee and a searching party was dispatched along the trail to Na-tsu-kite. The chief instructed the party to question carefully the Indians camped at Na-tsu-kite. This the searching party proceeded to do, doubtless employing the Indian equivalent of the "third degree." After a day or two of questioning, the murderer confessed. Apparently he was a "bad actor."

When the writer asked what then happened to the murderer, Billy replied, "Oh nothing, after he confessed."

Proceeding south on the highway along the east shore of Ska-man-a Lake [Lenore Lake], Billy showed us the site of another camp on the west shore. South of Ska-man-a Lake and north of Soap Lake was another big camp, along an old trail that entered the mouth of the coulee from the west. A stop was made on the east shore of Soap Lake.

The lake was reported to have once dried up, long before Billy Curlew was born. In the center of the present lake, legend has it that there was once a big rock, with a fresh water spring nearby, where the Indians used to camp. Billy told us that Henry Covington's sister died at Soap Lake long ago and was buried somewhere east of the present highway. Subsequently the Indians have never been able to find her grave.

On the west side of Soap Lake was one of the ranches of Tony Richardson, the "Horse King." Tony Richardson entered the country two years after the Moses band moved to the Colville Reservation. At the old Stevenson ferry, on the south bank of the Columbia River, south of the present reservation, he traded the Indians flour for horses. One sack was traded for each year-old mare that the Indians would furnish. The flour was brought in by pack train from Walla Walla, via Sprague and Wilbur. In such manner Richardson raised a tremendous horse herd that ranged all through central Washington. Eventually he sold most of his horses and moved to points unknown to the Indians. Apparently Richardson made quite an impression on the Indians. According to Billy, he was a big tall "raw-boned" man. His riding chaps came up to Jake Weipa's chin once when he tried them on.

From Soap Lake the route led south past Grant Orchards and over the sagebrush plain towards Moses Lake. Billy said the plain use to be covered largely by bunchgrass, instead of sage, and that sage hens and antelope were plentiful. After unrestrained grazing by Tony Richardson's horses and by great herds of cattle and bands of sheep we now have a depleted range. The antelope disappeared entirely, long ago and few sage hens remain.

The next stop was made at the Drew and McCleary Fish Hatchery by the head of the large stream [Rocky Ford Creek] that flows south to Moses

Lake. This stream originates from three quite large springs and numerous small ones. The area of the springs was known by the Indians as Seattle-oft-kum. Below the present hatchery is a series of short channels through which smaller springs join the main channel from the east. Here the Indians used to trap suckers coming up from Moses Lake to spawn. The Indians built spillways of rock with narrow entrances at the mouths of the short channels. Then, when the fish entered a channel, the entrance was blocked by means of a gate constructed of brush and tules. The fish were then caught by hand in the shallow water.

Billy wanted to identify and name each of the channels in which the fish were caught. At the entrance to the channels farthest downstream was a big rock called Pea-cast. This rock Billy apparently identified to his own satisfaction. The intervening channels, however, were so obscured by weeds and tall grass that it was impossible to identify them without actually wading through. The channel farthest upstream, immediately adjacent to the fish hatchery, he called Sta-sta-wadle. The next he called Ska-wast. The rest, four or five of them, he would not name because it was impossible to see them . . .

From Seattle-oft-kum, the party proceeded south over an exceedingly rocky, rough road along the west bank of the stream. In a short distance we arrived on the site of a big camp called Cla-mow-is-kin. A short distance farther was the site of another old camp called Kick-la-cast. Crossing to the east bank of the stream is dangerous here because of quicksand, Billy indicated.

A short distance below Kick-la-cast we crossed the Ephrata-Moses Lake highway and entered a fenced field through a gate beside a "No Trespassing" sign. Down the field approximately one mile, where the hills to the west encroached on the narrow valley, it was necessary to open two gates and to go through a barnyard and past a ranch house. Obviously the ranch is headquarters for a sheep outfit. A short distance below the ranch house we opened another gate and drove into a field pastured by buck sheep. About the middle of this field we left the car and crawled through a tight barbed wire fence to the west. At approximately 100 yards from the car we arrived at the base of a hill to the west and a large rock about 10 feet high and 10 feet in diameter. This, Billy informed us, was the site of one of the most important camps of the Moses band. Its Indian name is Un-ta-pas-neat, meaning "rock on the hill side." About 75 or 80 feet east of the rock, Billy showed us a cleared, circular depression in the ground, the site of the lodge of Chief Moses. Immediately south is another circular depression, the site of the lodge of his brother. Here Chief Moses held court and received important visitors. For the convenience of Chief Moses and his guests a rope to which horses could be tethered was stretched about the big rock.

Here for a distance of 3/4 to 1 mile up and down the west bank of the stream, almost the entire Moses band camped during the months of May, June, and July of each year. Across the stream to the east the valley was reserved for visitors from the east, the buffalo Indians from eastern Montana. These Indians, representing several different tribes, came to trade buffalo hides for horses. The writer indicated to Billy that it was his impression the eastern Montana tribes did not get along well with each other, and asked how they behaved as visitors.

Billy replied, "Chief Moses told them not to get rough with each other while in his country."

After returning to the car and driving through another gate we arrived opposite another large round topped rock, projecting several feet above the valley floor, approximately 300 feet south of Chief Moses' lodge. This, said Billy, marked the starting point of the race course. The course leads north about two miles, along the west bank of the stream and through the present site of the sheep ranch, to a turning stake immediately south of the present Ephrata-Moses Lake highway, thence back to a starting point, a total distance of about 4 miles. As a boy Billy saw the starting rock often piled high with buffalo hides and other articles that were bet on the races. The rock was also the place at which trading activities were conducted. The standard rate of exchange was one buffalo hide for one horse. An especially fast horse, however, might command several hides.

The adjacent slopes and benches, according to Billy, used to be in bunchgrass, while the river flat was covered with salt grass. The salt grass still persists, very sparsely in places, while the lower slopes of the hills to the west are sparsely covered by cheat grass, with scattered sickly looking rabbit brush. Some bunchgrass still persists among the rocks on the upper slopes. The flats and benches above are covered with sage and rabbit brush, with cheat and bunchgrass very sparsely represented.

Billy said, "The rock is still here, but the people have gone."

Billy then told of a hoax once perpetrated on visiting Montana Indians when trading horses for buffalo hides at the rock. Apparently the race was the best means by which the buffalo Indians could judge the relative merits of the various horses offered for trade. One of the Moses Indians whipped his horse into the lead, and when he disappeared behind some cottonwoods along the stream about a half mile north of the starting point, he was well out in front. Once out of sight he stopped and rested his horse while the others continued on and rounded the turning stake, another mile and a half to the north. When the others were returning on the final lap he came charging out in front from behind the cottonwoods and crossed the finish line at the rock well in the lead. Meanwhile, the young man's father loudly extolled the virtues of the horse to several of the Indian visitors who had hides to trade. This performance made such an impression that they offered several hides for the horse.

Darkness was settling so the party retraced the route through the sheep ranch to the highway and then drove to Moses Lake for dinner. It was discovered that no hotel or auto camp accommodations were available, so we then drove to Soap Lake, where accommodations were had at a lake side hotel.

After getting established in our rooms, Billy, Jake Weipa, and Harry Nanamkin listened to the writer's transcription of the notes taken during the day and made suggestions for correction and improvement.

Billy then told us of the manner in which the Indians first acquired livestock. In the early days the father of Chief Moses went to Fort Vancouver on the lower Columbia to visit the white men. These men he found to be Frenchmen, who treated him well and gave him gifts on his departure for the return trip. These gifts included live chickens and potatoes. With the potatoes they included mattocks, to be used in preparing the ground for planting the next spring. The chickens roosted on the lodgepoles and crowed each morning, to the amazement of the Indians.

Billy indicated that the lodges were then oblong in shape, with a framework of crossed poles and covering, usually, of laced tules. It is possible that the later adoption by these Indians of the conventional circular lodge with skin covering could have resulted from their trading contacts with the Indians from Montana. The acquisition of the horses by the Indians undoubtedly facilitated trading and exchange of ideas.

With respect to the potatoes, Billy indicated that they were planted the next spring, after the father of Chief Moses called all of the Indians together at the mouth of the Wenatchee River. Since the mattocks furnished by the frenchmen were not sufficient in number, the Indians fashioned additional tools out of limbs and trunks of Hawthorn bushes. After the soil was turned over by the mattocks it was further pulverized by beating with poles. The first crop proved such a great success that within a few years potatoes were cultivated throughout central Washington by the Indians.

Additional trips to Fort Vancouver were made by the Indians. On the second trip the Frenchmen gave them a number of hogs. These animals were turned loose in a canyon west of the Columbia River. They soon became unpopular with the Indians, however, because of the manner in which they rooted up the grass and the edible roots. After a few years, therefore, the animals were all disposed of.

The most important acquisition, on the third and last trip, was a small herd of cattle, reported at 6 head. These animals started the Indians in the business of raising cattle. Eventually the herd grew quite large, ranging from the vicinity of Moses Lake west to the Columbia, on the plain in the vicinity of Ephrata and Quincy.

Doubtless, additional cattle were eventually acquired from other sources, since Billy mentioned the acquisition, at one time, of a herd of Texas longhorns from Flathead, Montana.

The talk then turned to the Wenatchee and Chelan regions. At Lake Wenatchee, Billy indicated, the Indians used to make most of their dugout canoes from big cedar trees. The canoes were then taken down the Wenatchee to the Columbia. To avoid the impassible rapids above Leavenworth, the canoes were dragged and skidded over a low pass by means of horses to the headwaters of a branch stream.

Lake Chelan is icy cold, he said, and bear and deer sometimes become exhausted and drown when trying to swim across it. He had never been to the upper end of the lake. Jake Weipa then told how Lake Chelan was formed. The Coyote, who apparently is an important personage in Indian legends, proposed to the Chelan Indians that they give him a nice young girl, in return for which he would send lots of salmon up the Chelan River. The Chelans thought it improper for anyone so old as the Coyote to have anything to do with a young girl, so they refused. This made the coyote very angry, so he blocked up the canyon with huge rocks, causing falls in the river that have always been impassible to the salmon. Behind the rocks Lake Chelan was formed.

Jake claimed that the only fish native to Lake Chelan were suckers until the white men planted trout. This appears in direct variance to statements of state fish and game men, who mention native, landlocked steelhead salmon in the lake.

The discussion finally broke up at midnight.

The party made an early start the next morning, October 16, intending to have breakfast in Ephrata. First, however, Billy wanted to visit the old home of Tony Richardson, northwest of town, on the shore of Soap

Lake. It was found that new residences have been built on the old home site and that not a trace of the old place remains. The point on the ridge west of Soap Lake, said Billy, is called Koc-skin. The marker of piles of rocks is still there. It then became apparent that the car radiator was frozen. It was necessary to return to Soap Lake to thaw out the radiator with hot water and a blanket. Meanwhile, breakfast was had at a local restaurant.

Ephrata was the first stop after leaving Soap Lake. A nice stream, lined with cottonwoods used to issue from the draw in the hills north of town. The Indian name is An-tuh-hi-pum. The father of Chief Moses used to raise potatoes here. There remains not a trace of the stream or cottonwoods.

The plain between Ephrata and Quincy, Billy said, as we drove along, used to be covered by fine bunchgrass. Away to the south of Moses Lake, however, there used to grow luxuriant, high sagebrush, where deer were plentiful. The Indians used to run these deer with horses. When the deer became exhausted, they would try to hide by kneeling with their forelegs and sticking their heads under the sagebrush. Their hindquarters with the conspicuous white rump remained erect, to the amusement of the Indians.

I tried to get Billy to tell me the names of the summit peaks of the Cascades, in sight as we approached Quincy. The high ragged one, I told him was called Mt. Stuart by the whites. What was the Indian name? Billy replied that it was better to wait until we got closer. Then he would tell me the names of all the high mountains. This fact was later commented on by Jake Weipa. He did name the long, timbered ridge that extends south from the vicinity of Wenatchee toward Vantage Ferry. Its name is Na-faith-kin.

The next stop was made on the floor of the first canyon, or coulee, west of Quincy. The name of this place is Na-ha-lot-skin. It marks the intersection of a trail to the east towards Quincy with a main north-south trail up which the whites used to travel to the gold fields of British Columbia. The trail came up from the south and to the east of the Columbia, then dropped to the floor of the coulee at this point and continued north. It passed to the east of Waterville and crossed the Columbia at Bridgeport. The Indians used to guide the whites on the trail. [This was Joel Palmer's route.]

North of the present highway is a spring called Han-ta-pon-isk.

At Trinidad we drove to a vantage point where we could overlook the Columbia. The valley bordering the Columbia to the east, at the mouth of the coulee above mentioned, is called Na-qua-lot-kis-um.

Shortly after leaving Trinidad, we left the highway at a gravel pit and drove to the left almost a quarter of a mile along a high bunchgrass covered ridge to a point where a magnificent view was had up and down the

Columbia. At our feet the slope dropped precipitously several hundred feet into a huge gravel pit developed by the Great Northern Railroad.

East of the river, upstream from Na-qua-lot-kis-um the valley is called Chas-ta-cuks. Most of the river opposite this point, the valley was called Coma-quat-ka. The Moses Band used to winter along the Columbia because of the abundance of driftwood for heating and cooking fires. West across the Columbia from this point and upriver from Coma-quat-ka a stream called Ta-pis-kin issues from a canyon extending back into Na-faith-kin mountain. One mile up this stream from the Columbia are some falls where there used to be good fishing for salmon. The Indians also raised potatoes and corn in the stream valley. Communication with Coma-quat-ka was by means of a trail that passed above a basalt cliff that drops precipitously into the Columbia. Downriver from Coma-quat-ka another stream called Na-qual-a-qual-main joins the Columbia from a canyon in the mountain to the west. This also used to be a fine fishing stream.

Shortly after returning to the highway we entered the mouth of Moses Coulee and proceeded north via the oiled road on its floor. Billy can remember when a fine stream full of trout used to flow down the coulee. Now, however, the stream is dry, except during periods of spring runoff or heavy storms. Billy thinks that it has dried up because of all the water that has been taken for irrigation.

At 6.3 miles up the coulee we passed the site of a summer camp called Ska-low-os. Here the Indians raised potatoes and corn. A dry side canyon, entering from the west, used to support a fine stream. Also on the west side of the coulee there was a cave, high enough to permit a man to ride in on horseback. It can still be seen.

Some distance above Ska-low-os we passed a low basalt rimrock, to the right, where one of the sons of Chief Moses used to hide his tobacco. Young men and boys, explained Billy, were not supposed to smoke until they were deemed to have reached the age of manhood by their elders. This boy frequently raided Chief Moses' supply and hid the tobacco in a crevice in the cliff. Smokes then were obtained on the sly when he and a boy companion used to ride past the rock, which was frequently.

At 14.9 miles the main Moses Coulee bends sharply to the east, while a side canyon, called Mus-ta-wak-in-nin enters at the bend from the north. Up this canyon goes a branch line of the Great Northern Railroad to Waterville. The canyon heads at Douglas, and it also used to support a fine stream in which were native trout. A short distance up the canyon from

Moses Coulee to the left is a big ledge called Ta-pa-kite. Below this ledge was a deep pool inhabited by a monster.

Below the side canyon, where the boulder fan intrudes on Moses Coulee is an Indian graveyard. Billy was not sure of its exact location but said that it was somewhere on the boulder fan.

At 15.4 miles we passed another summer camp that was occupied during planting and harvesting time. Potatoes and corn were raised. The camp is named Chuk-com-a-pas. A horse race course led for two miles east up the level coulee floor. Under the bluff to the south were ice caves. At 19.2 miles, where the coulee again forks and becomes much shallower, we turned back. Billy explained that all trails to the east, towards Grand Coulee and more distant points, used to funnel through Moses Coulee.

On returning to the mouth of Moses Coulee, Billy described the deer fence that the Indians constructed across the mouth of the coulee, long before his time, before the acquisition of the horse. It was approximately one mile long, across the mouth of the coulee and was constructed of cedar posts and a woven weed rope. From the rope, between the posts, were suspended bunchgrass and other weeds. These stirred and moved in the breeze and were calculated to scare or spook the deer as they were driven down the coulee. Cottonwood ashes were also placed in piles between the post. The scent of these ashes was supposed to be repugnant to deer.

The deer were driven south down the coulee to the fence, thence east towards the high bluff forming the east gate to the coulee. Most of the deer ascended the rough talus slope and climbed up the ledge that eventually led to a jumping off place. Once the deer were on the ledge they were stampeded over the brink by one of the fastest runners who chased them and rattled dry cedar sticks together. The Indians call such a deer trap "skee-ehh." [The Wanapam who inhabited the land just south of the Saddle Mountains also had a place where they chased deer off of a bluff; this area they called Tow-tom-ch-awa We-tosh, "the place where deer fall down."]

They were interested in the writer's description of a buffalo trap that he had seen on the Crow Indian Reservation in the Big Horn Mountains in southern Montana. There the buffalo were stampeded over a rimrock in somewhat the same manner. After leaving the Moses Coulee road, we crossed the highway and followed a dirt road until we came to another excellent view of the Columbia. On top of a mound, to the left of the dirt road, is buried the sister of Chief Moses, under a mound of rocks that are still plainly visible. She was the mother of Jim Chil-la-hat-ca.

Our vantage point overlooked another favorite camp spot of the Indians, on the east side of the Columbia called Squa-lat-ka. Downstream are rapids and an island called Tehuck-ita. Billy said that it used to be one of the best fishing places. Other rapids are visible in the Columbia about one mile upstream, toward Rock Island.

Opposite there entered a side stream from the mountains to the west. Harry pronounced this name as "Qua-la-kum," and mentioned that the whites still use the name. One of the maps available to the writer spelled this name as "Colockum." This indicated to the writer that his interpretation of the spelling of Indian names may not be too accurate.

Up Colockum Creek, the Indians used to fish for steelhead salmon. A trail, later a road, follows up the creek and over Na-faith-kin mountain to Ellensburg.

Apparently this is the canyon where the Indians kept the hogs for such short duration.

Billy said that the father of Chief Moses, who led the three expeditions to Fort Vancouver, was given by the Frenchmen at the post the name of Cras-an-ams. Billy Curlew's grandfather on his mother's side, named Pucks-pala-kin, was a nephew of Cras-an-ams.

Billy then took from a small suitcase an old paper that he asked me to read. It proved to be a certificate of good conduct, for some Indian, that was signed by a captain of the U.S. Cavalry at "Camp Wenatchee," in May 1885. Billy asked me how old the paper was.

When I replied "61 years," he said: "Then I can't be 87 years old. I was a boy when the paper was signed. If I was as old as they say, I would have had a wife and a bunch of kids at the time."

Billy also had a faded photo taken of himself on horseback, when a young man. I believe he said that the picture was taken at Wenatchee. He was dressed in the typical cowboy garb of the day. I believe that both the paper and the photo have considerable historical value, and that photographic copies should be made of each, with Billy's consent.

Before leaving, Billy told of a white man who met with extremely bad luck while attempting to cross the Columbia at this place in the early days. The white man, who had a fine big horse and an excellent saddle and clothes, declared it to be most necessary that he immediately cross the Columbia. One of the Indians attempted to cross him over by dugout canoe. The saddle and other equipment were ferried in the canoe while the horse, led by a halter, swam behind. Well out in the river the horse became panic stricken and began thrashing and striking the water with his forefeet. Soon he drowned. In his struggles he caused the canoe to capsize, pitching the Indian and the white man into the water. The Indian attempted to swim to shore but the white man elected to stay with the canoe. Men on the shore managed to reach a long pole to the Indians just at the brink of the rapids. Meanwhile the canoe went through the rapids, completely disappearing under the water at times, with the white man clinging to it. Below the rapids a big whirlpool sucked it under for fully a minute but when it bobbed up the white man was still with it. So he remained until the canoe drifted out of their sight around a bend in the river.

Later they found the canoe beached on the west bank of the river, far below. Of the white man they could find no trace. They surmise that he survived and, knowing that his horse and entire outfit was lost, he struck for Ellensburg on foot.

At 12:45 P.M. we arrived at Rock Island Dam and were escorted through by Mr. Maxwell, an employee of the Puget Sound Light and Power Company. Mr. Maxwell took quite an interest in the Indians and went to considerable pains to explain to them, through Harry, the manner in which the turbines and generators worked. After going through the powerhouse, we walked along the top of the dam to the spillway. Billy pointed to a place where an island or point used to project into the river from the east bank, below the dam. It was called Boen-te-aow-etz. Apparently it was completely blasted away during the construction of the dam.

Maxwell then directed Billy's attention to the high precipitous bluff, immediately east of the dam, asking if it were true that it used to be an Indian lookout point, and if a small spring is found near the top. Billy replied that it was true and there is a spring. He then indicated the route by which the ascent is made and a small grove of ponderosa pines growing about the spring.

He had never climbed it, but his wife had when a young woman, "one time when she had nothing better to do."

Maxwell then asked if it were true that the whites had lost a large herd of horses and cattle one winter in the 1840s or 1850s [1860s?] when they attempted to cross on the ice downriver from Rock Island. Billy replied that it was true; that his folks had seen it happen before his time. Apparently it was intended to drive the stock to the gold fields in British Columbia.

Maxwell next asked if he remembered the earthquake. Billy replied that he did, that it happened when he was a boy. The quake caused a whole mountain to slide into the Columbia above Entiat. About a day after the quake, the Columbia went almost completely dry. Then, after another day, high water came, higher than any that they had ever seen. The quake, together with fluctuations in the Columbia, caused the Indians to fear that the world was coming to an end . . . Later the writer discovered that A.J. Splawn, in *Ka-mi-akin: The Last Hero of the Yakimas*, dated the earthquake in the late fall of 1872 . . .

Billy told Maxwell that the Indian name of Rock Island was Ka-wah-chem. Then he asked how it happened that no more salmon came up the river past the dam. Maxwell said that during the past year 45,000 sockeye and 10,000 chinook went upstream over the fish ladders of the dam. Billy asked if the Indians could fish below the dam. Maxwell replied that anyone, white or Indian, could fish within 300 feet of the dam.

By this time it was late in the afternoon and, since we had had no lunch, Billy announced that it was time to go. He then expressed his appreciation to Maxwell and we left for Wenatchee. Immediately above the dam he indicated were No-own-sk Creek issued from the cliff and cascaded into the Columbia. The creek now is called Rock Island Creek and was called Ka-wah-chen creek by the Indians. Steelhead used to run up it to spawn. It heads on Badger Mountain.

After dinner in Wenatchee, the party started for home at 5 P.M. Billy pointed out that the first potato patch was at the mouth of the Wenatchee River. Above Entiat, when darkness was settling, he indicated the rapids where the quake caused the mountain to slide and temporarily dam the Columbia.

The winter after the "good conduct paper" was signed, in 1885, he indicated, the soldiers camped along the east bank of the Columbia, opposite Lake Chelan. The next winter they camped at Brewster. After that they occupied permanent quarters at Fort Spokane.

From marriages of the soldiers with the Indian women, he said there originated most of the mixed bloods now living on the Colville Reservation.

As interpreter, Harry expressed it: "Man needs woman, and woman needs man."

At 9:30 P.M. we returned Billy to his house on Little Nespelem Creek. Thus ended an exceedingly interesting but strenuous two-day trip. Before leaving the car, Billy indicated that he had lots more to show us on another trip and that the same men should go.

Endnotes

1. I located Weaver in Arkansas in the spring of 1982 and asked him if he had, in fact, made a second trip. He said they did, in the spring of 1947, covering the same area and a little more. Weaver wrote up an account of this second trip, but a short time later lost his notes and never found them again—Ron Anglin.
2. Harold Weaver, "A Tour of the Old Indian Camp Grounds of Central Washington," 1946. Unpublished manuscript in author's collection. The version presented in *Forgotten Trails* has been lightly edited.

Alfred Downing sketch of the Lower Grand Coulee, August 12, 1880. *Washington State Historical Society*

A view of Spring Creek near the location where Chief Moses's camp stood on the night of December 17, 1878, when the Indian leader was arrested by a posse. Moses eventually was released. The site now is inundated by the Potholes Reservoir. *U.S. Bureau of Reclamation photograph, June 10, 1946*

The Indian trading rock—located on Rocky Ford Creek approximately one hundred yards south of the site of Chief Moses's lodge. From left to right: Harry Nanamkin, Cleveland Kamiakin, and Billy Curlew. *Nat Washington photo, fall 1956*

"Brothers," by artist Keith Powell of Grand Coulee, WA (1984). In this fine painting, Sinkiuse men are depicted leaving the north end of the Grand Coulee. *Collection of Curt W. Campbell, Spokane, WA*

Ben Hutchinson's log cabin, built in 1888 on Crab Creek two miles west of Corfu. *Lloyd F. Nelson photograph, 1948*

Some of the many rock walls in the scabland country below O'Sullivan Dam that are attributed to Henry Gable's horse ranching operations. *Ron Anglin photograph, August 1985*

The Northern Pacific Railroad's notorious construction town known as Ainsworth (established 1879) stood on the north bank of the Snake River at the confluence with the Columbia. In this 1884 scene, the recently completed Snake River bridge is visible at left. The town largely was abandoned at about this time as Pasco was being founded. *Historical Photographs Collections, Washington State University Libraries*

Start of the "Last Grand Roundup" southeast of Ephrata, in 1906. Note the Great Northern Railway train to the left. The three riders in front from left to right are: (1) on the white horse, Owen Minton; (2) on the bay horse and wearing a coat, Tom Burgen, the boss of the roundup; and (3) on the blaze face, John Erickson. *Grant County Historical Society*

The 1906 "Last Grand Roundup"—two outfits camped close together. Note the two chuck wagons, and the saddle horses being held off to the left. *Grant County Historical Society*

The 1906 "Last Grand Roundup"—horses watering on Lower Crab Creek. *Grant County Historical Society*

The 1906 "Last Grand Roundup"—chuck wagon stalled in Crab Creek on Lower Crab Creek. *Grant County Historical Society*

Appendix 1
White Bluffs Trail

By Professor George F. Beck (1949)[1]

I N THE EARLY DAYS . . . the White Bluffs Trail . . . connected White Bluffs
with both The Dalles in Oregon and Fort Colville. It was a road hurriedly laid out in the late [1850s] to connect these military posts which
grew out of the Yakima Indian war. In my boyhood it was still the primary
highway of traffic from Black Rock southward to the Columbia. But by
1905, or thereabouts, it had vanished behind fences and beneath the plow.

Starting at White Bluffs, the Big Bend section of the road worked up
the steep bluffs and headed directly for the "saddle" in the Saddle mountains west of Othello. First camp out was made at Lower Crab creek at the
foot of the Saddle mountains. The next day's journey led westward up the
Frenchman hills and back to camp on Crab creek at about the site of the
present O'Sullivan dam.

The third day's travel covered the most difficult stretch of the road,
for it not only invited contact with the sand dunes at the foot of Moses
Lake, but presented a waterless sage plain beyond to Black Rock spring 20
miles from the last camp. For horses this was reasonable, but for oxen the
march was a forced one and extremely hazardous in hot weather. It was
found necessary, later, to dig a well at the Rocky Coulee crossing . . .

The fourth day found the trail veering sharply to the east, avoiding
the scablands of Crab creek until a few miles below Odessa, where it again
bore northward to the creek and fifth camp. Two days along the ridge
between Lake creek and Duck creek brought the road out at modern Davenport for the seventh camp.

Save Henry Marlin, who drove to Crab creek via this route in 1867
(according to Splawn), few other Big Bend settlers seem to have arrived
over this trail. The road saw some military movement, however, including
one classic tour of inspection in the late [1850s] which included Jefferson

Davis as secretary of war[2] and Phil Sheridan and U.S. Grant as young officers in his escort.[3]

In the [1860s], mining supplies began moving into the British Columbia and Rocky Mountain discoveries over the White Bluffs Trail, and for about five years the traffic built up considerably, culminating in a season of rush business when the Blackfoot diggings were opened in Montana and when steamboats pushed to the White Bluffs crossing of the Columbia . . . In the [1880s] a new gold rush and military movements revived use of the road. Ben Hutchinson told the writer he helped freight a military boat overland to Chelan. The craft had been sawed in two and loaded on strung out wagon running gears. The party was held up for hours in negotiating the sharp curves at the crest of Saddle Mountain pass.

Hutchinson, so he said, used to freight over this route with oxen, returning from the long trip in time to winter his cattle on Lower Crab creek. It was the fertile bunchgrass there that led him to settle in the general Othello area as a stockman . . .

With the coming of the railroads, the White Bluffs Trail no longer served any cross-country purposes. Donald Urquhart told me that in his time he knew of no regular traffic upon it, other than stockmen moving from one watering hole to the other. In the early days of the homesteading wheat farmers, stretches of the trail saw heavy service as "water roads" for family use. Today only some 10 miles of the White Bluffs Trail are still faintly visible in virgin sage.

Endnotes

1. Excerpt from George F. Beck's "The Four Old Wagon Trails" in the "Black Rock Pioneer Edition," Ritzville *Journal-Times*, 1949. George F. Beck was raised in the Big Bend country, and for many years served as a professor of geology at Central Washington State College (now Central Washington University), Ellensburg.

2. Regrettably, this sometimes repeated mentioning of a late-1850s inspection tour through the Big Bend country by Secretary of War Jefferson Davis (later, President of the Confederate States of America, 1861-65) is erroneous. The tale is a myth. Supposedly, Davis was accompanied by young officers (and future Union generals), Ulysses S. Grant and Philip H. Sheridan, in his escort. In actuality, Davis never visited the Pacific Northwest in any official capacity during his lifetime. Furthermore, though it is true that both Grant and Sheridan served in the Pacific Northwest, Grant had returned to the Midwest and resigned from the army in 1854, and Sheridan likewise was not on duty in Washington Territory after the mid 1850s. Both had departed the area long before the White Bluffs road was established in 1859. In addition, neither Grant, Sheridan, nor Davis mentioned such a trip in their memoirs. It is important to note that a career U.S. Army officer with a similar name, "Colonel Jefferson C. Davis," served in the Pacific Northwest in the post-Civil War era and particularly with distinction during the 1874 Modoc War. It is reasonable to assume that confusion, and false assumptions, have arisen due to the similarity of the two men's names.

3. I met Beck in a retirement home in Yakima in the fall of 1980 and asked him at the time where he acquired the information about this inspection tour. He told me it came from a letter written in 1927 by Mrs. Jennie Crawford Koppen (1858-1928), who lived at the old town site of Wahluke on the Columbia River. She had been told about this inspection tour by a Dr. R.O. Craig, who had been the family physician in Minnesota. It seems Dr. Craig once had been stationed at Simcoe, perhaps during the Indian agency days. Beck went on to say that before he could question Mrs. Koppen in person she tragically died in an automobile accident in Ephrata. One of Beck's daughters located the letter for me in Beck's papers after he died. However, it is a known historical fact that neither Grant, Sheridan, nor Davis were ever in the area when Fort Simcoe and Fort Colville were established and occupied, nor is there any official record of such an inspection tour taking place. Consequently, the tale certainly is a misunderstanding—Ron Anglin.

Appendix 2

MAP OF THE UPPER COLUMBIA RIVER,

FROM THE INTERNATIONAL BOUNDARY LINE TO SNAKE RIVER,

ON A SCALE OF ONE INCH TO TWO MILES.

25 SHEETS AND AN INDEX SHEET.

FROM SURVEYS AND EXAMINATIONS MADE IN 1881,

BY

LIEUT. THOMAS W. SYMONS, CORPS OF ENGINEERS,
Chief Engineer, Department of the Columbia,

AND

ALFRED DOWNING,
Topographical Assistant, U. S. Army.

Drawn by ALFRED DOWNING.

These sheets are numbered consecutively from the boundary to Snake River, and can be joined together into one sheet if desired, showing the river continuously.

While surveying the Columbia River in a 30-foot bateau, Symons and Downing were accompanied by an old HBC Iroquois boatman named "Pierre Agare" and four Colville-area Indian paddlers. They successfully completed their hazardous journey in September and October 1881. Reproduced here is that portion of Downing's maps extending from the mouth of the Snake to the mouth of the Okanogan. For the complete survey report, see *Senate Executive Document* 186, 47th Cong., 1st Sess., 1882, or *The Symons Report . . .* (Ye Galleon Press, 1967).

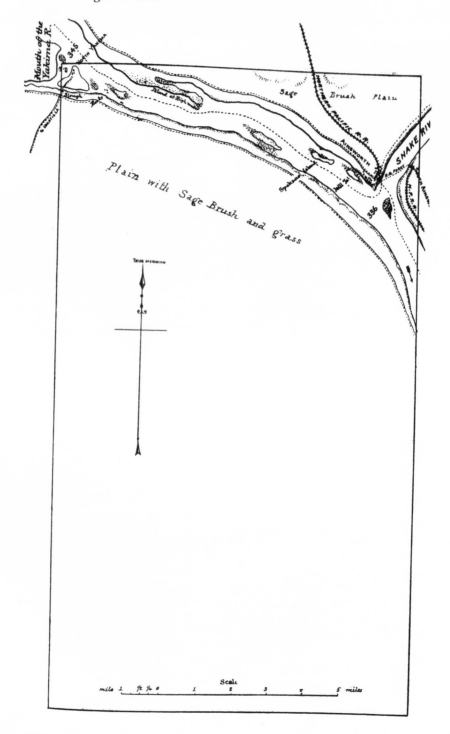

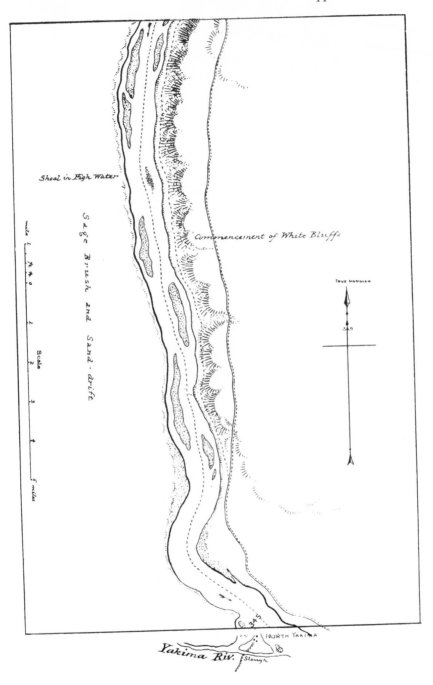

Shoal in High Water

Sage Brush and Sand-drift

Commencement of White Bluffs

TRUE MERIDIAN

miles 1 ½ ¼ 0 1 2 3 4 5 miles

Scale

NORTH YAKIMA

Yakima Riv. Slough

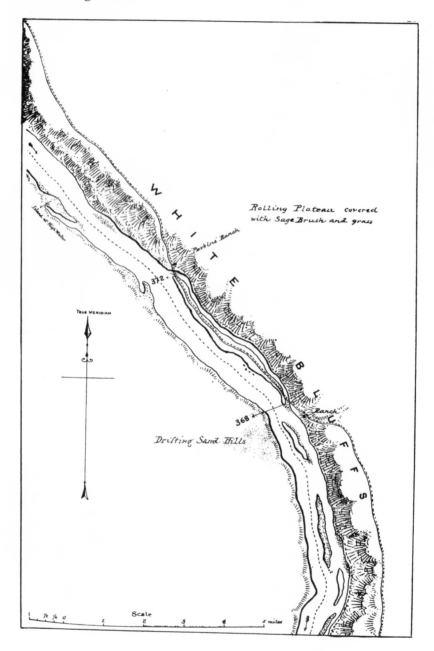

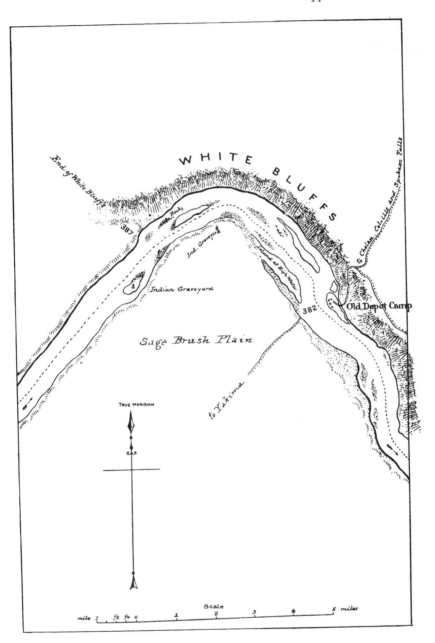

WHITE BLUFFS

End of White Bluffs

to Chelan, Colville and Spokane Falls

Rocks

387

Ind. Graveyard

Island at high water

Indian Graveyard

382

Old Depot Camp

Sage Brush Plain

to Yakima

TRUE MERIDIAN

Scale

mile 1   1/2 1/4 0   1   2   3   4   5 miles

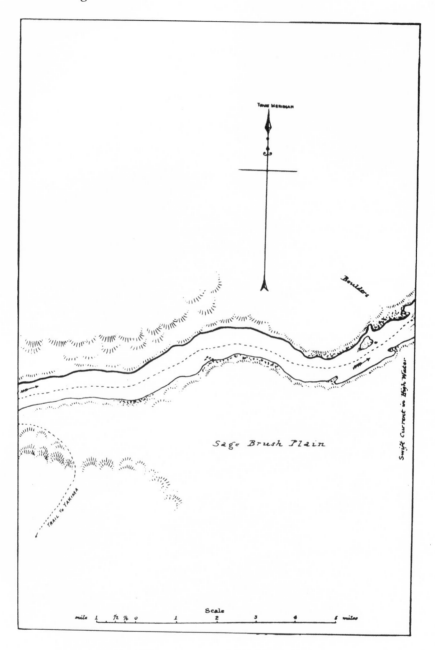

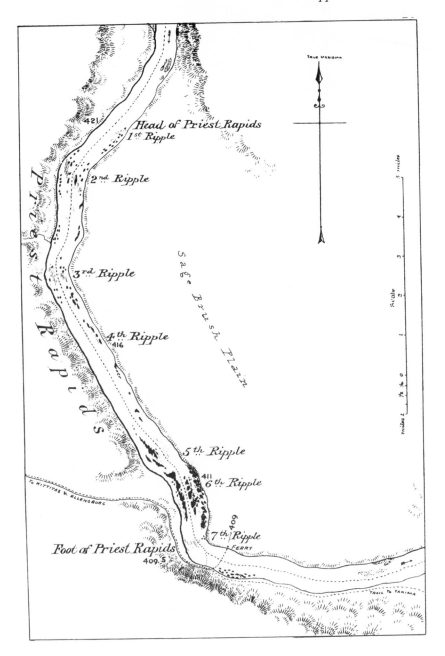

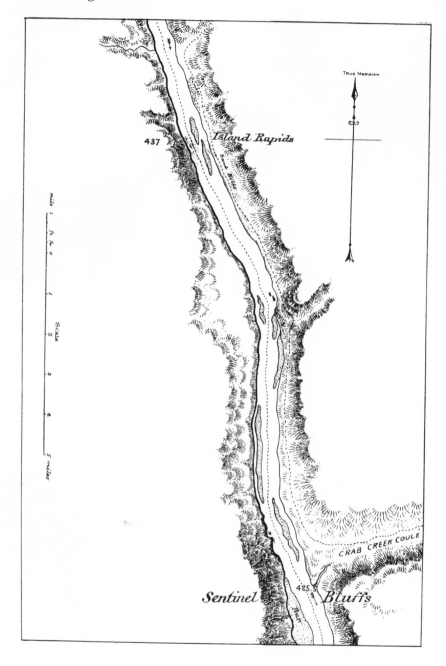

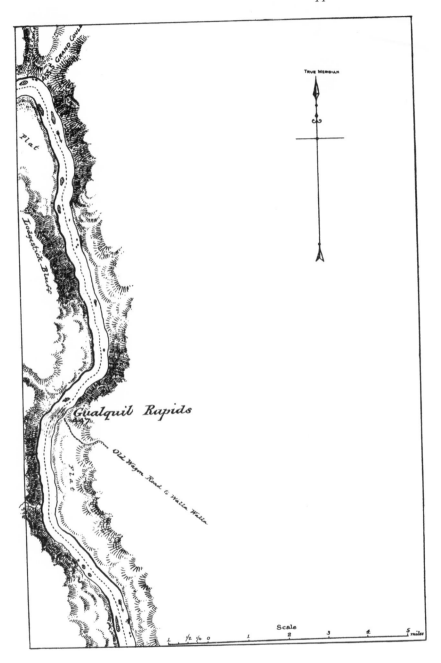

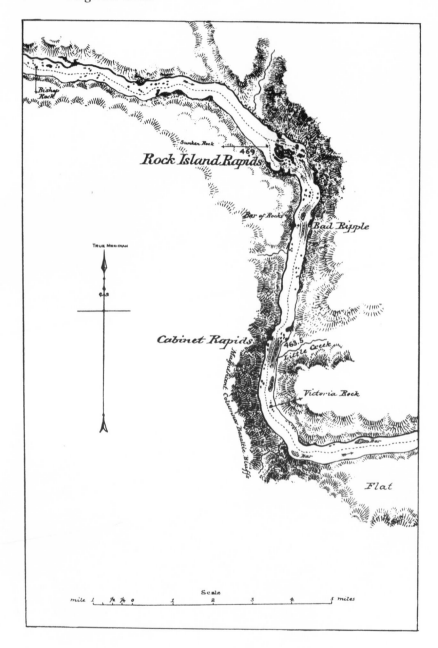

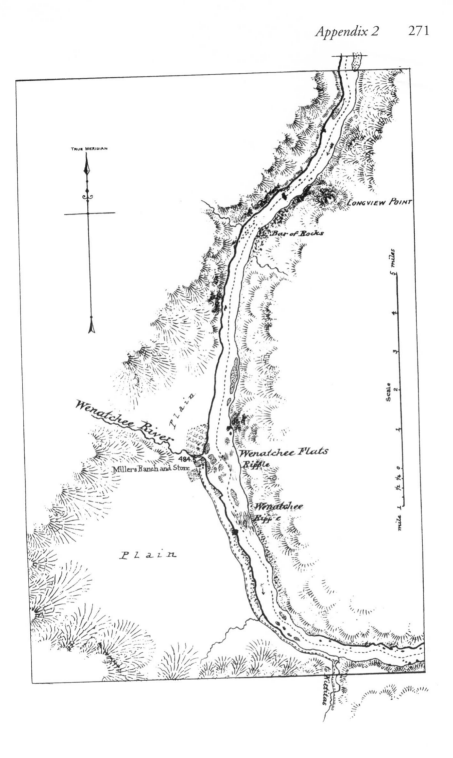

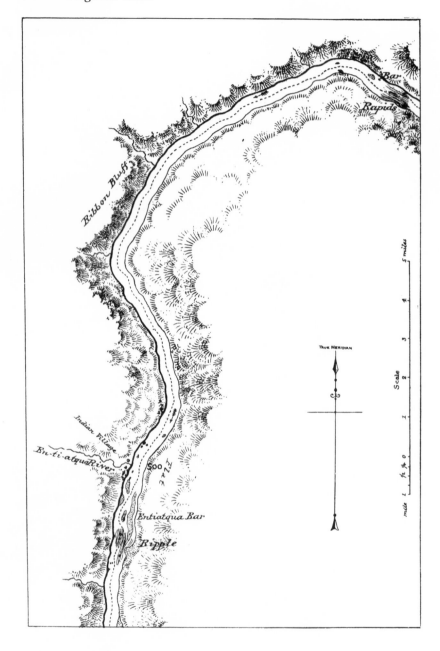

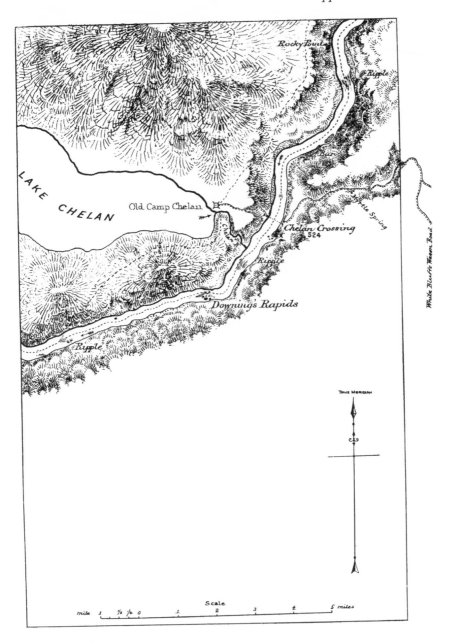

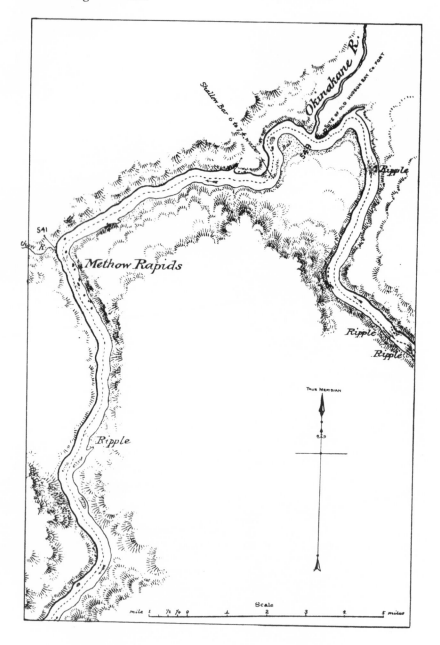

Bibliography of Historical Sources

Journal and Magazine Articles

"Barron Championed Inland Route North." *Okanogan County Heritage* 15 (Summer 1977).

Barry, J. Neilson. "Pickering's Journey to Fort Colville in 1841." *Washington Historical Quarterly* 20 (January 1929).

Beck, George F., compiler. "Black Rock Pioneer Edition." Ritzville *Journal-Times*, 1949.

Brown, William C. "Old Fort Okanogan and the Okanogan Trail." *Quarterly of the Oregon Historical Society* 15 (March 1914).

Buckland, F.M. "The Hudson's Bay Brigade Trail." *Sixth Report of the Okanagan Historical Society* ([British Columbia] 1935).

Camp, Dee. "An Account of a U.S. Exploration of the Okanogan Country." *Okanogan County Heritage* 26 (Winter 1987-88).

Coonc, Elizabeth Ann. "Reminiscences of a Pioneer Woman." *Washington Historical Quarterly* 8 (January 1917).

Crandall, Lulu Donnell. "The *Colonel Wright*." *Washington Historical Quarterly* 7 (April 1916).

Downing, Alfred. "A Brief Narrative of a Misadventure on the Columbia River [Washington Territory, 1880]." *Northwest Discovery* 4 (June 1983).

Elliott, T.C., ed. "Journal of David Thompson." *Quarterly of the Oregon Historical Society* 15 (June 1914).

_____. "Journal of John Work, June-October, 1825." *Washington Historical Quarterly* 5 (April 1914).

Esvelt, John P. "Upper Columbia Chinese Placering." *Okanogan County Heritage* 15 (Summer 1977).

"The First Steamboat on the Upper Columbia [*Colonel Wright*]." *Overland Monthly* 7 (1866).

"Fort Okanogan: Fur Empire Outpost." *Okanogan County Heritage* 15 (Spring 1977).

Freeman, Otis W. "Early Wagon Roads in the Inland Empire." *Pacific Northwest Quarterly* 45 (October 1954).

Frost, Robert. "Fraser River Gold Rush Adventures." *Washington Historical Quarterly* 22 (July 1931).

Garnett, Major R.S. "From Fort Simcoe to Fort Okanogan with the 9th Infantry." *Okanogan County Heritage* 12 (Fall 1974).

Glover, R. "York Boats." *The Beaver* (March 1949).

"Gold Trains North." *Okanogan County Heritage* 15 (Summer 1977).

Haines, Francis. "The Northward Spread of Horses among the Plains Indians." *American Anthropologist* 40 (January-March 1938).

"Handwritten Record: Ambush at McLoughlin Canyon and other Adventures of Francis Wolff." *Okanogan County Heritage* 2 (June 1964).

Harvey, A.G. "David Stuart: Okanagan Pathfinder and Founder of Kamloops." *British Columbia Historical Quarterly* 9 (October 1945).

Ireland, Willard E. "Simpson's 1828 Journey." *The Beaver* (September 1948).

Layman, William D. "Hawkbells: David Thompson in North Central Washington." *Columbia: The Magazine of Northwest History* (Winter 1991).

Lewis, William S. "The Camel Pack Trains in the Mining Camps of the West." *Washington Historical Quarterly* 19 (October 1928).

Lewis, William S., and Jacob A. Meyers, eds. "John Work's Journal of a Trip from Fort Colvile to Fort Vancouver and Return in 1828." *Washington Historical Quarterly* 11 (April 1920).

"Lt. Robert E. Johnson, 1841." *Okanogan County Heritage* 6 (December 1967).

Mansfield, R.H., "When David Thompson Passed By." *Okanogan County Heritage* 5 (March 1967).

Meagher, Thomas Francis. "Rides Through Montana." *Harper's New Monthly Magazine* 35 (1867).

Meany, Edmond S. "Grand Coulee in History." *Washington Historical Quarterly* 15 (April 1924).

Mehringer, Peter J., Jr. "Clovis Cache Found: Weapons of Ancient Americans." *National Geographic* 174 (October 1988).

Meyer, Bette E. "The Pend Oreille Routes to Montana, 1866-1870." *Pacific Northwest Quarterly* 72 (April 1981).

Neal, E.H. "Blythe: He Built Manor House in the Desert." *Okanogan County Heritage* 15 (Spring 1977).

Oliphant, J. Orin. "Old Fort Colvile." *Washington Historical Quarterly* 16 (April 1920).

Ray, Verne F. "Native Villages and Groupings of the Columbia Basin." *Pacific Northwest Quarterly* 27 (April 1936).

Ruby, Robert H. "Blythe: Gentleman Cowboy." *Okanogan County Heritage* 15 (Spring 1977).

Scheffer, Theo. H. "Voyageurs and Explorers in the Grand Coulee: The First Adventurers Striking into the Far West Scouted this Natural Phenomenon and Marveled at Its Grandeur." Spokane *Spokesman-Review*, January 29, 1950.

Scott, Leslie M. "The Pioneer Stimulus of Gold." *Quarterly of the Oregon Historical Society* 27 (September 1917).

Spaid, Stanley S. "The Later Life and Activities of General Joel Palmer." *Oregon Historical Quarterly* 55 (December 1954).

Sperlin, O.B., ed. "Document—Our First Horticulturist—The Brackenridge Journal." *Washington Historical Quarterly* 22 (April 1931).

Van Arsdol, Ted. "End of Track Town." *Frontier Times* (Spring 1961).

_____. "Pioneer Cattle Outfit: Phelps & Wadleigh." *Okanogan County Heritage* 4 (June 1966).

_____. "Pioneer Riverboats." *Okanogan County Heritage* 6 (March 1968).

_____. "Trail North—1858." *Okanogan County Heritage* 7 (March 1969).

Wilson, Bruce A. "Hudson's Bay Brigade Trail" and "Early Map Shows the Brigade Trail." *Okanogan County Heritage* 4 (September 1966).

_____. "University Library: Okanogan County in California [fur-trader John Work's journal]." *Okanogan County Heritage* 2 (June 1964).

Wood, C.E.S. "An Indian Horse Race." *Okanogan County Heritage* 2 (December 1963).

Books and Monographs

Anderson, Alexander C. *Hand-Book and Map to the Gold Region of Frazer's and Thompson's Rivers, with Table of Distances.* San Francisco, 1858.

Appelman, Roy E. *Lewis and Clark: Historic Places Associated with Their Transcontinental Exploration, 1804-06.* Washington, D.C.: National Park Service, 1975.

Barker, Burt Brown, ed. *Letters of Dr. John McLoughlin: Written at Fort Vancouver, 1829-1832.* Portland: Binfords and Mort, 1948.

Bonn, Marjorie Faulkner. *Hogback.* New York: Vantage Press, 1954.

Coues, Elliott., ed. *History of the Expedition under the Command of Lewis and Clark*, Vols. 2 and 3. New York: Dover, 1965.

_____. *The Manuscript Journals of Alexander Henry, Fur Trader of the Northwest Company, and of David Thompson, Official Geographer and Explorer of the Same Company, 1799-1814.* Minneapolis, 1897.

Cox, Ross. *The Columbia River,* ed. by Edgar I. and Jane R. Stewart. Norman: University of Oklahoma Press, 1957.

Douglas, David. *Journal Kept by David Douglas during His Travels in North America, 1823-1827.* London: Royal Horticultural Society, 1914.

Drumheller, Dan. *"Uncle Dan" Drumheller Tells Thrills of Western Trails in 1854.* Spokane, 1925.

Ermatinger, C.O., ed. "Edward Ermatinger's York Factory Express Journal, Being a Record of Journeys Made Between Fort Vancouver and Hudson Bay in the Years 1827-1828," in *Royal Society of Canada Proceedings and Transcriptions*, Vol. VI, Sec. 2. Ottawa, 1912.

Franchere, Gabriel. *Adventure at Astoria, 1810-1814.* Norman: University of Oklahoma Press, 1967.

Frush, Charles W. "A Trip from the Dalles of the Columbia, Oregon, to Fort Owen, Bitter Root Valley, Montana, in the Spring of 1858," in *Contributions to the Historical Society of Montana*, Vol. 2. Boston, Massachusetts: J.S. Canner, 1966.

Gass, Patrick. *A Journal of the Voyages and Travels of a Corps of Discovery.* Pittsburgh, 1807.

Goetzmann, William H. *Looking at the Land of Promise: Pioneer Images of the Pacific Northwest.* Pullman: Washington State University Press, 1988.

Guie, H. Dean. *Bugles in the Valley: Garnett's Fort Simcoe.* Portland: Oregon Historical Society, revised ed. 1977.

Hales, Marjorie. "The History of Pasco, Washington, to 1915," MA thesis, Washington State University, Pullman, 1964. [Also serialized in the *Franklin Flyer* historical journal, Pasco.]

Harper, Russell, ed. *Paul Kane's Frontier: Including Wanderings of an Artist among the Indians of North America, by Paul Kane.* Austin: University of Texas Press, 1971.

Harris, Mary Powell. *Goodbye, White Bluffs.* Yakima: Franklin Press, 1972.

Hunn, Eugene S. *Nch'i-Wana "The Big River": Mid-Columbia Indians and Their Land.* Seattle: University of Washington Press, 1990.

Irving, Washington. *Astoria, or Anecdotes of an Enterprise Beyond the Rocky Mountains,* ed. by Edgeley W. Todd. Norman: University of Oklahoma Press, 1964.

Johansen, Dorothy O., and Charles M. Gates. *Empire of the Columbia: A History of the Pacific Northwest,* 2nd ed. New York: Harper and Row, 1967.

Kane, Paul. *Wanderings of an Artist among the Indians of North America: From Canada to Vancouver's Island and Oregon through the Hudson's Bay Company's Territory and Back Again.* Toronto: Radisson Society of Canada, 1925.

Lage, Laura Tice. *Sagebrush Homesteads.* Yakima: Franklin Press, 1967.

Lewis, William S. *The Story of Early Days in the Big Bend Country.* Spokane: W.D. Allen, 1926.

McDonald, Archibald. *Peace River. A Canoe Voyage from Hudson's Bay to Pacific by the Late Sir George Simpson, (Governor, Hon. Hudson's Bay Company.) in 1828. Journal of the Late Chief Factor, Archibald McDonald, (Hon. Hudson's Bay Company), Who Accompanied Him.* Ottawa, Montreal, and Toronto, 1872.

McIntyre, A.A. *Last Grand Roundup.* Wilson Creek, Washington: Chief Publishing Company, 1906 [reprinted as *The Last Grand Roundup*, by Stuart McIntyre, 3848 Cresta Way, Sacramento, California: The Chief Research Co., 1989].

Meinig, D.W. *The Great Columbia Plain: A Historical Geography, 1805-1910.* Seattle: University of Washington Press, 1968.

Merk, Frederick, ed. *Fur Trade and Empire: George Simpson's Journal . . . 1824-25*, revised ed. Cambridge, Massachusetts: Harvard University Press, 1968.

Mills, Randall V. *Stern-wheelers Up Columbia: A Century of Steamboating in the Oregon Country.* Palo Alto, California: Pacific, 1947.

Mitchell, Bruce. *By River, Trail and Rail: A Brief History of the First Century of Transportation in North Central Washington . . . 1811 to 1911.* Wenatchee: Wenatchee *Daily World*, 1968.

Notices and Voyages of the Famed Quebec Mission to the Pacific Northwest. Portland: Oregon Historical Society, 1956.

Oliphant, J. Orin. *On the Cattle Ranges of the Oregon Country.* Seattle: University of Washington Press, 1968.

Parker, Samuel. *Journal of an Exploring Tour beyond the Rocky Mountains . . . in the Years 1835, '36, and '37.* Ithaca, New York, 1842.

Quaife, Milo M., ed. *The Journals of Captain Meriwether Lewis and Sergeant John Ordway . . .* Madison: State Historical Society of Wisconsin, 1916.

Relander, Click. *Drummers and Dreamers.* Caldwell, Idaho: Caxton, 1956.

Rice, Harvey S. "Native Dwellings of the Southern Plateau," in *Spokane and the Inland Empire: An Interior Pacific Northwest Anthology*, ed. by David H. Stratton. Pullman: Washington State University Press, 1991.

Rich, E.E., ed., *Part of Dispatch from George Simpson . . . to the Governor and Committee of the Hudson's Bay Company, London, March 1, 1829.* Toronto: Champlain Society, 1947.

Richards, Kent D. *Isaac I. Stevens: Young Man in a Hurry.* Pullman: Washington State University Press, 1993.

Rollins, Philip Ashton, ed. *The Discovery of the Oregon Trail: Robert Stuart's Narratives.* New York: Charles Scribner's Sons, 1935.

Ross, Alexander. *Adventures of the First Settlers on the Oregon or Columbia River.* London, 1849.

_____. *The Fur Hunters of the Far West*, ed. by Kenneth A. Spaulding. Norman: University of Oklahoma Press, 1956.

Ruby, Robert H., and John A. Brown. *The Cayuse Indians: Imperial Tribesmen of Old Oregon.* Norman: University of Oklahoma Press, 1972.

_____. *Ferryboats on the Columbia River: Including the Bridges and Dams.* Seattle: Superior, 1974.

_____. *Half-Sun on the Columbia: A Biography of Chief Moses.* Norman: University of Oklahoma Press, 1965.

Schmitt, Martin F., ed. *General George Crook: His Biography.* Norman: University of Oklahoma Press, 1960.

Simpson, George. *Narrative of a Journey Round the World, during the Years 1841 and 1842.* London, 1847.

Splawn, A.J. *Ka-Mi-Akin: The Last Hero of the Yakimas.* Portland, 1917.

Steele, Richard F., and Arthur P. Rose. *An Illustrated History of the Big Bend Country: Embracing Lincoln, Douglas, Adams and Franklin Counties, State of Washington.* Western Historical Publishing Company, 1904.

Stern, Theodore. *Chiefs and Chief Traders: Indian Relations at Fort Nez Perces, 1818-1855.* Corvallis: Oregon State University Press, 1993.

Symons, Thomas William. *The Symons Report on the Upper Columbia River and the Great Plain of the Columbia* [1882]. Fairfield, Washington: Ye Galleon Press, 1967.

Thwaites, Reuben Gold, ed. *Original Journals of the Lewis and Clark Expedition, 1804-1806,* Vols. 3, 4, 7, and 8. New York: Antiquarian Press, 1959.

Timmen, Fritz. *Blow for the Landing: A Hundred Years of Steam Navigation on the Waters of the West.* Caldwell, Idaho: Caxton, 1973.

Trafzer, Clifford E., and Richard D. Scheuerman. *Renegade Tribe: The Palouse Indians and the Invasion of the Inland Pacific Northwest.* Pullman: Washington State University Press, 1986.

Tyrrell, J.B., ed. *David Thompson's Narrative of His Explorations in Western North America, 1784-1812.* Toronto: Champlain Society, 1916.

Victor, Frances Fuller. *The River of the West.* Hartford, Connecticut, 1870.

Wilkes, Charles. *The United States Exploring Expedition*, Vol. 4. 1844.

Wilson, Bruce A. *Late Frontier: A History of Okanogan County, Washington, 1800-1941.* Okanogan: Okanogan County Historical Society, 1990.

Wilson, Fred W., and Earle K. Stewart. *Steamboat Days on the Rivers.* Portland: Oregon Historical Society, 1969.

Wright, E.W., ed. *Lewis & Dryden's Marine History of the Pacific Northwest.* Lewis & Dryden Printing Co., 1895 [reprinted 1967 by Superior Publishing Company, Seattle, Washington].

Special Series and Cultural Resources Reports

Chance, David H. "Influences of the Hudson's Bay Company on the Native Cultures of the Colvile District." *Northwest Anthropological Research Notes Memoir No. 2,* 1973.

Galm, Jerry R., Glenn D. Hartmann, Ruth A. Masten, and Garry Owen Stephenson [Bonneville Cultural Resources Group]. *A Cultural Resources Overview of the Bonneville Power Administration's Mid-Columbia Project, Central Washington.* Eastern Washington University Reports in Archaeology and History, No. 100-16, Cheney, Washington, 1981.

Leonhardy, Frank C., and David G. Rice. "A Proposed Culture Typology for the Lower Snake River Region, Southeastern Washington." *Northwest Anthropological Research Notes* 4 (Spring 1970).

Masten, Ruth A. *A Report on Archaeological Testing at Salishan Mesa (45GR455), Grant County, Washington.* Eastern Washington University Reports in Archaeology and History, No. 100-54, Cheney, Washington, 1988.

Osborne, Douglas. *Archaeological Tests in the Lower Grand Coulee, Washington.* Occasional Papers of the Idaho State University Museum, No. 20, Pocatello, Idaho, 1967.

Smith, William C. *Archaeological Explorations in the Columbia Basin: A Report on the Mesa Project, 1973-1975.* Department of Anthropology, Central Washington University, Ellensburg, Washington, 1977.

Spier, Leslie. *Tribal Distribution in Washington.* General Series in Anthropology, No. 3, Menasha, Wisconsin, 1936.

Teit, James H. *The Middle Columbia Salish.* Seattle: University of Washington Publications, 1928.

Archival Collections and Private Papers

Corless, John. Diary, May 27-October 8, 1880, Oregon Historical Society Library, Portland.

Graham, Robert. Papers, Box 2, File 30, Eastern Washington State Historical Society Library, Spokane.

Masiker, George. Diary, 1862, University of Oregon Library, Eugene.

Merrill, G. Diary, 1866, property of Vera Holm, Iowa; copy in author's collection.

Oregon Montana Transportation Company. Record Book, 1866, Oregon Historical Society Library, Portland.

Palmer, Joel. "Pocket Diary for 1860" (typewritten copy), Oregon Historical Society Library, Portland.

Washington, Nat W. "Mesa Top Cliff Dwellers of Eastern Washington," 1973. Unpublished report, Ephrata, Washington.

————. "The Nomadic Life of the Tsin-Cayuse as Related by Billy Curlew (Kul Kuloo) in the Fall of 1956 to Nat Washington, Jr." Unpublished typewritten manuscript, Ephrata, Washington.

Weaver, Harold. "A Tour of the Old Indian Camp Grounds of Central Washington," 1946. Unpublished manuscript in author's collection.

White, Cull. "The Steamer Chelan." Unpublished manuscript in author's collection.

Williams, Christina MacDonald McKenzie. To William S. Lewis, May 28, 1921, Eastern Washington State Historical Society Library, Spokane.

Government Documents

House Bill 33. "An act to authorize Thomas Howe to establish and keep a ferry across the Columbia River at White Bluffs," Laws, Eighth Session of the Territorial Legislature, Olympia, Washington Territory.

"Lieutenant Arnold's Report." *Pacific Railroad Explorations and Surveys, to St. Paul and Puget Sound,* Vol. 12, *Senate Executive Document* 46, 35th Cong., 2nd Sess., 1859 [992].

McGill, Henry M., Acting Governor. Message to the Eighth Annual Session of the Legislative Assembly, December 1860, Olympia, Washington Territory.

National Archives, Washington, D.C. Assorted U.S. Army records, including War Department, Letters Received; Records of U.S. Army Commands, Department of Pacific.

Pacific Railroad Explorations and Surveys, to St. Paul and Puget Sound, Supplement to Volume I, *Senate Executive Document* 46, 35th Cong., 2nd Sess., 1859.

Record Group 98. Records of the United States Army Commands (Army Posts), Post Returns Camp Chelan, Washington Territory, August 1879-September 1880.

"Report of Lieutenant Richard Arnold, U.S.A., of His Route from the Mouth of Clark's Fork, by Fort Colville, the Grand Coulée, and the Mouth of Snake River, to Wallah-Wallah." *Pacific Railroad Explorations and Surveys, to St. Paul and Puget Sound,* Vol. 1, *House Executive Document* 91, 33d Cong., 2nd Sess., 1855 [791].

Symons, Thomas William. "The Upper Columbia River and the Great Plain of the Columbia," *Senate Executive Document* 186, 47th Cong., 1st Sess., 1882.

Thomas, Captain George. To J.J. Abert, Chief, Corps of Topographical Engineers, Washington, D.C., October 6, 1859, U.S. Congress, *House Executive Documents*, 1859-60.

Index